Shaw
and Other Matters

Stanley Weintraub
Evan Pugh Professor of Arts and Humanities
The Pennsylvania State University

Shaw and Other Matters

A Festschrift for Stanley Weintraub on the Occasion of His Forty-Second Anniversary at The Pennsylvania State University

Edited by
Susan Rusinko

Selinsgrove: Susquehanna University Press
London: Associated University Presses

© 1998 by Associated University Presses, Inc.

All rights reserved. Authorization to photocopy items for internal or personal use, or the internal or personal use of specific clients, is granted by the copyright owner, provided that a base fee of $10.00, plus eight cents per page, per copy is paid directly to the Copyright Clearance Center, 222 Rosewood Drive, Danvers, Massachusetts 01923. [1-57591-008-X/98 $10.00+8¢ pp, pc.]

Associated University Presses
440 Forsgate Drive
Cranbury, NJ 08512

Associated University Presses
16 Barter Street
London WC1A 2AH, England

Associated University Presses
P.O. Box 338, Port Credit
Mississauga, Ontario
Canada L5G 4L8

The paper used in this publication meets the requirements of the American National Standard for Permanence of Paper for Printed Library Materials Z39.48–1984.

Library of Congress Cataloging-in-Publication Data

Shaw and other matters : a festschrift for Stanley Weintraub on the occasion of his forty-second anniversary at the Pennsylvania State University / edited by Susan Rusinko.
    p. cm.
    Includes bibliographical references and index.
    ISBN 1-57591-008-X (alk. paper)
    1. Shaw, Bernard, 1856–1950—Criticism and interpretation.
2. Shaw, Bernard, 1856–1950—Contemporaries. 3. Criticism.
I. Rusinko, Susan. II. Weintraub, Stanley, 1929– .
PR5367.S474   1998
822'.912—dc21   97-27975
                                                                               CIP

PRINTED IN THE UNITED STATES OF AMERICA

Contents

Acknowledgments	7
Introduction	9
The Dreaded Weintraub FRED D. CRAWFORD	15

On Shaw

"Oh, the Dreaming, the Dreaming": *Arms and the Man* RODELLE WEINTRAUB	31
Bernard Shaw's Bonaparte: Life Force or Death Wish? MICHEL W. PHARAND	41
Arnold Bennett: Shaw's Ten O'Clock Scholar KINLEY ROBY	53
The Evolution of Human Virtue: Precedents for Shaw's "World Betterer" in the Utopias of Bellamy, Morris, and Bulwer-Lytton JULIE SPARKS	63
Heartbreak House and the Trojan War KAY LI	83

On Shaw's Contemporaries

Family Dynamics in George Gissing's Novels MELISSA WITTE ANTINORI	95
The Curious Affair of the Lady Venus M. D. ALLEN	110
Additional Verse by Hilaire Belloc: An Edition MIKE MARKEL	121

On Speculative Fiction

The Golem-Robot Intersection MILTON T. WOLF	133

Octavia Butler Writes the Bible JOHN R. PFEIFFER	140

On Modern Drama

Joe Orton's Bookends: *Head to Toe* and *Up Against It* SUSAN RUSINKO	155
More Than Noises Off: Marsha Norman's Offstage Characters TRACY SIMMONS BITONTI	166
Murder Most Civilized: The Stage Thrillers of Frederick Knott ARTHUR NICHOLAS ATHANASON	180

On Military History

Memoirs, Fiction, and Paradox: A Reflective Essay on the Memory of War ROBERT C. DOYLE	191
Stanley Weintraub: A Select Bibliography COMPILED BY FRED D. CRAWFORD	204
Contributors	214
Index	217

Acknowledgments

For their constant and instant availability whenever a question arose, I am grateful to Fred Crawford and Kinley Roby, without whose editorial expertise this volume would not have been possible. Despite their busy schedules, the former as editor of *SHAW* and professor and the latter settling into retirement in Florida even as he continues field editing for Twayne Publishers, they have contributed unstintingly to this Festschrift for Stanley Weintraub.

I thank Shirley Rader, longtime secretary to Stanley Weintraub and to the Institute for the Arts and Humanistic Studies at The Pennsylvania State University for manuscript preparation and invaluable help in obtaining necessary information. Having worked with Stanley Weintraub on his manuscripts and with a number of his students on their dissertations (including mine), she appropriately concludes her years of loyal service by her participation in the Festschrift, her retirement in 1995 enabling her to contribute time and effort indispensably.

My thanks also go to Mary Anne Cahir, Sue Reighard and the Institute for the Arts and Humanistic Studies for their valuable assistance in a variety of ways; to H. A. Radar for providing photographs for the book jacket; to Hans and Barbara Feldmann at Susquehanna University and Michael Koy at Associated University Presses for their willing responses to my questions. Last, but far from least, I am grateful to the contributors for making editing so rewarding an experience for me.

Introduction

IN a variety of subject matter and critical approaches (among the latter: text, style, biography, psychoanalysis, sociology, cultural history, source/analog, archetype), this collection of essays demonstrates the influence of one scholar-teacher on his students and on others who have worked with him. The articles are extensions of the broad research interests of Stanley Weintraub, a faculty member at The Pennsylvania State University since 1956 and Evan Pugh Professor of Arts and Humanities since 1986. His many awards include a 1968 National Book Award nomination for *Beardsley*, the American Theatre Library Association's 1972 George Freedley Award for *Journey to Heartbreak*, a Freedoms Foundation Award in 1980 for *London Yankees*, and Pennsylvania's Distinguished Humanist Award in 1985. *The Last Great Victory: The End of World War II, July-August 1945* is doubly honored as his sixth Book-of-the-Month selection and as a History Book Club selection. The double honor was accompanied by many appearances on national and international radio and on national television during the fiftieth anniversary celebrations of the end of World War II. Among the many reprints/revisions of his books, *Victoria: An Intimate Biography* is the latest to be so honored in 1996 by John Murray Ltd., London.

With George Bernard Shaw at the hub of his literary interests, Weintraub's scholarly output is nearing fifty books and hundreds of articles and book reviews. Wherever his curiosity led, he has followed. That curiosity was first aroused in his reading of Shaw's plays during military service in Korea in the early 1950s. He followed up on that interest in his doctoral dissertation at Penn State. Work on the dissertation, as noted by Fred Crawford in his biographical essay, led to Weintraub's discovery of that other Shaw (Lawrence of Arabia), Arnold Bennett, Reginald Turner, Oscar Wilde and his fin de siècle circle, as well as the D. H. Lawrence group in Florence. Curiosity and serendipitous discoveries have always been his starting point. Always, as well, his involvement in several concurrent writing projects—each at a different stage of development—characterizes his incessant research activity. Thus 1996 witnessed publication of *Shaw's People: Victoria to Churchill*; 1997 witnesses his biography of Albert, and the following year or so will witness his Korean War book.

In 1956, he edited the first issue of the *Shaw Bulletin*, which became the *Shaw Review* in 1959, and then *SHAW: The Annual of Bernard Shaw Studies* in 1981. The annual continues today under the editorship of his former graduate student, Fred Crawford.

Weintraub's first book, an edition of *An Unfinished Novel by Bernard Shaw* (1958), was followed by *Private Shaw and Public Shaw: A Dual Portrait of Lawrence of Arabia and G.B.S* (1963). The scholarly pattern for the rest of his career was set, with biography and history constituting the primary thrusts of his publications. His early books on C. P. Snow, *The Yellow Book*, the Royal Court Theatre, Beardsley, the Spanish Civil War intellectuals, and Oscar Wilde led to what may be seen as a defining event in his career, the two-volume autobiography of Bernard Shaw (1970 and 1971). More and more individual and collective biographies (Whistler, Beardsley, the four Rossettis, London Yankees, Frank Harris) took over his writing interests; *Victoria* (1987) and *Disraeli* (1993) were among his latest. Two works in progress reflect a continuation of his biographical-historical bent: a biography of Albert, a companion volume to *Victoria*, and yet another "war" book, this one on the Korean War.

His Korean War experience, always there to be drawn on, as was his boyhood interest in World War II, surfaced in *The War in the Wards: Korea's Unknown Battle in a Prisoner-of-War Hospital Camp* (1964, rev. 1976). Later he launched into what can be seen as a trilogy of cultural histories involving World War I and World War II: *A Stillness Heard Round the World: The End of the Great War, November 1918* (1988); *Long Day's Journey into War, December 7, 1941* (1991); and *The Last Great Victory: The End of World War II, July-August 1945* (1995). His next venture into twentieth-century wars, the Korean conflict, involves a return to the war of his own military service.

Always, however, Shaw remains a central research interest, as witnessed in the long list of books that include editions of Shaw's work, an autobiography of Shaw, a transcription of Shaw's diaries, and the many studies of Shaw's works, times, and contemporaries. In 1993, he and his wife, Rodelle, edited a Bantam-edition-paring of Shaw's *Arms and the Man* and *John Bull's Other Island* and in 1995, a Bantam-edition pairing of Shaw's *Misalliance* and *Heartbreak House*, prefaced with their "The Enchanted Country House." In 1996, combining his interests in Shaw, biography, and cultural underpinnings, he published *Shaw's People: Victoria to Churchill*.

It is his own breadth of curiosity that is mirrored in the essays in this collection. Without one centralizing thematic concern, but with Shaw as the literary center of the book, the subject matter is as varied as is the prolific scholarship of Weintraub himself. The encouragement of interest in Shaw is present in articles that illustrate a variety of approaches to the work of Shaw: Michel Pharand's tracing of Shaw's changing views on Napoleon, Rodelle Weintraub's dream analysis of *Arms and the Man,* Kinley Roby's discussion of Shaw's frequent exchanges with Arnold Bennett on the matter of playwriting, Kay Li's archetypal exploration of characters in *Heartbreak House,* and Julie Sparks's contrast of Shaw with Bellamy, Morris, and Bulwer-Lytton as world-betterers.

Weintraub's inevitable pursuit of Shaw's contemporaries is reflected in Melissa Witte Antinori's tracing of the relationship between daughters and parents in the 1890 novels of George Gissing. Adding a playful note are some previously unpublished poems by Hilaire Belloc, on whose writings Mike Markel has engaged in extensive research at the Boston College Libraries. Weintraub's work on T. E. Lawrence is taken up by M. D. Allen, whose dissertation on "Ross" was published as *The Medievalism of Lawrence of Arabia* (1991). Allen's continued research into intriguing figures is represented here in his investigation of yet another mysterious, albeit minor, person known as the "Lady Venus."

The recent forays of Weintraub into cultural histories of twentieth-century wars take a personal turn in the article by Robert Doyle, whose concern with war memoirs is an outgrowth of his dissertation, published as *Voices from Captivity: Interpreting the American POW Narrative* (1994).

Weintraub's editing legacy has fallen in part to Kinley Roby, who, in addition to his own books on Arnold Bennett, T. S. Eliot, Joyce Cary, and Edward VIII, has edited nearly one hundred fifty books on British literature for G. K. Hall—among these, four of mine—and to Fred Crawford who continues in the general editing of *SHAW.* In his biographical essay here, Crawford, also the author of books on British novelists and poets of the early twentieth century, conjoins the personal and professional aspects of Weintraub's life and career, the latter continually reinvigorated by discoveries of the old and the currency of the new, both always meticulously researched for accuracy.

Guest editor of a recent special-topics issue of *SHAW,* sub-titled *Shaw and Science Fiction,* Milton Wolf in his commentary on golems and robots links a centuries-old topic to the computer age. Writing about a particular genre of speculative literature, John Pfeiffer recreates the fictional world of Octavia Butler's rewriting of the Bible in her fantasy-futuristic novels.

Not to be excluded in this variegated collection is Weintraub's work in modern drama, particularly his editing of several volumes of twentieth-century British dramatists in the *Dictionary of Literary Biography* series. Among his many former doctoral students, Arthur Athanason and I, contemporary advisees who wrote our respective dissertations on John Osborne and Harold Pinter, have continued to write about modern drama. Athanason, a frequent actor/director on radio, stage, and television, probes the drawing power of Frederick Knott, a popular writer of mystery plays. My piece on two of Joe Orton's posthumously published minor works, a novel and an unproduced film script for the Beatles drawn from the novel, compares the two, the former written before his stage successes and the latter just before his death. Tracy Simmons Bitonti reinvents her earlier published article on Shaw's offstage characters in an analysis of the practical and aesthetic effects of the use of such characters in the plays of Marsha Norman.

Weintraub's legatees have become his colleagues, and the exchange of ideas and interests between him and them continues. This *Festschrift* is a tribute not just to one man but to a longstanding American academic tradition involving the passing on of intellectual inquiry from mentor to students, a rite acknowledged immediately in the spontaneity and enthusiasm with which the latter responded to my call for papers and ultimately in their respective scholarly pursuits.

SUSAN RUSINKO

Shaw
and Other Matters

The Dreaded Weintraub
Fred D. Crawford

By September 1971, Stanley Weintraub had already published more than twenty books. These had nothing to do with my decision to enroll in his Literature of Victorian England seminar since I knew nothing about him or his work. Despite the warnings of a few graduate students who had been at Penn State for a while and who, for the most part, were still there when I left with my doctorate, I enrolled in the Dreaded Weintraub's seminar.

"Weintraub," they had explained, "assigns an impossible amount of reading and requires a research paper." They had also pointed out that unlike most professors, Weintraub was prone to put Cs on the transcripts of graduate students who fell short of his expectations. Forewarned, I braced myself.

On the first day of class, about a dozen of us appeared in the seminar room on the first floor of Burrowes, but the professor was not there. Instead, there arrived Shirley Rader, who informed us crisply, "Dr. Weintraub will not be here today due to a religious holiday. He wants me to tell you that the class will meet at Ihlseng Cottage and to give you these." "These" turned out to be a thick course syllabus and schedule, complete with reading/discussion questions for each class session.

The seminar would focus on the late Victorians—Wilde, Shaw, Gissing, Moore, Conrad, Hardy, Wells, and sundry Aesthetes and Decadents—and the course syllabus confirmed the warnings. There were hundreds of pages of assigned reading for each weekly meeting, not only from the texts available at the bookstore but also from books in the maw of Pattee Library. There would indeed be a research paper, for which a prospectus that "should include a statement of the problem and a survey of the local resources for research on the problem" required Dr. Weintraub's approval "during the sixth week (or earlier)."

As we soon discovered, his casual tweed jacket and turtleneck attire and his relaxed demeanor belied the intellectual rigor that he expected of his students. He proved to be a forceful presence at the head of the conference table. All other places at the table constituted the foot. When the more courageous among us asked questions intended to demonstrate their own sophistication and intellectual prowess, he disposed of these quickly, exhaustively, and authoritatively as if he had been expecting them and had spent hours preparing polished responses.

After reading *The Portable Oscar Wilde* and the required supplementary works from the stacks, I felt sufficiently prepared for the first session. Within minutes, enlightened as to the meaning of adequate preparation, the entire class was busily scribbling, next to reading notes hastily scrawled on that session's question sheets, the notes that we should have taken. His first question had come as no surprise, since we already had it on that session's list, but we were not prepared for his incisive follow-up questions. An answer to any of his questions might have formed the thesis of a thoughtful essay. By the end of that session, we had a fuller appreciation that behind each question there lurked "obvious" implications that were our responsibility to identify and to consider in depth. The reading questions were merely springboards for discussion, not ends in themselves.

It was clear that this would be an intensive and serious seminar in which insincere or ill-conceived comments had no place. He reinforced this with his precise distinction between the words *scholar* and *critic*. A scholar might also be a critic, but a critic was not necessarily a scholar. This news was not entirely welcome to a roomful of fledgling critics.

Dr. Weintraub's approach to graduate seminars differed markedly from that of the other professors whose courses I had taken, or would later take, at Penn State. The most striking contrast was his focus on professional research. "If you know what you're going to find, you're not doing research," he told us more than once. We soon realized that those who did not begin research for the prospectus well before the sixth-week deadline were already behind, since the prospectus alone could demand as much actual research as completed papers acceptable in other seminars. Dr. Weintraub also made it clear that when he evaluated seminar papers, he paid close attention to editorial matters as well as to substance.

His seminar departed from the norm in other ways as well. He was sufficiently enthusiastic about his own research to assume that graduate students were both eager and able to aspire to his level of expertise, regardless of the amount of work that this might involve. He frequently referred to subjects for books or articles that he himself did not have time to write, as well as to topics for dissertations that might eventually be publishable. Another revelation was the readiness with which he could suggest profitable directions for research that, in addition to gratifying curiosity, might actually be fun. He made it clear that a Ph.D. is not an end in itself but a hunting license. In his courses he emphasized approaches and methods that could enable his students to maintain standards in a profession where the phrase "academic discipline" is rapidly becoming oxymoronic.

Two years later, with his seminars on Late Victorians, Bernard Shaw, and Between-the-Wars Novels behind me, as well as the doctoral-comprehensive pentathlon, I embarked on my dissertation. It soon became obvious that Dr. Weintraub had been pulling his punches during those demanding and sometimes daunting seminars. His criticism of draft chapters of the dissertation, which he read as I produced them, was not only blunt, but regrettably valid. His response to the third or fourth chapter began, "Like most of your chapters to date, this one is too long" before moving rapidly to an enumeration of revisions required by the shortcomings of what I had done and what I had left undone. He then concluded with words of encouragement and inexplicable optimism about where the dissertation was headed.

When the dissertation failed to progress as rapidly as he would have liked, he did not send notes exhorting action or calling attention to the passing of time. Instead, my pigeon-hole in the department mailroom would begin to sprout newspaper and article cuttings relevant to my subject, usually marked with a neutral statement such as "You may find this useful." Within a day or two of his response to one chapter, my pigeon-hole would begin to fill with clippings relevant to the next one. This goading, although indirect, was effective.

In April 1975, as we walked back to Burrowes from my dissertation defense in Ihlseng's conference room (where, it turned out, I *still* seemed to be at the foot of the table), the once-dreaded Dr. Weintraub remarked offhandedly, "By the way, you'll have to cut out the doctoring and professoring. You're a colleague, not a student." "Colleague" was certainly stretching the point, since I then had no prospects for academic employment, but "Stan" he has been since that day.

One of my lesser ambitions as a graduate student had been to submit a paper to Stan in which he would not find a misspelled word or grammatical botch. Once I nearly succeeded, but *contraversy* did me in. Now I pinned my hopes on the final typed version of the dissertation. An improbably short time after I dropped the copy off for Stan's final perusal, he sent a short note: "Perhaps I'm the only one who will notice it, but on p. 20 *Apollodorus* has two *p*'s." At least I did not have to retype the page.

He did insist that I retype my dissertation's vita to delete a sentence in which I had declared, describing myself with the third-person pronoun, "He has developed a strong aversion to manual labor." Stan refused to sign his name to register his official approval until he had seen the revised page. An extra *p* in *Apollodorus*, if noticed, was a trivial matter, but among the stodgy and narrow folk who review academic job applications, an inappropriate statement in a vita might do actual harm.

Stan's commitment to his students does not end when they graduate. He does what he can to help find university positions for his students, sending them copies of job announcements, writing letters of recommendation, and offering inside information about a specific job search that he has acquired from his vast network of correspondents. He has ushered several seminar papers through the review process to help students publish articles, and when Stan's students are writing their own books, he reads their draft chapters, provides a wealth of information and material from his own files, and helps them find a publisher. Stan has remarked that he regards the résumés of his students as extensions of his own. That seems fair enough, given how much of his own effort has gone into those résumés.

Stan himself has had quite a variety of jobs, many far removed from the ivory tower. In fact, he may owe much of his distinction as teacher, scholar, and writer not to a traditional academic background, but to the lack of it.

Born in Philadelphia on 17 April 1929, he was the eldest child and first son of Benjamin Weintraub and Ray Segal Weintraub. His father had emigrated from Romania as a child, completed his formal education through the fourth grade, and supported the family by collecting five- and ten-cent insurance premiums in the Lithuanian and Polish communities of Philadelphia. His mother had emigrated from Poland. Stan and his younger siblings, Herbert ("Hershey," born 1932) and Gladys ("Cookie," born 1937), are first-generation Americans.

His first decade coincided with the Great Depression. Although his parents were necessarily frugal, they found the means to develop and gratify his early curiosity about the world. He recalls that his father would buy back issues of *National Geographic* for a nickel apiece. His family had a radio and, something of a rarity in South Philly during the 1930s, a telephone.

The seven-year-old Stan became more aware of the outside world when he first heard of Ethiopia following Mussolini's 1936 invasion. He began collecting the then-popular bubble-gum war cards although he failed to recognize the propaganda implicit in their depiction of the wars in Ethiopia, Spain, and China. One neighbor was not appreciative of the youngster's burgeoning interest in world affairs when Stan scratched a misspelled "Ethiopia" into the wet cement of a nearby sidewalk. In 1939, his father applied for a library card so that the ten-year-old Stan could check out adult books. The first such book that he borrowed was *I Broadcast the Crisis* by radio commentator H. V. Kaltenborn.

Stan's primary interests were history and international politics, and he began to write his first book, a chronicle of World War II, in 1939. He abandoned it in 1940. When he came down with scarlet fever and spent some weeks of April and May 1940 in bed, he followed the European conflict through radio, magazines, and newspapers. Among the radio news broadcasters he heard were Edward R. Murrow from London, William Shirer from Berlin, and Eric Sevareid from Paris. This was of much greater interest to him than the experimental approach of his sixth-grade class, which tied all academic areas, including mathematics, to a central project on ancient Rome.

He took an early interest in domestic politics as well. F.D.R. was his idol. Outside the 1940 Republican Convention in Philadelphia, when the crowd began to chant "We want Willkie!" Stan could not resist shouting "We want Roosevelt!" Later he felt sorry for Willkie when F.D.R. buried him in the November election.

Stan focused more intently on world events after the Japanese bombing of Pearl Harbor. His bar mitzvah in April 1942 coincided with Jimmy Doolittle's bombing of Tokyo. A continuing interest in bubble-gum war cards provided an early lesson in what happens to truth in wartime. He began to notice that the patriotic cards contradicted the reality, which was that the United States seemed to be losing everywhere.

The meaning of war came to Stan in various ways. Many of his cousins were in uniform. At school, one teacher began to insist that the junior high school boys in his charge master the rope climb to prepare themselves for their turn in the war and, also with regard to their future as soldiers, oriented the boys to the horrors of venereal disease. In 1942, Stan began to put together model warplanes to hang from the ceiling of his bedroom. To his mother's dismay, these included German aircraft authentically embellished with swastikas.

Stan's first editorial position was as the humor editor for the Thomas Junior High *Herald* in 1942. His first work to see publication was not a prose biography or history but a verse marking the December 1941 Japanese capture of Wake Island. Another poem in a similar vein, "The Battle of Bataan," published in the December

1942 issue, seems to have comprised the other half of his Complete Poetical Works.

In the fall of 1942, at South Philadelphia High School, he tried his hand as a playwright, writing and directing a school play/historical pageant called "The Spirit of America." Disaster interrupted the production when a vagrant melodeon on wheels slipped its moorings and rolled across the stage. It took some time for the teachers to quiet the students before the final soloist could perform. As Stan later put it, "This was my first and last production. My show business career was over."

In 1943, Stan's homeroom supervisor was a mechanical-drawing teacher who began the fifteen-minute period reading ten verses from the Bible, as mandated by Pennsylvania law. He then spent the rest of the fifteen-minute period sermonizing on the ten verses. When the teacher began to expatiate on the text, Stan turned to his homework. The teacher eventually caught him and demanded to know why he was not paying attention. Stan responded, "State law says that you may read ten verses from the Bible *without* comment. You're violating the law." Laughter from the other students did not improve the mood of the teacher, who called Stan a "shyster lawyer" and gave him an after-school detention slip.

When Stan complained to the assistant principal and implied that the detention would interfere with a part-time job (he had no job but was looking for one), he found an ally, who counseled him simply to ignore the slips without telling the teacher or talking back. After some weeks the teacher realized what was happening and stopped handing out the daily slips. Stan recalls that although the teacher "kept on sermonizing, the armed truce lasted out the war."

During his adolescence, Stan held a succession of odd jobs, ranging from fetching neighbors to the telephone at the candy store for tips to working for a summer in an uncle's clothing store in Marcus Hook for forty cents per hour. For a short time, he was also a small link in a chain that made condoms available to servicemen. Since it was illegal to send such material through the U.S. mail, Stan's job was to carry the packages to the railway express office.

As a sixteen-year-old in wartime, Stan could work as long as forty-four hours a week. When he found that his schooling interfered with his work hours, he resolved the problem by cutting the last class of the day. In September 1944, this had worked, since the teacher did not take roll, but in September 1945, another teacher was more attentive to his charges. Stan failed trigonometry. Despite this lapse, in 1989 he was named a distinguished alumnus of South Philadelphia High School, an honor he shares, as he likes to point out, with

Fabian, Chubby Checker, Mario Lanza, and the final soloist of his ill-fated pageant, Eddie Fisher.

In the fall of 1946, Stan went to West Chester State Teachers College, living at home and rising at 5:00 A.M. to commute the twenty-five miles from Philadelphia, which took ninety minutes each way. Then he reported to his job, selling records at a Sun Ray Drugstore. In 1949, he received his B.S. in education. In 1968, his alma mater, which had become West Chester University, presented him with its Distinguished Alumnus Award, and on 11 November 1982, West Chester, in honor of its most distinguished alumnus, inaugurated the "Stanley Weintraub Room," an archive of his books, papers, and memorabilia. One item at West Chester is the plaster head sculpted by Samuel Sabean. On Stan's retirement from the directorship of the Institute for the Arts and Humanistic Studies, the Fellows presented him with a bronze head cast from this sculpture.

In 1949, he became a master's candidate in English at Temple University. Although Temple awarded the degree in 1951, Stan has called his master's "suspect," since he had to leave before completing examinations, having been called up for the Korean conflict two months before graduation. Temple awarded his degree "in absentia."

West Chester, a teacher's college, had no R.O.T.C. program, and for a time it appeared that Stan would wind up as a foot soldier in the infantry. Failing trigonometry made him ineligible for a commission in the Navy or Air Force. The Army was awarding direct commissions only to those whose degrees were in science, but according to Army logic, a B.S., even one in education, was a science degree. Thus, he received his commission as an Army Second Lieutenant. He served as the admissions officer for a United Nations hospital for Korean POWs. While he was there, some eleven thousand patients rioted over the issue of repatriation. After being promoted to First Lieutenant and awarded a Bronze Star, he was separated from the Army in 1953. Forbidden by military regulations to keep a journal, he had recorded his Korean experiences in letters home, which he used to write *The War in the Wards* (1964).

Stan's brother, Herb, was responsible for two major influences on Stan's subsequent career. The first was to provide Stan, who was in Korea at the time, with a paperback book of Bernard Shaw's plays. The second, shortly after Stan's return to civilian life, was to introduce him on 8 May 1953 to Rodelle Horwitz, a Philadelphian who would earn her degree in elementary education at Temple, where she had been Herb's classmate. She was twenty, four years younger than Stan. Their first date was to attend a performance of Shaw's *Man and Superman* in a production that included the *Don Juan in Hell* third act. Rodelle recalls, "I was late, I fell asleep during the play, and I left my umbrella in his car. But he returned it the next day and offered to teach me to drive, which he did every Saturday morning." Six months later, "He drove through an early November blizzard, despite my advising him that it wasn't a good idea, to give me my engagement ring, November 7, 1953. Was he that eager to see me or not to waste the tickets we had for *Kismet*?"

Stan, with the help of the G.I. Bill, enrolled at Penn State in September 1953. Although his department was English, he was more interested in history. Pattee Library was Stan's first experience with open stacks, and he did a good deal of browsing. When he learned that Shaw had written novels before turning to plays, he decided to combine literature with history by making his dissertation a biography of Shaw's years as a novelist.

On 6 June 1954, Stan and Rodelle married. During their honeymoon week in Lake Placid, Stan joined the local library and on their return home, they stopped in New York City to visit then-editor of the *Shaw Bulletin*, Dan H. Laurence.

Later in 1954, Stan spent weekends visiting the homes of two Pennsylvania collectors of Shaw, LaFayette Butler in Hazleton and T. E. Hanley in Bradford. Both Butler and Hanley (who had accumulated thousands of letters and manuscripts by G.B.S. that later went to the HRHRC at Texas) had cheerfully given Stan access to their Shaw holdings. As a result, his dissertation, "Bernard Shaw, Novelist," directed by Bruce Sutherland and formally approved on 6 May 1956, included so many extensive quotations of previously unpublished material that acquiring permission to publish it in book form was virtually impossible. Still, so many have borrowed the dissertation from Pattee that it has required rebinding.

When he received his doctorate on 10 June 1956, Stan did not know that he had an academic job. Later he learned that Penn State had already "hired" him without bothering to inform him and had been telling other places making inquiries that he already had a job. After he had turned down offers from the University of Massachusetts and from a small college in Nacogdoches, Texas, Penn State informed him that he could have an instructorship. By then, Stan and Rodelle had planned to leave State College and had notified their landlord that they were vacating the premises. There would be no paycheck from July through September, they had no place to live, and they had an infant. One of Stan's jobs that summer was to run a day camp for children of rabbis attending a Hillel conference. In September, he began his instructorship of four courses per term, a teaching load that seemed to mandate against research.

There were other demands on his time as the family began to increase. Mark Bennett Weintraub (30 June 1956), David Andrew Weintraub (25 June 1958), and Erica Beth Weintraub (4 May 1961) quickly filled the duplex that the Weintraubs, and the bank, owned at the corner of South Atherton Street and Westerly Parkway. Both Weintraubs were also active in the Jewish Community Council (Rodelle was president in 1962, Stan in 1964). Rodelle recalls that "Stan was wonderful with the kids when they were young—took them canoeing, swimming, played baseball with them." David, a gymnast in high school and in college, remembers that his parents "came to all my meets, in and out of town, even up in New England."

Teaching four courses per term and spending time with his family slowed, but hardly stanched, Stan's scholarly activity. In November 1956, he edited his first issue of the *Shaw Bulletin*, which in 1959 metamorphosed into the *Shaw Review* and then in 1981 into *SHAW: The Annual of Bernard Shaw Studies*. His first published book, an edition of *An Unfinished Novel* by Bernard Shaw, appeared in 1958. Stan did not realize at first how difficult it would be to secure the permission of the Shaw Estate to publish, and on what terms. The book was limited to 1,025 copies (525 for the U.S., 500 for the U.K.), and instead of royalties, Stan received a small fee for preparing the edition.

The book and his editorship of the *Shaw Bulletin* were enough for his promotion to assistant professor in 1960 and to associate professor with tenure on 1 July 1962. He became full professor in 1965, research professor in 1970 (when he also began his twenty-year tenure as Director for the Institute for the Arts and Humanistic Studies), and Evan Pugh Professor of Arts and Humanities in 1986. At Stan's suggestion, the Evan Pugh Professor title specified Arts and Humanities rather than English.

Stan wanted to make his first trip to England in July 1961, but the third child, Erica Beth, was expected around the end of May. Apparently sensitive to problems of scheduling, she obligingly arrived three weeks early. Immediately after her birth, Stan brought a draft chapter to Rodelle to edit in the hospital. Six weeks later, after borrowing $600 from a local bank, he left for England, where he remained for two months.

While researching his dissertation, Stan had discovered another Shaw, better known to the world as Lawrence of Arabia, and had wondered whether there was any connection with the playwright. There was. Stan had also seen an unpublished letter from Arnold Bennett to one Reginald Turner that piqued his interest, particularly when he learned that Turner was part not only of the fin de siècle circle of Oscar Wilde but also of the between-the-wars D. H. Lawrence group in Florence. As always with Stan's books, the starting point was curiosity. The results of his first research trip to England were *Private Shaw and Public Shaw* (1963) and *Reggie: A Portrait of Reginald Turner* (1965).

Private Shaw and Public Shaw was Stan's first attempt at writing a biography of a relationship. Despite the numerous discoveries that have appeared in print about both Shaws during the intervening three decades, no new information has emerged to contradict any of that book's statements. This is even more remarkable in view of the role of A. W. Lawrence, T. E. Lawrence's younger brother and literary executor, who vetted the manuscript with an eye to protecting his brother's reputation and who had rigid control over what Stan might or might not quote.

Stan did not stint his students in the interests of his own research. He received the PSU Class of 1933 Award for Outstanding Teaching in the Humanities in 1964.

Stan commented in 1986, "Every writer needs a good editor, and I had prudently married one." In 1991, Stan wrote in a letter, "I am also trying to write the Disraeli bio, but Rodelle says the first fifty pages are lousy and need much work. So I won't show her the next twenty until they are a lot better!" Rodelle has been the first editor for all Stan's books, and he describes her as his toughest critic, with considerable justice. In addition to aiding in his research, critiquing his drafts, typing manuscripts, selecting titles, and suggesting projects, she has been his co-author on four books.

Rodelle frequently conveys her views of what projects are worth Stan's time, "especially," as Stan wrote in 1993, "if it's a subject she deplores my wasting time upon!" Editing *Bernard Shaw: The Diaries, 1885–1897,* which appeared in 1986, cost Stan more than $100,000 in time and expenses without returning a cent. Research can be an expensive hobby.

One historical event that has fascinated Stan for some time involves the Christmas Truce of 1914. Both his U.S. and U.K. agents feel that the book will not reach a large enough market. Nevertheless, although it may be a while before the book appears, it is probable that Stan's desire to write the book will again prevail over economics.

In connection with Stan's research, the family has done a good bit of traveling to various collections and locations—UCLA in 1963, England for some months in 1968, Hawaii in 1973. In addition to annual (and sometimes more frequent) trips to England, Stan's research has taken him around the world twice and the length of the Pacific, from New Zealand to Japan.

The three children, following their father's example, have earned doctorates, married, and started rearing families of their own. Mark, J.D., is with the Federal Public Defender's Office in Eugene, Oregon. David, Ph.D., is an assistant professor of astronomy at Vanderbilt. Erica, Ph.D., is an associate professor of communication at Washington State University. There are now eight grandchildren.

On a visit to Nashville in 1994, Stan took with him the first proofs of his book about the last month of World War II, *The Last Great Victory*. Granddaughter MaryAlison, a second-grader, noticed that the partial calendars illustrating various chapter headings had weeks of eight and even nine days instead of seven. She used her computer to design an appropriate seven-day calendar, a copy of which Stan faxed to his publisher.

During the early 1960s, the children clamored for a Christmas tree, which Stan refused to permit. As a way to circumvent him, Rodelle conceived the idea of the Stanley Tree, a spruce branch onto which the children hung miniature match-box books that they had illustrated to look like Stan's. The Stanley Tree has grown some four feet, its branches laden with miniature books that now include several made by the Weintraub grandchildren.

He has long had recognition as a foremost world authority on Bernard Shaw, but "Shaw scholar" does not describe the range and diversity of his research and publications. Rather than confine himself to one "field," Stan has always pursued his own interests, each book leading him to another figure or event that becomes the subject of a later book. Bernard Shaw led first to T. E. Shaw and then to others. Reggie Turner led to Beardsley, who in turn aroused interest in the 1890s periodicals *The Yellow Book* and *The Savoy*. Beardsley also led to Whistler and, through him, to several British and American figures, the subjects of *The Four Rossettis* and *The London Yankees*. This has even been true of the one book that he wrote on consignment, his biography *Victoria,* timed to appear on the 150th anniversary of her accession to the throne. He was already aware of connections between G.B.S. and the Widow of Windsor, and *Victoria* led directly to two other books—a biography of Disraeli and a life of Victoria's consort, Albert.

A 1995 Associated Press release erroneously but aptly identified Stan as a professor of "Arms and Humanities." His early interest in World War II and his service in Korea, combined with his studies of various Victorian and modern literary lives, resulted in *The Last Great Cause* (focusing on the cultural and literary responses to the Spanish Civil War), *Journey to Heartbreak* (Bernard Shaw during World War I), *A Stillness Heard Around the World* (an exhaustive treatment of the five days culminating in the 11 November 1918 Armistice—the publisher vetoed the original, and better, title *When the Shooting Stopped*), *Long Day's Journey Into War* (a narrative covering the forty-eight hours, due to the international date line, of 7 December 1941), and *The Last Great Victory* (a history of the last month of World War II—the publisher vetoed Stan's original "bookend" title, *Journey's End*). His early work with T. E. Lawrence resulted in two works co-authored with Rodelle, *Evolution of a Revolt* and *Lawrence of Arabia: The Literary Impulse*.

His four decades at Penn State have included thirty-five years editing *SHAW* and its predecessors, seven years editing the *Comparative Literature Studies Journal*, twenty-one years on the Penn State Press executive committee (one year as acting director), and twenty years as Director for the Institute for the Arts and Humanistic Studies. He is a senior professor in both English and Comparative Literature. To devote more time to research and to make it easier to spend time playing with and reading to the grandchildren, he has recently withdrawn from the press committee and has passed on the directorship of the Institute and the scholarly editorships to successors. He became sixty-five in April 1994, but his withdrawal from various activities is not a retirement as much as an attempt to prioritize his activities.

Stan usually works on three or four book projects simultaneously. In June and July 1982, for example, he was reading proofs for *The Playwright and the Pirate*, a *Dictionary of Literary Biography* volume, and *The Unexpected Shaw*, as well as transcribing and annotating Shaw's 1880 diary. He constantly finds material for various projects in highly unlikely places. He wrote to me in 1979, "Found an Armistice Day reference in Zelda Fitzgerald's *Save Me the Waltz*. Bet you couldn't have predicted that, let alone that I would have read it!"

His writing has brought him several awards, including a 1968 National Book Award nomination for *Beardsley*, the American Theatre Library Association's 1972 George Freedley Award for *Journey to Heartbreak*, and a Freedoms Foundation Award in 1980 for *London Yankees*. The Pennsylvania Humanities Council granted him its third Distinguished Humanist Award in 1985. *Whistler* was named one of the "30 Notable Books of the Year" in 1974. In 1991, *Long Day's Journey into War* made the "best" list of *Publishers Weekly, Library Journal*, the *New York Times Book Review*, and the New York Public Library.

Phil Young, who co-edited *Directions in Literary Criticism* with Stan in 1973, once remarked to me, "Everybody knows how many books Stan has written, but nobody seems to notice that each one is better than the one before." One reason for this is that Stan has never been one to shrink from the challenges of new approaches. Early in his career, he chose to develop the biography of a relationship, a form with few models, and when he decided to document the cultural response to the Spanish Civil War, the vastness of that enterprise did not deter him. When he embarked on his history of the Armistice, drawing upon hundreds of responses to his request for reminiscences, he called it "the hardest writing task I've given myself," and later he could have said the same about his history of the bombing of Pearl Harbor and later yet about his history of the last month of World War II, both of which draw upon even greater numbers of respondents.

Stan once defined his ambition as a writer: "I want to be read." He has certainly achieved that goal. Many of his works have gained wide readership, and his books remain reliable and invaluable sources of information long after their initial publication. *The Last Great Victory* has been the sixth of his books (the first was *Whistler* in 1974) selected by the Book-of-the-Month Club, and it went into its third printing within a month of its release date. For some weeks, Stan was making three or four radio appearances a day to talk about *Last Great Victory*, and on 16 August 1995, a station in Massachusetts canceled the Rush Limbaugh broadcast to extend Stan's time to an hour.

Stan's interest in his students involves him in quite a bit of correspondence. This is all the more amazing, since he is a two-finger typist who shifted to hitting the keys with the eraser ends of two pencils when arthritis made typing painful. As Stan's correspondents can attest, he is not one to waste paper. He has typed many letters on long-outdated *Shaw Review* stationery and on the backs of the galley proofs of his various books. During 1977, he took to using the blank side of unused copies of Penn State Form G5.6 (12–14–56), the purpose of which was to attest "unequivocally" that a candidate for employment at the university "is not a subversive person as the term 'subversive person' is defined by the Pennsylvania Loyalty Act."

How he can attend to correspondence on top of everything else that he does remains a mystery. He wrote to me on 7 December 1989 that "my stamina isn't what it was. For me a 14-hour day used to be easy. Now it's hard to do 10 hours." There is no question that he puts in long hours, but the combination of the concern, enthusiasm, and genius that distinguish Stan probably has more to do with his productivity.

Sources

Since this festschrift honoring Stan was to be a surprise, I could not approach him directly for information. I have relied heavily on his letters of the past two decades, and I am particularly grateful to Rodelle for answering my questions and for vetting this essay.

Stan's autobiographical writings include *The War in the Wards: Korea's Unknown Battle in a Prisoner-of-War Hospital Camp* (Garden City, N.Y.: Doubleday, 1964; revised, San Rafael, Calif.: Presidio, 1976); "Confessions of a Bookworm's Apprentice," *Town & Gown* (September 1984): 24–54; "Research as Fun" (unpublished typescript of a talk delivered to a local chapter of Phi Beta Kappa, April 1986); and "A Kid's War," *Contemporary Authors Autobiography Series* 20 (Detroit: Gale Research, 1994): 297–317. Helpful interviews are John F. Baker, "Stanley Weintraub," *Publishers Weekly* 205 (4 February 1974): 8–9; and Jean W. Ross, "The Practice of Biography: An Interview with Stanley Weintraub," in *Dictionary of Literary Biography Yearbook: 1982* (Detroit: Gale Research, 1983), 34–46.

Jo Chesworth, "Biography of a Biographer," *Town & Gown* (August 1990): 66–76, has some factual errors but quotes interviews with Stan, Rodelle, Mark, David, and Erica Weintraub, as well as with Shirley Rader and Charles Mann. John J. Conlon, "Stanley Weintraub (17 April 1929–   )," *Dictionary of Literary Biography, Volume III: American Literary Biographers, Second Series* (Detroit: Gale Research, 1991), 285–99, presents a useful overview of Stan's career, with particular attention to his biographical and historic works.

On Shaw

"Oh, the Dreaming, the Dreaming": *Arms and the Man*

RODELLE WEINTRAUB

EVEN the earliest of Shaw's plays demonstrate an understanding of dream theory that not only preceded Freud's interpretations but could be considered, in the words of Barbara Bellow Watson, "an early literary parallel" to Freudianism.[1] Although Freud's *Interpretation of Dreams* had been published in a small edition in German in 1899, this espousal of the significance of dreams had not yet received much attention by an English-speaking audience outside the ranks of the earliest Freudian disciples prior to Freud's lecture trip to the United States in 1909. After the 1909 lecture trip, Freud's theories were known on both sides of the ocean, and a "veritable wave of dream plays hit Broadway."[2] His impact on the more traditional British stage was yet to come.

Critics, in general, excepting Watson, Sidney Albert (who in his article "Reflections on Shaw and Psychoanalysis" pointed out some important, yet generally overlooked, relationships of Shaw to psychoanalysis),[3] and myself, have not only not seen any Freudian elements in Shaw's plays but have categorically denied them. Maurice Valency went so far as to say that "there is not the slightest evidence that Shaw had any inkling of what was being said" at the first International Psychoanalytic Congress in 1908.[4] That Shaw does not make any specific reference to Freud until 1923, however, does not mean that Shaw was unaware of psychoanalysis nor that he made no use of Freudian-like situations in his plays.

Exactly when and if Shaw read Freud's *Interpretation of Dreams* can only be speculative. He did know Ernest Jones, a fellow Fabian and early Freud disciple. Jones was later Freud's biographer. Shaw met frequently with Jones, read his articles on psychoanalysis, and is even referred to by Jones in his 1910 article, "The Oedipus Complex as an Explanation of Hamlet's Mystery."[5] Not having read Freud's interpretation of dreams does not preclude Shaw from intuitively understanding the dream theories about which Freud would write. Freud himself claimed to have learned from the poets and philosophers who had "discovered the unconscious before I did," and he included playwrights among those poets and philosophers.[6] Whatever Shaw's specific acquaintance with Freudian dream insights, some general awareness of their import seems to be suggested in his lengthy 14 March 1911 letter to Gilbert Murray. "I am not very appreciative of the psychiatrists," Shaw wrote, "but there may be something in their theory that repressed instincts, though subconscious, play a considerable part in our lives . . . and . . . the suppression apparently vanishes in sleep."[7] It would be surprising if a playwright as prolific and intuitively knowledgeable as Shaw would not have written any dream plays other than conventional literary dream plays such as the *Don Juan in Hell* interlude in *Man and Superman* and the epilogue to *Saint Joan*.

It is now generally accepted, whether or not one be a Freudian, that dreams function as a problem-solving mechanism. To Freud the dream begins with some unfinished business that arouses conflicts from all periods of life. It functions as an adult version of the childhood fantasy battles about oral, anal, phallic, or childishly oedipal wishes.[8] The dream unites the conflicts and presents them in a condensed but ambiguous manner without regard to logical niceties. The conflict can then be settled along the lines of a wish fulfilled.[9]

In a wish fulfillment dream play, the underlying fantasy reflects upon and illuminates the manifest surface of the play in much the same way as the latent dream represents the thoughts and feelings of the manifest dream (152). As we watch the play unfold, the subtext illuminates the narrative and aids us, consciously or otherwise, in comprehending it. To Freud the manifest dream is "composed of various fragments . . . held together by a binding medium, so that the designs that appear on it do not belong to the original [meaning]" (73). It is, therefore, important that the latent content of the dream, or the dream play, not be judged solely by its manifest content, even when it tells a well-organized story. "It must be seen as containing a hidden meaning which needs to be unscrambled to find its original meaning" (74). The stories in the manifest dream and the latent dream, or in the manifest play and the underlying fantasy, need not be totally separate. Each contains the same idea expressed in different forms, and the feelings in the manifest dream or play may be undistorted and accurately represent the feelings of the latent dream (73). The resolution of one character's problem in the manifest play is not totally unrelated to the solving of the dreamer's problem in the dream play. It may even be a means to the solution of that problem. As the episodes in the manifest dream help unravel the conflicts hidden in the latent dream, the dreamer's frustrations and feelings are paralleled in each.

A brief look at what I believe to be Shaw's earliest dream play will demonstrate how, in 1894, Shaw intuitively made use of a wish fulfillment dream to write his first fantasy play, the farcical *Arms and the Man*. Although theoretically set in Bulgaria, Shaw did not select an actual locale and war for the play until after he had completed a draft of it. Thirty years after the play was first performed, the Bulgarian minister to Germany protested a Berlin revival of *Arms and the Man*. Shaw wrote to the *Berliner Tageblatt*, reminding its readers that it was "the business of the writer of a comedy to wound the susceptibilities of his audience." Real comedy, he explained, was possible "only in a highly civilised country; for in a comparatively barbarous one the people cannot bear to have their follies ridiculed.... Barbarous Bulgarians ... behave exactly as my own countrymen behaved when Synge's *Playboy of the Western World* was performed in Dublin; they were infuriated by what seems to them to be a personal insult."[10] What Shaw didn't add was that a dozen years before Synge had written *Playboy*, most likely Shaw himself had his own native Ireland in mind when he wrote *Arms and the Man* and had been satirizing impoverished, gentility-ridden Ireland. But he did it subtly and safely by claiming to have set his scene in remote Bulgaria, much as, in his adaptation of *Fathers and Sons*, Brian Friel's Russia seems more early twentieth-century Ireland than mid–nineteenth-century Russia. The imposition by the English National Theatre of an English class system on a Russian society again makes one think of a British Isles setting. Ireland, like the Bulgaria of Shaw's play, had deliberately been kept a century behind the times, often by absentee English landlords. Underdeveloped but aspiring Ireland was just beginning to enter the modern world of regular baths, of a population that could read books, of electric bells and other symbols of emergence from feudalism. The romantic notion of fighting for freedom from colonial domination, though real in a Balkan setting, could in 1894 still be only an Irish dream to be realized by a later generation.

In *Arms and the Man*, Raina, a bored immature young woman, a member of the newly risen aristocracy, whose mother claims she can trace her ancestry at least twenty years, is engaged to a handsome cavalry officer whom her father, Major Petkoff, has selected for her. Even though her family considers him a wonderful match, he bores her. Her mother is more enamored of the idea of having Sergius as a son-in-law than Raina is of having him as a husband. Raina admits that her romanticized ideas about him are just that. Louka, Raina's maid, is also bored with her fiancé, the servant Nicola. Louka, who accuses Nicola of having the soul of a servant whose aspirations are limited to having his own shop one day, wants to become a lady. The pompous Sergius is the man who can make her one. Into this household comes Captain Bluntschli, the "chocolate soldier," a Swiss mercenary fighting for the Serbs. Having escaped the battle, he has found refuge in Raina's bedroom. The rest of the story progresses as a farce should, until the mismatched couples are correctly matched with the mates of their choice. Raina gets Bluntschli, whose given name she never learns but whose rank is the highest known in Switzerland—free citizen—the irony of which could be immediately understood in Ireland. Louka gets Sergius. Bluntschli, who ran away from home to escape going into his father's hotelier business, has now inherited it and has two hundred horses; seventy carriages; thousands of sheets; eiderdowns; knives, forks, and spoons; six palatial establishments; four medals; and the rank of an officer and standing of a gentleman. Mrs. Petkoff gets a son-in-law whose wealth is beyond anything she could have imagined, or dreamt. Nicola will no longer be a servant and may even become the manager of one of Bluntschli's hotels. The war is ended. Bulgaria is free. All the men are heroes. Everyone gets what he or she has wanted, even if it is not what had been desired at the beginning of the play.

But the most unlikely things occur. Bluntschli, having sought refuge by climbing up a drain pipe, has no interest in raping Raina. All he wants to do is sleep. Raina, who should be terrified at having this intruder in her bedroom, is delighted by his presence and disappointed at his indifference. Raina's mother, soldiers, and Louka enter the bedroom where Bluntschli is not very well hidden. In fact his pistol is in plain sight. But no one, except for Louka, sees him or the pistol. Rather than calling attention to the presence of an enemy soldier in the Major's daughter's bedroom, Louka notes the pistol's presence and does not mention it. Raina gives Bluntschli her father's coat to wear and puts her picture in its pocket, and, with the assistance of her mother and Louka, she helps him make his escape. Bluntschli, who meets with the Major to arrange the peace, does not find the picture. He then tries to return the coat, which causes much confusion, and is encountered by the Major who welcomes him into his home as the hero the Major thinks he is. Major Petkoff is very confused by all that is happening, especially about his coat. At first he cannot find it. Then it mysteriously appears in his closet with burst seams, and he finds the picture of Raina in the pocket. To the father, the inscription, "Raina, to her Chocolate Cream Soldier: a Souvenir," is nonsensical. When Petkoff reaches into his pocket for the picture, it has disappeared. It is now Bluntschli who possesses the picture. Sergius, tired of the strain of the "higher love" with Raina seeks relief with Louka. The wily maidservant tricks him into promising that the next time he touches her, she will be his affianced wife. When she reminds him of his promise but permits him to back out of it, he stolidly refuses, his refusal hardly a realistic action for a member of the aristocracy, even in primitive Bulgaria. Bluntschli agrees to marry Raina only after he discovers that she is much older than he had first thought. And all through the play the characters talk of dreams and dreaming.

Could this farce then, at one level, be a dream? If so, whose dream might it be, for there must be a dreamer. In some way the dream must work out an unresolved problem for the dreamer. And what clues has the playwright given to enable us intuitively to understand the subtext of this dream play? We meet Raina in her bedroom, preparing for bed. She is—or is she?—awakened to find Bluntschli in her room. In the beginning of the play, Raina seems to us, and to Bluntschli, not yet to be a woman. She is her father's child, living in his house, cared for by servants as if she were still a child, engaged to a man selected for her by her father. She confesses that her head is full of romantic notions. But when she hears of the battle, her first thought is not for Sergius but for her father. By the end of the play, Raina has freed herself from her father and his choice of a husband for her. She has grown up and can at last leave her father's household. In the process of doing so, she actually dresses Bluntschli in her father's coat, thereby effecting the transformation before us. So we have a possible dreamer, a problem in the manifest play (who will Raina marry?), and a related problem in the latent play (can Raina outgrow her oedipal attraction for her father and replace it with a mature woman's sexuality?).

What clues has the playwright given us to enable us to discern the subtext of this dream play? In a dream play, as in a dream, there is an air of unreality, of fantasy, about the proceedings. Events seem sharply divorced from one another. Strindberg, explaining his 1901 *Dream Play,* described "a medley of memories, experiences, free fancies, absurdities and improvisations."[11] William Archer, reviewing the play in 1894, wrote that the reader

> must not expect a humdrum, rational, steady-going farce . . . bearing a well-understood conventional relation to real life. Let him rather look for a fantastic, psychological extravaganza, in which drama, farce, and Gilbertian irony keep flashing past the bewildered eye, as in a sort of merry-go-round; so quickly that one gives up the attempt to discriminate

between them. . . . By attempting to fix his action down to solid earth [Bulgaria] he simply emphasizes its unreality. . . . At the end of the first act we do not quite know where the play is coming in.[12]

The play opens in a lady's bedchamber. The first word of the stage directions is "*Night.*"[13] A distant peak, "*wonderfully white and beautiful,*" framed by a window, though miles away, seems close at hand. "*The interior of the room is not like anything to be seen in the west of Europe.*" The room is lighted by only two candles and whatever light the night sky sheds. On a chest of drawers is a pile of novels, a box of chocolates, and a photograph of an extremely handsome officer, whose lofty bearing and "*magnetic glance can be felt even from the portrait,*" and one of the two candles. A young woman is gazing at what Shaw called the snowy "*Balkans.*"[14] Her "*reverie is interrupted.*" The play has not yet begun, but we are already being prepared for an illusionary world, one in which reality is but an assumption of daylight awakening. Before a word is spoken, we are presented with an array of Freudian-like dream symbols that startle the critic almost a century later, for how could Shaw have intuitively "known" what psychiatrists would later tell us:

> . . . in the dream, human anatomy is symbolized by buildings, with windows and doors corresponding to the body orifices. . . . Symbolization borrows heavily from nature to represent anatomical parts and zones: . . . mountains frequently appear. . . . All articles that enclose space or are capable of being entered qualify as symbolic representation of female genitalia. . . . Stoves, closets and cupboards refer more to the uterus than to the vagina. . . . The street, too, is a sexual symbol—the place for traffic with women. . . . The phallus is symbolized by anything resembling it in form, function, or general properties."[15]

So here we have, rather heavy-handedly, a phallus—the candle—erect upon a uterus—the chest of drawers, the scene framed by a symbolic vulva in which the labia surround a clitoris—the mountain within the window frame. The mouth can also represent a vagina, eating can represent intercourse, and even the chocolate of the "chocolate-cream soldier," which is in a box upon the chest of drawers, has immediate sexual symbolism that increases throughout the play.

Our dreamer, who has had her reverie interrupted by her mother, has a head full of romantic notions. She confesses to her mother, "I sometimes used to doubt whether [our heroic ideals] were anything but dreams" and wonders whether they might not have come into our heads, "because we are so fond of reading Byron and Pushkin and because we were so delighted with the opera that season at Bucharest. Real life is seldom like that." Only fourteen speeches into the play, the playwright has overtly suggested that what we are seeing may be other than it first appears. Several times in the first act stage directions, Shaw uses *dream:* "her *dreams* of glory rush back on her"; "*dreamily,* lulled by her voice," and the scene ends after Bluntschli has hypnotically repeated "sleep, sleep, sleep, sleep, slee— . . . danger, danger, danger, Where's danger? Mus' find it . . . . What am I looking for? Sleep—danger—dont know." *A blissful expression comes into his face. . . . he . . . falls fast asleep instantly.* In the first speech of the second act, Shaw again uses *dreams:* "she never *dreams.*" Later in this act, Raina tells Sergius that while he was at battle proving himself, she was "at home—*dreaming*—." In the first stage direction for Raina in act 3, Shaw has her "*suddenly coming out of her reverie,*" and her father says, "She's *dreaming,* as usual."

Dreams are often triggered by some incident that occurs just before retiring. Here Shaw gives us not one incident but a veritable glut. Raina goes to bed after being told by her mother that there has been a great battle in which Sergius, her fiancé, had been a splendid hero, and after being warned by the maid Louka that there are Serbian soldiers wandering the town. By her bed is the picture of the over sentimentalized lover about whom Raina has doubts and a box of chocolates that will play a prominent role in the rest of the scene. She retires with knowledge of a glorious battle in which Sergius has been the hero and with a warning about strange soldiers wandering the town. Gazing at her hero's picture, Raina utters, "I shall never be unworthy of you any more, . . . never, never, never"; she either falls asleep and dreams the rest of the play or is instantly unfaithful, whether or not she be unworthy, to Sergius. A man enters her bedchamber, having mounted the drainpipe to do so. He takes her cloak, and first having threatened to shoot her if she makes any noise, he throws his pistol onto an ottoman. Hearing soldiers approach, he hides behind a curtain. Louka, but no one else, sees the pistol, and she says nothing. After everyone leaves, Raina sits on the pistol, jumping up with a scream. When Raina asks Bluntschli to leave as he came, sliding down the waterpipe, he protests, "Stop. Wait. I cant! I darenot! The very thought of it makes me giddy." Could he be expressing a Freudian fear of castration?

We are now only seven printed pages into the first scene, and the dream allusions and dream symbols are overwhelming. The snowy white peak in the night sky, the upright drainpipe that can be mounted but which Bluntschli cannot descend, and the exposed pistol that only Louka sees and on which Raina sits cannot be mere accidents. In fact when Shaw first wrote the play, only Raina, like Louka in the final version, saw the pistol, but when he later revised it, he had Raina actually sit on the exposed but unloaded penis symbol. This last change suggests that Shaw had at first used Freudian symbolism intuitively, but later he consciously made the parallels more obvious.

Strindberg notes that characters in a dream, "split, double, multiply, vanish, solidify, blur, clarify."[16] Are there any characters in *Arms and the Man* who could fit Strindberg's definition? Raina and Louka are about the same age, and both are attractive to the same man, Sergius. Raina, the aristocratic woman, appeals to Sergius's higher love, but it is Louka whom he finds sexually appealing. By marrying Bluntschli, Raina will become a commoner, whereas Louka, in marrying Sergius, becomes an aristocrat. Of some Freudian import, however, is that Louka, in marrying Sergius, the father substitute, can act out the forbidden father-daughter incest. By doing so she frees her other self, Raina, who can move on to a more mature relationship with Bluntschli. A third person who may be part of the Raina-Louka trilogy is Mrs. Petkoff, the mother-woman who is married to Raina's father and who finds Sergius more attractive than her daughter does. All three women participate in hiding Bluntschli, his escape, and in the deception of both the Major and Sergius.

Sergius and Major Petkoff could be cut from the same cloth, both upstart aristocrats and officers in the Bulgarian army. Neither man regards Raina as a mature woman. Sergius has placed her on a pedestal. She is his queen, his lady, and his saint. But his higher love for her is very tiring for both of them. Petkoff thinks of her as a child and addresses her as "my little pet girl." Raina tells her mother, "I know Sergius is your pet. I sometimes wish you could marry him instead of me." If Sergius is another form of the father character, Raina's mother *is* married to him, and Raina is recognizing her own need to be released from oedipal conflict.

Another possible character split occurs in Bluntschli-Nicola. Both are outsiders in this aristocratic household: Nicola, as a commoner working as a servant but keeping the household in running order; Bluntschli as the Swiss mercenary who actually commands the war and organizes the peace. Both are examples of Shaw's practical men of business, and both are instrumental in changing the status of Louka-Raina. Nicola makes Louka's marriage to Sergius possible, as well as her becoming an aristocrat—first by educating her in the proper appearance and behavior of a maidservant and then by releasing her graciously from her engagement to him. Bluntschli will elevate Raina from the status of daughter of an aristocrat to wife of a citizen, and he will release her from her prolonged childhood in the Petkoff household. There is the suggestion at the end of the play that Bluntschli the hotel chain owner will make Nicola a hotel manager. It seems of little importance that Nicola has no surname—he is only a servant—and that Bluntschli has no given name, about which his wife-to-be seems not in the least curious.

In both the manifest play and the latent play, Raina has gained maturity and the husband of her choice. The play's mischievous laughter delights audiences as much now as it did when the play was Shaw's first commercial success in 1894, and it conceals its dream dimension.

Notes

1. Barbara Bellow Watson, *A Shavian Guide to the Intelligent Woman* (New York: Norton, 1964), 132–33. Watson hypothesizes about Shaw's having created an early literary parallel to Freudianism.
2. W. David Sievers, *Freud on Broadway* (New York: Hermitage Press, 1955), 48.
3. Sidney P. Albert, "Reflections on Shaw and Psychoanalysis," *Modern Drama* 14 (September 1971): 176–77.
4. Maurice Valency, *The Cart and the Trumpet* (New York: Oxford University Press, 1973), 293.
5. Ernest Jones, *Hamlet and Oedipus* (Garden City: Doubleday Anchor Books, 1954), 82–83. Originally printed as an exposition of a footnote in Freud's "Traumdeutung" under the title of "The Oedipus Complex as an Explanation of Hamlet's Mystery," in *The American Journal of Psychology* (January 1910).
6. Meredith Ann Skura, *The Literary Use of Psychoanalytic Process* (New Haven: Yale University Press, 1981), 1.
7. Dan H. Laurence, ed., *Bernard Shaw, Collected Letters, 1911–1925* (New York: Viking, 1985), 18. In *Collected Letters 1926–1950* (1988), Laurence states, "It is doubtful if Shaw had more than a second-hand acquaintance with the works of Sigmund Freud (1856–1939), though he made frequent references to him in the later correspondence" (391). This volume includes five letters in which Shaw mentions Freud or Freudianism. There are no references to Freud in the earlier three volumes of *Collected Letters*.
8. Skura, *Literary Use*, 67.
9. Walter A. Stewart and Lucy Freeman, *The Secret of Dreams* (New York: Macmillan Co., 1972), 73. Further references to this work will be cited in the text.
10. "Ein Brief Bernard Shaws," *Berliner Tageblatt*, 6 (October 1924): 2.
11. Quoted in Margery Morgan, *The Shavian Playground* (London: Methuen and Co., 1972), 200.
12. William Archer, initialed notice, *World*, 25 April 1894.
13. All quotations from the play are from volume 1, *Bernard Shaw Collected Plays with Their Prefaces* (London: Max Reinhardt, 1972), 389–472.
14. Apparently Shaw did not realize that it was not the mountains that were called the "Balkans."

15. Leon L. Altman, *The Dream in Psychoanalysis* (New York: International Universities Press, Inc., 1975), 24–25. Some commonly accepted Freudian dream symbols used by Shaw include:

airplane, gun, drainpipe: penis
flying, rhythmic activity, exercise: intercourse
rooms, windows: uterus, womb
breaking of glass: intercourse, penetration, defloration
mouth: vagina
landscape, woods: pubic hair

16. Morgan, *Shavian Playground*, 200.

Bernard Shaw's Bonaparte: Life Force or Death Wish?

Michel W. Pharand

Many early stage treatments of Napoleon Bonaparte portrayed him as the oversimplified hero of popular mythology, or, in the words of one critic, as "an illustrative example, chosen for powerful emotional effect, of the precariousness of human happiness in the face of a hostile destiny."[1] But with characteristic mischief, Bernard Shaw debunked this icon in a one-act play, *The Man of Destiny*,[2] a not so trivial playlet in which the twenty-seven-year-old general is outmaneuvered and outwitted by a woman. In fact one might say that Shaw's Bonaparte is the antithesis of the hero of those "romanticist" playwrights who preferred their history diluted with equal parts of myth and fantasy. Moreover, in *The Man of Destiny*, he is also the first of two demystifications of French military leaders. Shaw's version of Joan of Arc's trial was still three decades away.

Shaw dismissed his playlet as "ridiculous," "a mere stage brutality," "a silly little play," a "baby comedietta," a "bravura piece to display the virtuosity of the two principal performers," "a display of my knowledge of stage tricks," and "a harlequinade."[3] William Archer agreed: his review published one month after the play's three performances calls it "a piece of mechanical and meaningless claptrap."[4] Whatever its shortcomings, *The Man of Destiny* is a gem of characterization in miniature, perhaps even "one of the great *jeux d'esprits* of dramatic literature" (Berst, 85). Not only is it Shaw's most developed—albeit whimsical—characterization of the French hero; it is also his very first stage portrayal of any famous historical figure. More importantly, Shaw's Bonaparte is an early seriocomic embodiment of the Life Force, an incarnation that bears a striking resemblance to Shaw himself.

But the play is only one of Shaw's attempts to come to terms with an historical figure who seemed to embody the Life Force. Over time Shaw found himself in an increasingly painful dilemma. As he matured he saw Bonaparte increasingly as a monster, and if Bonaparte did embody the Life Force, then the Life Force was also monstrous. In the end Shaw could not confront the full implications of his discovery, for to have done so would have required an extensive and disorganizing personal redefinition. His solution, as we will see, was to revert to a bellicose defense of the French hero. Therefore, if we examine briefly what Shaw's Bonaparte owes to biography and art, compare him with one famous contemporary French stage Napoleon, and analyze how Shaw's estimate of the historical Bonaparte varied with the times, we will better understand why the very idea of a Napoleon in the world remained essential to Shaw's worldview, and why this Great Man continued to fascinate Shaw to the end of his life.

Aside from the lighthearted trivialization of his play and despite its subtitle "A Fictitious Paragraph of History," Shaw was more than a little intrigued by Bonaparte the man. He doubtless knew Arthur Lévy's *Napoléon intime* (1893), translated the next year as *The Private Life of Napoleon*. He was also familiar with the history behind his "fictitious paragraph": the Empress Joséphine once admitted in a letter that if she were to marry the general, Vicomte Paul François de Barras would have her husband named as commander of the army in Italy.[5] However, because there is no evidence that Napoleon obtained the promotion by means other than military competence, the episode in *The Man of Destiny* remains pure invention.

Moreover, although Shaw claimed to have written his play "out of the vacacitude of the densest historical and geographical ignorance" (*Letters 1874–1897*, 552), there is evidence to the contrary. On 27 August 1895, three days after completing the first version of the play, Shaw wrote to T. Fisher Unwin to obtain the issues of *Century Magazine* (New York) in which William Milligan Sloane's *Life of Napoleon Bonaparte* was being run serially (from November 1894 to October 1896). Shaw was still reading Sloane as late as 30 December,[6] and Charles Berst has convincingly shown how Sloane's *Life* played a greater part in the delineation of Napoleon's character than was hitherto believed, demonstrating that Shaw "adapted materials from the biography to strengthen and refine the play's historical references, characters, dramatic values, and theme" (Berst, 110). By close scrutiny of the "extensively, almost chaotically revised" facsimile manuscript, he demonstrates how Shaw incorporated some of Sloane's ideas on Napoleon's personality, the Napoleon-Josephine-Barras love triangle, and especially the "theatre-of-life" metaphor, wherein Napoleon (in Sloane's words) was a "leading actor" who played out "a human tragicomedy" (cf. also 112–14). That Shaw consulted whatever documents were available is not surprising, because he typically used historical materials to suit his purpose. He would do so to an even greater extent with the translated transcripts of the trial of Joan of Arc while writing *Saint Joan*.

Shaw not only examined published sources for his psychological portrait of Bonaparte, but to a degree he based his physical portrait on artistic ones, although he was careful to dissociate his general from the common heroic representations. One stage direction cautions that his general is not the Napoleon of Paul Delaroche or Jean-Louis Meissonier, whose well-known paintings are the usual mid-nineteenth-century apotheoses of a successful conqueror "which later ages expect of him" (*Plays* 1: 618). Shaw was recalling Meissonier's *Napoleon in 1814* (1863) and *Campaign of France* (1864), and Delaroche's *Napoleon at Fontainebleau* (1845), *Napoleon Crossing the Alps* (1848), and *Napoleon at Saint Helena* (1852), all exhibited in London in Shaw's day.[7] These dignified and military scenes are far removed from our first glimpse in *The Man of Destiny* of a young man seated at a table hard at work while finishing a meal, his map under a clutter of dishes and glasses, his long hair trailing into the risotto. It has been suggested that Shaw's tableau may have been partially inspired by an untitled painting (ca. 1875–85) by the historical artist François Flameng, depicting a youthful, long-haired Napoleon working at a table piled with books and papers. Shaw's diary for 31 March 1894 notes the opening of "François Flameng's Napoleon pictures at the Goupil Gallery" (*Diaries*, 1023). Although he missed the opening, it is likely that Shaw returned to the Goupil later and remembered the painting (*Unexpected Shaw*, 70).

Despite the playlet's debt to historical and artistic sources, Shaw's man of destiny thrives not on verisimilitude but on domestic discord: the general is fighting in the boudoir rather than on the battlefield, trying to avert at all costs a personal, not a military, defeat. The discovery of a billet-doux from Joséphine to his *Directeur* Barras—with whom she has some influence in advancing her husband's career—would force him to fight a duel for his wife's honor. Bonaparte realizes that "by taking care not to know" (*Plays* 1: 638), as he puts it, he could avoid being ridiculed as a cuckold, alienated by his future benefactor, and embroiled in a public scandal that could ruin his career. A recent performance of the play was followed by a symposium in which it was observed that *The Man of Destiny* is precisely about being realistic, about Napoleon's "various intersections" with the truth.[8] Shaw's young Napoleon is involved in a battle of wits for personal and political survival, as well as in a fight to preserve his dignity in the face of scandal: his posturing and theatricality, combined with a vicious streak and nervous energy, often make him behave like a man on the edge. He refers to himself as a "vile vulgar Corsican adventurer" (642), and when he is informed that there is no red ink, he facetiously tells the innkeeper, "Kill something and bring me its blood" (612). The wit does not altogether mitigate his heartlessness, however, which emerges later in his willingness to sacrifice the foolish Lieutenant to safeguard his public image. Shaw's Bonaparte may be somewhat ruthless, but we will see that this is often the only way that embodiments of the Life Force can carry out its design for the eventual improvement of the human race.

But can this madcap avatar really be in earnest? Is this young Bonaparte, as was so often the case with Shaw, too much the posturing actor for his pronouncements to be taken seriously? Shaw has chosen to involve him in what has been called "a long mutual seduction, a play of sexual titillation" (*SHAW* 14: 59) in which posturing and theatrics prevail. It may be precisely the paradoxical nature of this cruel-yet-comic figure that Shaw wishes to underline by the Great Man's Shavian histrionics and hyperbole. According to Berst, some of the key elements in *The Man of Destiny* include role-playing, pretense, deception, bluffing, trickery, masking and unmasking, and a life-as-theater theme that is the play's "one continuous dominating issue" (Berst, 87, 94). For example Napoleon "deliberately poses for an oration" on fear, which he calls the only "universal passion" and "the mainspring of war," even denying there is any such thing as a real hero when the Lady calls him one (*Plays* 1: 630). "I win battles for humanity: for my country, not for myself," he says (631). "Self-sacrifice is the foundation of all true nobility of character," he proclaims (632). There is some truth to these rather pompous pronouncements, and it is clear that Bonaparte embodies for Shaw the essence of Creative Evolution: "You teach us what we all might be," the Lady tells him, "if we had the will and courage" (633). Unfortunately young Bonaparte is also caught in the grip of the Life Force itself by the extravagant Joséphine, a woman who has lied to him about her age and income and who is incapable of fidelity to people or principles (640). Yet he cannot help loving her. The ultimate irony is that despite his ambition, talent for warfare, flair for public posturing, and a certain ruthless temperament, Shaw's Bonaparte is nonetheless a slave to his own passions. One must take him seriously precisely because he is human and not the godlike icon of historical romance.

One must also take him seriously because he is very much like Shaw. He has been called "one of Shaw's masterful realists, unhampered by idealism or altruism, by conscience or morality."[9] For Bonaparte heroism is a matter of survival, by trickery if necessary. To avoid dishonor, he must rid himself of the bundle of dispatches as if they had never existed, and at the very end of the play, the incriminating billet-doux is destroyed: "Caesar's wife is above suspicion. Burn it" (661).

In doing what is most expedient, Bonaparte resembles Shaw himself. Maurice Valency goes so far as to observe that in the young general "it is far easier to recognize Shaw at the age of thirty-nine than Napoleon at twenty-six."[10] For although he is powerless against the Life Force, Bonaparte can at least try to explain it: the underlying premise of his final, grandiloquent diatribe against the English is Creative Evolution, Shaw's credo of human perfectibility. In this light, *The Man of Destiny* concerns two issues of some interest to Shaw: religion and nationality. One could say that Napoleon is outwitted by heredity itself, because the Lady's grandfather was English—which accounts for her "conscience," "devotion," "self-sacrifice," and "goodness"—and her grandmother Irish, which accounts for her "brains" (657, 659). The English, whom Bonaparte criticizes as a race chained to its rigid principles and moral convictions (657–59), seem a lost cause entirely. In fact, one might almost believe that Shaw's admiration for the Napoleon figure owes something to his own exasperation with the English. "It seems hardly possible," Shaw wrote three years later, "that the British army at the battle of Waterloo did not include at least one Englishman intelligent enough to hope, for the sake of his country and humanity, that Napoleon might defeat the allied sovereigns."[11] As we shall see, this is one of Shaw's less radical statements.

Thus did Shaw create a Bonaparte in his own image, and the stage directions complete the self-portrait: an "original observer" with "prodigious powers of work, and a clear realistic knowledge of human nature in public affairs," "imaginative without illusions, and creative without religion, loyalty, patriotism or any of the common ideals" (607–8). What is this if not the Life Force in action? The essential feature of Shaw's Napoleonic ideal is that only someone capable of changing the destiny of nations is of any value to Shaw who, in his own struggling way, considered himself capable of doing so. Jack Tanner's "Revolutionist's Handbook," for example, goes so far as to claim that real change is impossible "until there is an England in which every man is a Cromwell, a France in which every man is a Napoleon, a Rome in which every man is a Caesar, a Germany in which every man is a Luther plus a Goethe" (*Plays* 2: 751). Of course this is Tanner, not Shaw. Nevertheless, Shaw firmly believed that an individual will to power is necessary for world progress. He may have overstated his case when he wrote to Gilbert Murray in 1915, but he leaves little doubt as to how far thought can reach: "Not like Napoleon, who said 'I make circumstances' or like me, who, going one better than Nap, say '*I* am a circumstance'" (*Letters 1911–1925*, 301, Shaw's emphasis).

In contrast to Shaw's Bonaparte, it is instructive to examine the stage Napoleon of a playwright whom Shaw was forever berating as the nadir of French drama: Victorien Sardou, whose *Madame Sans-Gêne* (1893) represented for Shaw yet another example of French incompetence in writing effectively for the stage. Shaw had begun his own Napoleon play on 10 May 1895 and was still working on it when he saw the French version of Sardou's play on 8 July. Although Shaw may have "adopted or paralleled" some of Sardou's plot or prop devices in later stages of his draft, *The Man of Destiny* is not so much an "answer" to Sardou as a touchstone for his theater reviews (Berst, 92–93). "I have never seen a French play of which I understood less," he wrote, calling it "a huge mock historic melodrama which never for a moment produces the faintest conviction," a work in which Sardou managed to combine "the maximum of expenditure and idle chatter with the minimum of drama."[12] When he reviewed the 10 April 1897 performance of the English version, he was no less scathing: Ellen Terry had sailed "the Lyceum ship into the shallows of Sardoodledom," and Sardou's Napoleon was reduced to "nothing but the jealous husband of a thousand fashionable dramas, talking Buonapartiana" (*Drama Observed*, 827, 831). The roles were unchallenging, settings were garish, and the literal translation was an odd mixture of ready-made locutions and artificial eloquence. Nonetheless, Shaw defended Terry from critics who accused her of portraying a vulgar character, on the grounds that Madame Sans-Gêne, a washerwoman, must needs be coarse and that slang befits a laundress-turned-duchess.

Sardou's play is eminently forgettable, but Shaw's defense of Ellen Terry's Sans-Gêne shows that he recognized even in a Sardou character certain worthy (that is, Shavian) traits: realism, iconoclasm, a determined will, and a passion for survival. In fact, Shaw was even approached to write an English version of Sardou's Napoleon play as an opera, but he refused for lack of time, "time meaning will," he noted. But he added that if they had asked him to do it for Ellen Terry, he "would have obliterated them from the surface of the globe" (*Letters 1874–1897*, 565). Such an opera could have become Shaw's most ironic triumph: with his own adaptation of a Sardou melodrama on the English stage—perhaps even on the Parisian stage—once and for all he could have taught the French in a most pragmatic way a lesson he believed they desperately needed to learn: how to write a good play.

What is interesting is that these two "Napoleon plays" focus on two different characters: Shaw's is mostly Napoleon, Sardou's mostly Catherine, Madame Sans-Gêne. In her use of idioms and slang amidst the aristocrats at court, Catherine recalls the faltering Eliza Doolittle. But unlike Shaw's flower girl, who is merely playing the part of a princess and dissimulating her lowly origins and cockney accent, Catherine has married into the nobility and has no qualms about her old profession or rough language. Because she is now legitimately part of the aristocracy, she can boast: "Blanchisseuse, oui, princesse. Et j' m'en cache pas, vous voyez! Y a pas d' sot métier, y a que de sottes gens! Qu' si j' parle l' jargon du peuple, c'est que j'en suis, du peuple, et en belle compagnie, j'peux l'dire, . . ." (Laundress, yes, princess. And as ya can see, I don't hide it! There ain't no stupid occupations, they's only stupid people! 'Cause if I speak the lingo of the people, it's 'cause I'm part o' the people, and in good company, I'll say).[13] If Sardou's Napoleon is merely a stereotypical jealous husband, there is something endearing about his feisty young Catherine, a woman who used to air "dirty linen" in public—and who metaphorically still does.

The differences between the two plays do not eclipse resemblances that may or may not be due to Shaw's having seen *Madame Sans-Gêne* while writing *The Man of Destiny*. Arthur Ganz points out that in both plays, "Napoleon flirts with and loses his temper with a clever woman trying to protect a secret of his wife's, and in both he intrigues for and intercepts a letter concerning her fidelity."[14] But the resemblance ends there. Like other successful historical comedies, *Madame Sans-Gêne* is an example of historical events "reduced to the level of domestic trivia" (Howarth, 139). On the other hand, *The Man of Destiny*, as a parodic interpretation of romantic comedy, is "openly subversive of the established tradition" (Valency, 146). In the end, Sardou's melodrama is little more than a flourish of period costumes and settings, whereas Shaw wanted "to present something of Napoleon's spirit and will, the human qualities that raise a Man of Destiny above the ordinary jealous husband."[15] It remains to be seen how long Shaw would continue to uphold that "spirit and will" in the turbulent years that followed.

Shaw's stage coda to the Napoleon theme occurred immediately after the Great War. It took the form of the "saturnine and self-centred" general in military uniform of *Back to Methuselah* (1918–20), Cain Adamson Napoleon, whose opening line reveals him to be an incarnation of Shaw's earlier Bonaparte: "I am the Man of Destiny," he proclaims. And although his encounter with the Veiled Woman is also reminiscent of the younger Napoleon's scene with the Strange Lady two decades earlier, there is a note of anguish and anger in Shaw's attitude to the Napoleon figure now. One senses in this new portrayal a disillusionment stemming from Shaw's struggle to master his own postwar bitterness. The result is a pronouncement on the folly of warfare and an account of the now-dubious role of the Great Man in history.

Shaw's new, futuristic Bonaparte is an arch-realist: "I do not believe in metaphysical forces" (*Plays* 5: 532). Shaw may be endowing his creation with some of his own beliefs (or lack thereof). One critic quotes Shaw as affirming that the historical Napoleon was an atheist, but she cites two pieces of evidence to the contrary: the Emperor's last will and testament, in which he writes, "Je meurs dans la religion apostolique et romaine" (I die in the apostolic and Roman religion), and a letter of Napoleon to his surgeon, which begins: "Je suis loin d'être athée" (I am far from being an atheist) (Moore, 126–27). Nonetheless, the "atheist" Cain Adamson Napoleon embodies the Life Force to such a degree that there seems to be even more of Shaw in him than in the younger general of *The Man of Destiny:* "The truth is that my talent possesses me. It is genius. . . . I am great when I exercise it. At other moments I am nobody" (534–35).

But this talent for organizing the slaughter of warfare "to give mankind this terrible joy which they call glory" does not make him happy. There is more Cain than Adam in his Life Force: "I have the virtues of a laborer: industry and indifference to personal comfort. But I must rule, because I am so superior to other men that it is intolerable to me to be misruled by them. Yet only as a slayer can I become a ruler" (535). "I matter supremely: my soldiers do not matter at all," he says, realizing that he is invincible only at the cost of "the demoralization, the depopulation, the ruin of the victors no less than of the vanquished" (538). This is a Bonaparte conscious that ultimately there are no winners in warfare. His megalomania is tinged with lucidity, and it is possible to see here something of Shaw's own pellucid worldview: nine-tenths "common humanity" but "the other tenth is a faculty for seeing things as they are that no other man possesses. . . . I mean that I have the only imagination worth having: the power of imagining things as they are, even when I cannot see them" (535–36). In light of these gifts, how does Napoleon come to terms with the fact that warfare causes bloodshed and death? The Veiled Lady, revealed early on as the Oracle, shows him the way out of that quandary: "To die before the tide of glory turns" (539). To this end, she shoots at him at close range but misses. It would appear that Napoleons are necessary evils after all—and difficult to get rid of.

Shaw's views on Napoleon continued to be cautionary. In 1921, as a witty response—but also as a critical rebuttal—to *The Outline of History*, Shaw sent H. G. Wells the Napoleon scene from *Back to Methuselah*. Clearly the war had done something to alter Shaw's admiration for the man of destiny, whose egotism and pettiness had been encroaching upon his heroism: in wartime, Cain was beginning to overtake Adam. This is evidenced by Shaw's unsent letter to Wells, for which he had substituted the Napoleon scene. A quarter of a century after *The Man of Destiny*, although Shaw still considered the general an incredible tactician with an amazing memory, the historical Bonaparte emerges more flawed than great:

> If he hadn't been a soldier he would have been a nobody. He tried writing and everything else that he could try in his youth, and failed at them all. He was useless even as a subaltern: only for the revolution he would have been kicked out of the army as a disgrace to it. But from the moment when he got a military command he never looked back until he was defeated, and then he was nothing. All the other things he did could have been better done by other men. Peace was fatal to him. . . . He spoke as an artist when he described a field strewn with corpses as a beautiful sight. (*Letters 1911–1925*, 724–25)

"Peace was fatal to him." At times it is difficult to tell if the above passage is praise or censure, but the ambiguity is typical of Shaw's attitude toward Bonaparte in later years, during which he continued to be preoccupied by the Napoleon figure. He used him to great effect in a toast to Albert Einstein in 1930, where he received "laughter and applause" from his Savoy Hotel audience when he stated: "I could say many flattering things about Napoleon. But the one thing which I should not be able to say about him would be perhaps the most important thing, and that was, that it would perhaps have been better for the human race if he had never been born."[16] The following year Shaw used the name "Napoleon" on the stage one last time in *Too True to be Good* (1931): the Lawrence of Arabia figure who runs the army from the ranks and who rides about the desert on a motorcycle is called Private Napoleon Alexander Trotsky Meek. First Cain, now Trotsky; what next?

In 1935 he ridiculed Bonaparte outright as "a very ordinary snob in his eighteenth-century social outlook," citing his assumption of the imperial diadem, his remanufacturing of a titular aristocracy, and "his silly insistence on imperial etiquette" at Saint Helena as evidence that "for all his genius, he was and always had been behind the times." As the disastrous march to Moscow had proved, he was "fundamentally a commonplace human fool." But once again, this is the paradox of greatness: that a "shabby-genteel Corsican subaltern" could eventually place on his own head the crown of Charlemagne. In Shaw's opinion, Napoleon's apotheosis was the result of the idolatry of a nation who had been taught "to measure greatness by pageantry and the wholesale slaughter called military glory" (*Plays* 6: 856–58, 876). The French got the hero they deserved.

Shaw's penultimate volley came in 1944 with the publication of *Everybody's Political What's What?*—his attempt to make sense of the second great upheaval of the century. With the rise of fascism, Shaw had already been making controversial statements. As early as 1927, he had written that "Mussolini . . . has done for Italy what Napoleon did for France" (*Letters 1926–1950*, 69). But by 1944, Napoleon had fallen from grace utterly. In Shaw's estimation he had been "a scourge and a tyrant," "a snob, a cad, an assassin, and a scoundrel," even a precursor to Adolf Hitler: "our contemporaries die for their upstart Führer as Frenchmen used to die for their upstart Emperor."[17] Such dictators demonstrate that "barbarism, surviving in a disguise of chivalrous heroism, has ended in an idolatry of famous warriors." Hence the necessity of recognizing that military heroism thrives less on nobility of character than on "popular pugnacity, idolatry, and glory worship," which are the bulwarks of all conquerors in any age (*Everybody's*, 134). In the aftermath of two world wars, Shaw's Bonaparte had degenerated from Life Force to Death Wish.

But not entirely. It must be emphasized that Shaw's postwar condemnation of Napoleon the glory-seeking "upstart" did not lessen the Emperor's importance for him as an idea and a symbol, as an embodiment of what every individual is capable. Whatever his flaws, Bonaparte was a man, "not an anthropomorphic god" (*Everybody's*, 339). More importantly, he was a man with a mission capable of nothing else but the accomplishment of that mission, even at the expense of human lives—which is precisely the way the Life Force wields its power through a superbeing: progress requires sacrifices.

Even at the age of ninety-two, Shaw was still vigorously defending Napoleon against those who persisted in treating him as the mythical hero of a glorious military romance. His letter to *The New Statesman and Nation* of 9 October 1948, entitled "The Acquired Habits of Napoleon," reveals that Shaw still thought of Napoleon as an avatar of the Life Force in action. He maintained that the historian A. J. P. Taylor's essay on Napoleon was "farther off the mark than H. G. Wells's *gaffe* on the same subject in his *Outline of History*." He ascribed Napoleon's "extraordinary natural aptitude for the tactics dictated in his technical schoolbooks" to his "overwhelming habit of mind," decrying as "schoolboy romance" Taylor's claim that Napoleon supposed he "could master the world by will alone" (in Taylor's words). He concluded that "Napoleon's professionalism is the key to his whole career."[18]

Which brings us full circle to the Napoleon Bonaparte of *The Man of Destiny:* an original observer with prodigious powers of work, a realistic knowledge of human nature, and imaginative without illusions. If we add to these qualities a professionalism, natural aptitude, and habit of mind, we have listed the characteristics of an avatar of the Life Force—and certainly of Shaw himself. Moreover, although his esteem for the Great Man was tempered in later years by political turmoil, Shaw's continued interest in the Bonaparte figure shows that his "vile vulgar Corsican adventurer," for all his shortcomings, formed an integral part of Shaw's worldview.

Notes

1. W. D. Howarth, "Bonaparte on Stage: The Napoleonic Legend in Nineteenth-Century French Drama," in *Themes in Drama: Historical Drama,* ed. James Redmond (Cambridge: Cambridge University Press, 1986), 139.

2. Written in 1895, performed in 1897, published in 1898. Further references to Shaw's plays are from *The Bodley Head Bernard Shaw: Collected Plays with Their Prefaces,* ed. Dan H. Laurence, 7 vols. (London: Reinhardt, 1970–74) and noted in the text as *Plays.*

3. Charles A. Berst, "The Man of Destiny: Shaw, Napoleon, and the Theatre of Life," in *Shaw: The Neglected Plays,* ed. Alfred Turco, Jr.; *SHAW: The Annual of Bernard Shaw Studies,* vol. 7, ed. Stanley Weintraub, (University Park, Pa.: Penn State Press, 1987), 93, 86, 88.

4. Dan H. Laurence, ed., *Bernard Shaw: Collected Letters 1874–1897* (New York: Dodd, Mead, 1965), 791; references to *Letters 1911–1925* and *Letters 1926–1950* (New York: Viking, 1985) will be noted in the text.

5. Mina Moore, *Bernard Shaw et la France* (Paris: Champion, 1933), 122.

6. Stanley Weintraub, ed., *Bernard Shaw, The Diaries, 1885–1897, with Earlier and Later Diary Fragments from 1875–1917* (University Park, Pa.: Penn State Press, 1986), 2: 1102–3.

7. Stanley Weintraub, *The Unexpected Shaw: Biographical Approaches to G.B.S. and His Work* (New York: Ungar, 1982), 68.

8. "From Symposium: *The Shewing-Up of Blanco Posnet* and *The Man of Destiny,*" in *1992: Shaw and the Last Hundred Years,* ed. Bernard F. Dukore; *SHAW* 14, Fred Crawford, ed., (1994), 60.

9. Martin Meisel, *Shaw and the Nineteenth-Century Theater* (Princeton, N.J.: Princeton University Press, 1963), 358.

10. Maurice Valency, *The Cart and the Trumpet: The Plays of George Bernard Shaw* (New York: Schocken, 1983), 144.

11. Dan H. Laurence, ed., *Shaw's Music: The Complete Musical Criticism*, 3 vols. (New York: Dodd, Mead 1981), 3: 466–67.

12. Bernard F. Dukore, ed., *Bernard Shaw: The Drama Observed* (University Park, Pa.: Penn State Press, 1993), 2: 389, 390.

13. Victorien Sardou, *Madame Sans-Gêne*, in *L'illustration théâtrale* 75 (21 décembre 1907), n.p. Catherine's lines are from the end of act 1, scene 14. My translation.

14. Arthur Ganz, *G. B. Shaw* (London: Macmillan, 1983), 74.

15. J. L. Wisenthal, *Shaw's Sense of History* (Oxford: Clarendon, 1988), 62–63.

16. Bernard Shaw, "Toast to Albert Einstein," in *SHAW* 15 (1995), 233.

17. Bernard Shaw, *Everybody's Political What's What?* (New York: Dodd, Mead 1944), 34, 338, 131. For other remarks, cf. 32, 123.

18. Bernard Shaw, "The Acquired Habits of Napoleon," *New Statesman* 36 (9 October 1948), 304.

Arnold Bennett: Shaw's Ten O'Clock Scholar
Kinley Roby

In *Table Talk* (1925), Bernard Shaw is quoted as having stated categorically that a person could not be taught to write plays unless nature had done 99 percent of the work and that "if an author cannot write an effective stage play without teaching, nothing he can learn will be of any use to him: he has mistaken his profession."

He was equally emphatic in denying any interest in teaching playwriting, insisting that he was "a practitioner, not a professor."[1] His single concession to those who asked for his help in writing or in marketing their plays was an open letter, printed in galley proof form, which he sent in response to all such inquiries. The letter gave directions for preparing and submitting a script and warned the aspiring dramatist not to let rejections stop him from writing.[2] With Arnold Bennett, however, Shaw broke his rule, and over a period of ten years, he tried—sometimes publicly, sometimes privately, and always without success—to teach Bennett what a play should be.

Shaw's involvement with Bennett had its beginning in a sharp but good-natured exchange between the two men over the relative difficulty of writing a play and writing a novel. In 1914, Bennett published *The Author's Craft*, in which he insisted with a brashness that had become his hallmark that it was easier to write a play than to write a novel, basing his assertion on the fact that since he had written about twenty of each, he was in a position to know what he was talking about.[3]

It required six plays, he insisted, to make up the "matter" of one novel, adding that a play did not need to have either atmosphere or description written into it and demanded only a mild degree of subtlety in any of its parts. The exaggeration was laid on in part for effect, but it also gave away Bennett's sensitivity concerning his long list of theatrical failures. His denigration of the playwright's art was a defense against his own lack of success in writing plays. Out of those twenty plays which he had written by 1914, only *Milestones*, written in collaboration with Edward Knoblock, and *The Great Ad-*

venture, adapted from his novel, *Buried Alive,* had caught the public's fancy and become box office hits.

Shaw may or may not have read *The Author's Craft* in 1914, but in 1916, when Henry W. Massingham, editor of *The Nation,* asked him to review the book, Shaw was delighted to do it. His review, which appeared in *The Nation* on 11 March 1916, took as its point of departure Bennett's remarks on playwriting. The piece contains a brilliant parody of the prose styles of Bennett and John Galsworthy, which is inserted in the review as a demonstration of how those two writers might have written act V, scene viii, of *Macbeth* and was intended as a counterblast to Bennett's assertion that a play was easier to write than a novel. The parody is some two thousand four hundred words in length; and having reached the end of it, Shaw states that he could write that sort of thing by the hundred thousand words "on his head" and with a little effort could devise a "typewriter attachment that would do it." He added that when his faculties had decayed a little further, he would go back to writing novels and that Arnold Bennett could fall back on writing plays.[4]

Bennett did not respond to Shaw's jibe, and the argument died with the score about even. Writing the parody, however, may have reawakened Shaw's interest in *Macbeth,* because later in the year he wrote a playlet based on *Macbeth,* I, v, which he titled "Skit for Lillah McCarthy and Gerald DuMaurier." Shaw left Lady Macbeth's lines almost unaltered, but he rewrote Macbeth's speeches, transforming that powerful character into a maundering nincompoop with a manner of expression very like that of the narrator in the "Macbeth novel," which Shaw had written to make fun of Bennett and Galsworthy. Unfortunately the skit was never performed, and Shaw noted satirically in the margin of the manuscript that "Gerald would not burlesque himself. Probably he considered himself an ideal Macbeth."[5]

The parody in *The Nation* was the first of Shaw's efforts to correct Bennett's misconceptions about playwriting and brought to an end two years of public exchanges in which the two writers confronted one another in print on political issues and on the question of England's participation in the war. The dissimilarity of their views and of their temperaments might well have led them into genuine hostility, but instead their disagreements only brought them closer together.

Their collisions formed the basis of a friendship that became sufficiently solid to allow Bennett, who was very reluctant to let anyone see his plays before they were bought, to send Shaw a copy of *The Bright Island* for his comments and to lead Shaw to abandon his rule against helping authors to write plays. Before the two men reached that degree of intimacy, however, they had clashed publicly on most of the major issues of the day. A glance at some of those controversies will demonstrate how remarkable it was that Bennett sought Shaw's advice on the construction of *The Bright Island* and how equally remarkable it was that Shaw gave it.

Their first clash occurred in November 1914 over Shaw's *Common Sense about the War*, in which he charged England with being as much to blame for the conflict as Germany.[6] Bennett, who had just published a propaganda piece, *Liberty—A Statement of the British Case*, defending England's innocence in the events leading to the outbreak of war, responded to Shaw's charges in *The Daily News and Leader* and the *New York Times* on 18 November.[7] After praising Shaw's article for containing in its best sections "the most magnificent, brilliant, and convincing common sense that could possibly be uttered," he accused Shaw of having failed to realize the solemnity of the occasion and Shaw's own importance. "The present is no hour," Bennett scolded, "for that disingenuous, dialectical bravura which might easily relieve a domestic altercation."

Shaw responded on the following day, justifying his stand by pointing out that he and other writers like him were the "mouthpieces of many inarticulate citizens, who are fighting at home against the general tumult of scare and rancor and silly cinematograph heroics for a sane facing of facts."[8] He then invited Bennett to pay him some more nice compliments and to "reserve his fine old Staffordshire loathing for my intellectual nimbleness until the war is over." It was a pleasant piece of verbal tilting, but neither man had taken the guard from the point of his lance.

A less public confrontation occurred when Bennett joined the board of directors of the *New Statesman* in March 1915. Shaw was a member of the board, and he and Clifford Sharp, editor of the *NS*, were in violent disagreement over the attitude the *NS* should be taking toward Asquith's government and that government's war policies. Shaw wanted the *NS* to attack Asquith and to denounce England's continued participation in the war. Sharp was equally insistent that as long as the war lasted and he remained editor of the *NS*, the journal would support the nation's war aims. Bennett was a staunch supporter of Asquith and a true "hawk" regarding the war, as his articles in the *Daily News* for that period demonstrate.

He and Shaw managed, however, to disagree without unpleasantness. In his journal entry for 17 November 1915, he recorded a heated exchange between Shaw and Sharp over Asquith and wrote that Shaw "had no conception of public opinion at all"; but he added that the "fundamental decency and kindness of Shaw were evident throughout."[9]

In 1916, they clashed over politics for the last time. The point at issue was Shaw's complaint that the government was being remiss in not utilizing the available brain power in the nation in the task of running the government. Shaw's article appeared in the *NS* on 12 February, and in it he challenged Bennett to say why he supported Asquith. Bennett responded with "Mr. Shaw v. the Prime Minister."[10]

Ignoring Shaw's demands for reasons why Asquith should be supported, he wrote that one could imagine the results of putting Shaw into the prime minister's post or of staffing the government with inexperienced men drawn from Shaw's "intelligencia." He concluded by insisting that Shaw was naive if he thought that men in power would relinquish that power voluntarily and that to put such a scheme forward implied "an almost sensational lack of the sense of reality." In the journal he dismissed Shaw's plan as "idiotic."

Whatever their political differences during the war years, these two fundamentally different men gradually formed a friendship that survived every confrontation, a fact that is heartening evidence of their tolerance, humanity, and largeness of spirit. The essential good humor of their exchanges is demonstrated in Shaw's *Back to Methuselah*, Part III, "The Thing Happens." The Archbishop, recounting his own feigned deaths, says, "At first I used to attend my own funeral in disguise, because I had read about a man doing that in an old romance [*Buried Alive*] by an author named Bennett, from whom I remember borrowing five pounds in 1912."

Although they disagreed politically, they were in agreement on the state of English drama from 1914 to 1918. Shaw withheld *Heartbreak House* from production in 1917 for the reason that he thought it would not be well received by the wartime audience. In the Preface to *Heartbreak House*, he wrote that the war had "completely upset the economic conditions which formerly enabled serious drama to pay its way in London."[11] He was referring to the new audience, made up chiefly of soldiers on leave and their companions, who knew nothing about the theater and were not capable of responding intelligently to a serious play.

Bennett was equally critical of the theater after 1914, but he was considerably less understanding than Shaw in his comments on the fare being offered the public. His objections were not leveled at the audience but at the cynicism of the theater managers who chose the plays. In two of his novels, *The Roll-Call* (1918) and *The Pretty Lady* (1918), he describes two imaginary but typical plays being performed in the West End; and the descriptions give a clear indication of what he found wrong with the theater of the period.

In *The Roll-Call*, he described the play in question as pivoting "unendingly on the same twin centers of alcohol and concupiscence."[12] Of the play in *The Pretty Lady*, he wrote that "in fullest publicity it was licensed to say that which in private could not be said where men and women meet, and that which could not be printed."[13] His references in the journal to contemporary drama are even more scathing.

His distaste was not sufficiently strong, however, to keep him from trying to have his own plays produced. In *Judith*, which he wrote in late 1918 and early 1919, he allowed Lillah McCarthy, who was playing the title role, to appear on stage in a costume that he feared might provoke a police action. No police action was provoked by the costume, and it was not sufficiently shocking to provoke much box office activity either. The play collapsed in the second week of its London appearance.

Bennett's only other play to be produced during the period was *The Title* (1918), a wholly innocuous comedy that had a moderately successful run. Between 1914 and 1918, on the other hand, Shaw wrote *Heartbreak House*, four playlets on war themes—*O'Flaherty, V.C.* (1915); *The Inca of Perusalem* (1915); *Augustus Does His Bit* (1916); and *Annajanska, The Bolshevik Empress* (1917)—and began *Back to Methuselah* in 1917, completing the play in 1921.

Neither Bennett nor Shaw was very enthusiastic about one another's plays, and their agreement on the decline of the drama during the war did not dispel that lack of enthusiasm. Either by inadvertence but more probably by design, Shaw omitted Bennett's name from a list of seventeen contemporary playwrights who he thought justified A. B. Walkley and William Archer's contention, advanced before the turn of the century, that English drama had a bright future (Henderson, 67).

In 1907, Shaw had as conspicuously omitted Bennett's name from another list. This earlier list was made up of the names of novelists whom Shaw had "tried hard" to persuade to "leave their safe and dignified position as masters of the art of fiction" and write for the theater. The writers named were Galsworthy, Wells, Kipling, Conrad, and Maurice Hewlett, two of whom, Galsworthy and Hewlett, had already turned their talents to playwriting.[14]

By 1907, Bennett had published eleven novels and had clearly earned a place on Shaw's list; but Shaw was probably aware that Bennett had also written a number of plays, none of which had been produced. Bennett had, in fact, written almost as many plays as novels, although he did not succeed in having one produced until 1908, when his *Cupid and Commonsense* opened at the Shaftesbury Theatre. Because there is no evidence that Shaw had read any of Bennett's plays, it cannot be stated definitely that he omitted Bennett from his list on the basis of firsthand knowledge of the poor quality of Bennett's plays. Given the intimate character of the London theatrical world, however, it is reasonably safe to assume that Shaw had heard enough about them to be convinced that Bennett did not have a bright future as a playwright.

On his side, Bennett wrote to his nephew in 1921 that *Heartbreak House* was "three hours fifty minutes of the most intense tedium."[15] In the journal he did, however, praise an early revival of *Arms and the Man*, adding that he was astonished that Shaw's plays found a public at all, and closed with the observation that his plays "must have immensely educated the public" (*Journal*, 285). Slowly and almost grudgingly, Bennett was won over to a highly qualified liking for some of Shaw's plays.

In 1903, Bennett had judged Barrie to be Shaw's superior as a playwright (*Journal*, 120), but in 1920, he wrote that *Arms and the Man* now seemed to him much better than it did twenty-five years earlier and that Shaw's title to be the modern Molière was not so "rocky" as he had thought (*Journal*, 696). Five years later he gave the highest praise to Shaw's adaptation of Trebitsch's lightweight *Jitta's Atonement*, describing the play as containing "some of the most brilliant work, some tender, some brutal, and lots of the most side-splitting fun that Shaw ever did" (*Journal*, 807). Only a year earlier, however, he had seen *Back to Methuselah* and been very bored by it, finding "neither action nor character nor a sermon nor wit" in the play. He went to sleep in the second act and had to be wakened for fear that his snoring would be heard on stage (*Journal*, 767).

Bennett's reaction to *Heartbreak House* was certainly known to Shaw, because Bennett and Nigel Playfair had refused to produce the play at the Lyric Theatre, Hammersmith. Their stated reason for the rejection was that they objected to Ellen O'Malley's being cast in the role of Ellie Dunn. They insisted, with justification, that she was too old for the part. The objection may have been only a convenient excuse for refusing the play, because Bennett did not like it and would have preferred not to tell Shaw that he thought it dull. Shaw grew weary of the debate, so that when James Bernard Fagan asked if he could have the play for the Court Theatre, Shaw gave it to him.

St. John Ervine, the playwright and critic, was equally upset with Shaw's stubborn insistence on Ellen O'Malley's being cast in the role of Ellie Dunn. After the reviews of the play were out following its opening on 18 October 1921, Shaw wrote Ervine a letter rebuking him for saying that O'Malley was miscast. "You give a dig at poor Ellen O'Malley," he wrote, "which I connect with the fact that you were talking to Arnold Bennett between the acts."[16]

Bennett's refusal to produce *Heartbreak House* did not interrupt his friendship with Shaw, and in 1925, he sent Shaw a copy of *The Bright Island* for comment before its production. Shaw responded immediately with a warning concerning the play's hopes for success:

> Humanity cannot stand one hundred fifty minutes' unrelieved scoffing no matter how witty it is. There must be refuges for the affection, the admiration, the detestation of the audience; or else you must fill the gaps with refuges for its concupiscence and ferocity, as the Restoration playwrights did, or enchant it with all the art of the opera and the ballet.[17]

Bennett thanked Shaw for having read the play but dismissed his advice with a cool "I daresay there is a great deal in what you say, but I have definitely arranged with the Stage Society to do the play, and I shall now let them do it."[18]

The Bright Island went onto the boards at the Aldwych just as he had written it, and Shaw's doubts about the play's chances for success were well founded. With bald honesty Bennett recorded in the journal that it received the worst press ever accorded one of his plays, some of the reviewers having gone so far as to demand that he be stopped from writing such plays (*Journal*, 811). Following the play's cold reception, Shaw wrote to Bennett again, making a second attempt to tell his friend what was wrong with his playwriting technique. The letter is an appealing mixture of kindness and irritation and is written in the tone of a schoolmaster lecturing a promising but bungling student:

> There are gleams and strivings in that play which seem to indicate destiny. But like all inveterate novelists you will not take the theatre seriously enough. And you will study the wrong models. You have nothing to learn from Scribe & Co., and everything to learn from Beethoven. A play should go like a symphony; its themes should be introduced emphatically at the beginning and then hit on the head again and again until they are red hot, the pace and intensity increasing to the end with every possible device of unexpected modulations and changes, and sudden pianisimos, as in the Priest Lied and the finale of Mozart's Figaro. You never think of this, you depend on your confounded invention, and keep ladling in primitive matter right up to the end without ever working it up, so that the last fifteen minutes of your play are exactly like the

first, and there is no reason why they should be the last rather than the first, or why you should not, like George Moore go on like that forever. A play must have a destination, even if it be to the bottom of an abyss, in which case the further it falls the faster it goes. Here endeth the first lesson. (Pound, 285)

It is not known what, if any, response Bennett made to Shaw's letter, but the criticism would have come as no surprise. Bennett was painfully aware of his inability to write consistently successful plays. In March 1922 after the failure of his play, *The Love Match*, he confessed sadly to Hugh Walpole that the failure of the play was due to his having attempted to write "modern, otherwise new-fangled plays consisting of realism delicately enveloped in wit." Then he added ruefully that the real tragedy was that he was "unteachable" (Pound, 286).

But if he could not be taught, neither could he be discouraged. Nothing demonstrates more clearly his stubborn persistence in clinging to a false hope than his determination to find a producer for his pretentious and ineffective play, *Don Juan de Marana*. He had completed the play in 1914 and was looking forward to a fall premiere when the war intervened, canceling all plans for a production. For the next sixteen years, Bennett tried unsuccessfully to have the play produced, resorting to such desperate devices as making it a condition of sale of some of his later plays that *Don Juan* also be bought. He was always forced in the course of the negotiations to drop his demands concerning *Don Juan*, but he continued to be hopeful. Until 1930, his failure with the play was complete; and then he consented, in what must have been an act of despair, to convert the play into an opera for Eugene Goosens.[19] Bennett's faith in his play was pathetic rather than admirable and strongly suggests a blind spot in his critical faculties.

Shaw's instruction did nothing to correct that blindness. Of his three plays produced between *The Bright Island* and his death on 21 March 1931, only *Mr. Prohack*, adapted from his novel of the same name and written in collaboration with Edward Knoblock, could be called a success. The extent of Bennett's delight (and undoubtedly his relief) over the success of *Mr. Prohack* is expressed in a letter written by Dorothy Cheston Bennett to Reggie Turner shortly after the play's opening:

Arnold's play *Mr. Prohack* is a success. When we have to leave the Court Theatre, on the expiring of our short lease, we shall take it elsewhere, up in the West End. . . . It's rather a triumph for Arnold—everyone saying it is the most delicious comedy that's been seen for ages—as they've been pitying poor Bennett for imagining he could write plays for years, and this has been refused by several managers. I wish that you would be coming to London to see it—for I *think* . . . that it will run some time.[20]

In the same year, *Flora* was performed in Manchester, and in 1928, *The Return Journey*, his last play to be produced, opened for a brief run at the St. James Theatre. Bennett described the play as "harrowing" and watching it an "ordeal." The first of his plays to be produced had been *Cupid and Commonsense*, exactly twenty years earlier. He wrote of the first performance that it was "extremely depressing." He ended in the theater about where he began, a relative failure.

Shortly after the war, Bennett wrote to his friend Frank Swinnerton that he was aware that most people insisted his plays were not plays but something else: "My aim," he declared, "is and always has been to widen the meaning of the word 'dramatic.'" That is to say, I was determined to prove that the interest of an audience can be held by the presentation of material generally held to be undramatic" (Pound, 285). It had been his aim as a novelist to discover beauty where others had not seen it and to reveal the drama of life in the mundane details of daily existence.

The method that he employed to achieve those ends was the careful marshaling of details and incidents. It is a technique that requires the spaciousness of the novel in order to be effective and is ill-suited to the stage. Shaw was right in calling Bennett an inveterate novelist, and it was in reference to this "inveterateness" that Bennett's judgment on himself was most sound when he wrote that he was "unteachable." He was a novelist first and last, and not even the genius of Bernard Shaw was capable of making him a dramatist.

Notes

This article first appeared in *The Shaw Review* XIII, no. 3 (Pennsylvania State University Press, 1970): 96–104. (Reprinted by permission of the publisher.)

1. Archibald Henderson, *Table-Talk of G.B.S.: Conversation on Things in General between Bernard Shaw and His Biographer* (London: Chapman and Hall, 1925), 72–73, 74; hereinafter cited in text as Henderson.
2. Stanley Weintraub, "The Indefatigable Non-Correspondent: G.B.S.," *Texas Quarterly* (spring 1968), 113–25.
3. Arnold Bennett, *The Author's Craft* (London: Hodder and Stoughton, 1914), 69.
4. Bernard Shaw, "Mr. Arnold Bennett Thinks Play-Writing Easier Than Novel Writing," in *Pen Portraits and Reviews* (London: Constable and Co. Ltd, 1949), 43–52.

5. Bernard F. Dukore, "Macbeth Skit," *Educational Theatre Journal* 19 (October 1967), 344.

6. Bernard Shaw, *Common Sense about the War,* Supplement to *New Statesman* 14 November 1914.

7. Arnold Bennett, "Arnold Bennett Answers Shaw," *New York Times,* 18 November 1914.

8. Bernard Shaw, "Shaw in Rebuttal to Arnold Bennett," *New York Times,* 19 November 1914.

9. Arnold Bennett, *The Journal of Arnold Bennett,* ed. Newman Flower (New York: Cassell and Company Ltd., 1933), 574; hereinafter cited in text as *Journal.*

10. Arnold Bennett, "Mr. Shaw v. The Prime Minister," *Daily News and Leader,* 16 February 1916.

11. Bernard Shaw, *Heartbreak House* (New York: Brentano's, 1919), xlii.

12. Arnold Bennett, *The Roll-Call* (London: Hutchinson, 1918), 183.

13. Arnold Bennett, *The Pretty Lady* (London: Cassell, 1918), 1.

14. "The Complimentary Dinner to Mr. J. E. Vedrenne and Mr. H. Granville Barker: A Transcript of the Proceedings," *The Shaw Review* 2 (May 1959), 27. Introduction and notes to the transcript by Stanley Weintraub.

15. Arnold Bennett, *Arnold Bennett's Letters to His Nephew,* ed. Richard Bennett (New York: Harper and Brothers, 1935), 68.

16. St. John Ervine, *Bernard Shaw: His Life, Work and Friends* (New York: Morrow, 1956), 475.

17. Reginald Pound, *Arnold Bennett: A Biography* (London: Heinemann, 1952), 284; hereinafter cited in text as Pound.

18. Arnold Bennett, *Letters of Arnold Bennett: 1916–1931,* ed. James Hepburn (New York: Oxford University Press, 1970), 3: 229.

19. *Don Juan de Marana* was performed at Covent Garden on 24 June 1937, six years after Bennett's death. See Hepburn, 3, note, 342.

20. Quoted from a letter formerly in the Lafayette Butler collection.

The Evolution of Human Virtue: Precedents for Shaw's "World Betterer" in the Utopias of Bellamy, Morris, and Bulwer-Lytton

Julie Sparks

Despite the bustling technological progress and burgeoning prosperity that swelled British complacency in the Victorian period, those socialist reformers who rejected the materialists' definition of "progress" felt an urgent call to save modern humanity from itself. Bernard Shaw, one of the most perceptive and articulate of these reformers, acknowledged that it is essentially futile to focus on correcting the gross economic inequalities and the physical squalor produced by early industrialism, for he believed that the human animal itself must change before any real improvement in social conditions is possible. In the words of Jack Tanner, Shaw contended, "Unfortunately, the earnest people get drawn off the track . . . by the illusion of progress. Any socialist can convince us easily that the difference between Man as he is and Man as he might become . . . under millennial conditions of nutrition, environment, and training, is enormous."[1] Although Shaw the Fabian socialist reformer toiled alongside the "earnest people" Tanner mocks, Shaw the utopian writer strove to articulate just how the human animal might be improved through a sort of intellectual and moral evolution. Like all political philosophers before him, Shaw had to consider two questions: whether humanity could be improved, and (if so) how. He emphasized the importance of the first question in the first chapter of his book-length political treatise, *Everybody's Political What's What?* In answer to his own chapter heading, "Is Human Nature Incurably Depraved?" Shaw wrote: "If it is, reading this book will be a waste of time . . . if we have neither the political capacity nor the goodwill to remedy [the mistakes of our civilization] we had better not torment ourselves uselessly by making ourselves conscious of them. Better cling to our delusions and keep our hope and selfrespect, making the most of our vices and follies before they destroy us." However, Shaw continued, "[I]f this book is to be worth writing or reading, I must assume that all this pessimism and cynicism is a delusion caused, not only by ignorance of contemporary facts but, in so far as they are known, by drawing wrong conclusions from them."[2]

One example he could have cited was the opposing conclusions people drew from Darwin's theories, for, ever since *On the Origin of Species* forced us to reconsider the Original Sin theory, reaction was deeply divided. Some were dismayed to find humanity more closely related to the "angry ape" than to the angels, whereas others were encouraged by the suggestion that human nature might be evolving, along with our opposable thumbs, into something more noble. Clearly this controversy related directly to the question of human improvability. Shaw became an enthusiastic proponent of the more optimistic view, though he had to formulate the "metabiologic" religious doctrine of Creative Evolution to oppose what he considered the gross folly of what he labeled "Neo-Darwinism," evolution conceived as a series of blind accidents following the line of least resistance. Although Shaw's "metabiologic pentateuch," *Back to Methuselah*, stands as the grandest effort to transform Darwin's theory into a new vision of humanity's future that could provide both an explanation for humanity's apparent depravity and a reason to hope that this depravity can be overcome, earlier utopian theorists, most notably Edward Bellamy, William Morris, and Edward Bulwer-Lytton, had incorporated their own interpretations of Darwinism into their speculative fiction. Shaw's vision can be better understood by considering some of those literary precedents.

Although Shaw agreed on some points with Bellamy, who wrote one of the most influential socialist utopias of the Victorian period, *Looking Backward* (1887), and with William Morris, who responded to Bellamy's vision with his own very different socialist utopia, *News from Nowhere* (1891), the chief point of contention was what Shaw saw as the simplistic environmental determinism on which their conception of human nature rested. Bellamy and Morris both believed that, as Tanner put it, "millennial conditions of nutrition, environment, and training" would completely reform human nature, for both describe their utopias as states that have established those "millennial conditions" and thereby produced virtuous people. We see this in Bellamy's novel when the narrator, Julian West, a Rip van Winkle–like time traveler from the nineteenth century who wakes up in a utopian future, is told by his host, Dr. Leete, that "some persons nowadays . . . hold that we have entered upon the millennium, and the theory from their point of view does not lack plausibility."[3] Yet when Dr. Leete informs him that this society has managed to eradicate strife and corruption from politics, that all citizens work their hardest for the common good (even though all receive the same income), and that crime and even everyday lying have completely disappeared, West keeps insisting that "human nature itself must have changed very much. . . ." "Not at all," his host replies, "but the conditions of human life have changed, and with them the motives of human action" (60–61).

Although Morris does not develop the point as explicitly as Bellamy, there is a strikingly similar passage in which the time traveler from the nineteenth century who wakes up in a utopian future, is told by his host how crime and strife have disappeared with the establishment of the arcadian-communist commonwealth, and he replies in perplexity, "I have been told that political strife was a necessary result of human nature." He is asked "Human nature! . . . what human nature? The human nature of paupers, of slaves, of slaveholders, or the human nature of wealthy freemen?" He responds as one newly converted to the Socialist world view, "Well . . . I suppose there would be a difference according to circumstances in people's action about these matters."[4]

The relationship between sociopolitical environment and human morality is most fully developed in Bellamy's novel as part of a sermon (which is delivered over the airwaves in a remarkably prescient anticipation of radio). Marx may have denounced all religion as the "opiate of the people," but most socialist utopians of the nineteenth century considered traditional religious doctrine—properly interpreted—to be an essential part of human society. Consequently, Bellamy and Morris, like Shaw, do not banish religion from their utopias; they simply appropriate and reinterpret Christianity's tenets, imagery, and sanctifying aura to reflect their own worldview. As Warren Sylvester Smith noted, Shaw does just what his "Saint" Andrew Undershaft advises: if "you have made for yourself something that you call a morality or a religion or what not . . . [and] it doesn't fit the facts . . . scrap it and get one that does fit."[5] Bellamy rejected the Christian tradition that "the heart of Man is deceitful above all things and desperately wicked"—a passage that Shaw cites and contradicts in his "Incurably Depraved?" chapter of *Everybody's Political What's What?* In his "radio" sermon, Bellamy's preacher likewise emphatically repudiates this old idea when he explains:

> Now that the conditions of life for the first time ceased to operate as a forcing process to develop the brutal qualities of human nature . . . the nobler qualities showed a sudden luxuriance which turned cynics into

panegyrists and for the first time in human history tempted mankind to fall in love with itself. Soon was fully revealed, what divines and philosophers of the old world never would have believed, that human nature in its essential qualities is good.... The constant pressure, through numberless generations, of conditions of life which might have perverted angels, had not been able to essentially alter the natural nobility of the stock, and these conditions once removed, like a bent tree, it had sprung back to its normal uprightness. (287–88)

Clearly Bellamy adapted Darwin's theory to his own purposes, with much more sanguine results than those who follow the "juggernaut theory of human nature," which was defined in a recent *New York Times* article as the belief that "people are programmed by their genetic heritage to be so selfish that a sense of global responsibility will come too late" to prevent our self-destruction through overpopulation, pollution, murder of the rain forests, and so on.[6] In defiance of this sort of grim determinism that continues even to the present, Bellamy pointed out that despite "constant pressure, through numberless ages" human nature had *not* evolved into morally degenerate creatures who are now hurtling toward self-destruction—we had only acquired bad *habits* as survival tactics, not bad genetic characteristics. Regenerative moral evolution, therefore, was not necessary. Furthermore, Bellamy was so convinced that the Socialist program he had outlined was plausible that he wrote in the postscript that the novel "is intended, in all seriousness, as a forecast, *in accordance with the principles of evolution*, of the next stage in the industrial and social development of humanity" (334 [emphasis mine]).

Shaw explained why this cheerful interpretation of Darwin is embraced by so many Socialist utopians: it contradicted what Shaw called "perhaps the strongest moral bulwark of Capitalism . . . the belief in the efficacy of individual righteousness." Shaw told how a British reformer, Robert Owen, "made desperate efforts to convince England that her criminals, her drunkards, her ignorant and stupid masses were the victims of circumstance" rather than moral degenerates punished by God—but to no avail. "If you were rich," Shaw explained, "how pleasant it was to feel that you owed your riches to the superiority of your own character!" In addition, this comfortable belief relieved the complacent beneficiaries of capitalism from the arduous task of reforming a flawed system or even of ameliorating its cruelties—the task of world-bettering. But when Darwinism took hold in sociology as well as biology, and "made a clean sweep of all such self-righteousness . . . by discovering in the environment of an organism an influence on it more patent than Owen had ever claimed. . . . it threw the authority of science on the side of the Socialist who said that he who would reform himself must first reform society."[7]

Yet Shaw himself did not agree with the other Socialist reformers on this point. As Eric Bentley pointed out, Shaw had *begun* with a typical socialist orientation, "according to which you must change society in order to change man," but he came to realize that "the trouble was that unless you changed man he refused to change society."[8] Shaw put it another way: "poets who plan Utopias and prove that nothing is necessary for their realization but that Man should will them, perceive at last . . . that Man does not effectively will them" (*M&S*, 724). Thus the first task for the reformers must be to make the Will to Evolve more widespread in the race. In a speech he delivered to the Fabians in 1933, Shaw again addressed the problem, this time with an interesting twist: he asserted that "devising Socialist constitutions for unpolitical animals is like composing symphonies for the deaf and painting pictures for the blind." He remarked somewhat facetiously that one possible remedy for this problem has been suggested in the utopian romance of a very un-Fabian writer, whom Shaw nevertheless counted as an ally:

> Bulwer-Lytton anticipated the Fabians by a Utopia, called The Coming Race, in which all our difficulties were vanquished, because Man had been forced to become political by having developed a power of killing at sight, which made oppression or even irritating rudeness too dangerous to be practiced. . . . The attainment of this power, Bulwer Lytton saw, was the only hope of human civilization.[9]

Bulwer-Lytton's idea of "mutually assured destruction" is certainly a prescient suggestion, and as one critic noted, the society that he shows developing under the influence of this power contains most of the elements of utopian society advocated by the Socialists of the time: "peace, prosperity, personal liberty, full social equality of sex and class, scientific mastery over nature, great technological innovation, perfect physical well-being, and complete communal harmony."[10]

Nevertheless, Bulwer-Lytton did not write *The Coming Race* (1871) to provide his own blueprint for achieving a Socialist utopia; on the contrary, as he explained in a letter to his son: "If all the utopian dreams for human society could be achieved . . . it would be deadly to us, not from its vices but its virtue. Secondly, the realization of these ideas would produce a society which we would find extremely dull, and in which the current equality would prohibit all greatness" (Campbell, 56). From this one can only conclude that the narrator speaks for the author when he says, "Neither, on the other hand, have I the wish to represent the commonwealths of the Vril-ya as an ideal form of political society, to the attainment of which our own efforts of reform should be directed."[11] Campbell explained why Bulwer-Lytton was disinclined to strive for a "beatified community" such as the utopians of his time advocated: he foresaw that such a society "would produce no great soldiers and statesmen, no great orators and thinkers, and no great works of art. Consequently, Bulwer-Lytton urged man to remain content with his present condition and not strive for what he is *unfit by his nature* to achieve, sustain, or enjoy" (Campbell, 56 [emphasis mine]). Although Bulwer-Lytton was not among the stern moralists who believe human nature is "incurably depraved," he clearly believed human nature is immutable, which disqualified him from the work of the world-betterer as Shaw defined it. He belonged instead with those whom Shaw advised to "cling to [y]our delusions and keep [y]our hope and selfrespect, making the most of [y]our vices and follies before they destroy us." (*EPWW*, 1)

Despite his anti-utopian views, however, Bulwer-Lytton portrayed a society so appealing to Socialist utopian writers that it is easy to see how they might mistake him for a kindred spirit. Furthermore, although he presented a delightful satire of Darwin's suggestion that humanity shares a common ancestor with the other primates (the Vril-ya believe they are descended from a race of huge frogs), he was probably the first to show how a particular kind of evolution could lead to a utopian existence. Although Shaw cited many deeper thinkers as sources for his own interpretation of evolutionary theory that developed into Shaw's "scientific religion" of Creative Evolution, Bulwer-Lytton's early influence is worth noting.

In his preface to *Back to Methuselah*, his fullest treatment of Darwin's ideas, Shaw referred back to his first comment on Darwin and the confusion it had caused: "I had published my own view of evolution in a play called Man and Superman; and I found that most people were unable to understand how I could be an Evolutionist and not a Neo-Darwinian, or why I habitually derided Neo-Darwinism as a ghastly idiocy" (ix–x). Yet it *is* a little confusing to read in "The Revolutionist's Handbook," after a very un-Socialist denunciation of the efficacy of the "quackeries, political, scientific, educational, religious, or artistic" that are proposed as the agents of Progress to improve humanity and that "our only hope . . . is in evolution. We must replace the man by the superman" (*M&S*, 723).

This is puzzling, because mainstream scientific doctrine now concurs with some of the tenets of what Shaw derided as "Neo-Darwinian," especially the idea that evolution takes countless eons to produce noticeable changes and that evolution cannot be directed by human agency to produce specific results. Assuming these facts, "What hope is there then of human improvement?" as Shaw asks in his *Methuselah* preface. "According to the Neo-Darwinists, to the Mechanists, no hope whatever, because improvement can come only through some senseless accident which must, on the statistical average of accidents, be presently wiped out by some equally senseless accident." Shaw then offered a more hopeful interpretation of evolution: Neo-Lamarckian Evolution, or what Shaw calls Creative Evolution, which *can* be manipulated for specific ends. Shaw illustrated the theory with one of his simple but intriguing metaphors: "If the weight lifter, under the trivial stimulus of an athletic competition, can 'put up a muscle,' it seems reasonable to believe that an equally earnest and convinced philosopher could 'put up a brain.' Both are directions of vitality to a certain end" (*Methuselah*, xvii, xviii).

Shaw referred primarily to Lamarck as his source for this theory, but he may well have been influenced by Bulwer-Lytton's application of the idea in a utopian context. This is clearest in the scene in which Bulwer-Lytton's narrator visits a museum with his host's daughter, Zee. When the narrator expresses his wonder at the power Zee wields through her manipulation of the mysterious force called vril, something like electricity that can be focused and channeled like a laser beam, she compares her hand with his to point out the crucial differences: her larger thumb and a well-developed nerve that rises at the wrist and forks up to the bases of the fore- and the middle fingers. The narrator reports, with some dismay, "There is almost, in this, as great a difference as there is between the thumb of a man and that of a gorilla." This simile points to Darwin, but Zee's explanation of how the special power developed suggests Lamarck instead, for it is a *willed* acquisition that is transmitted hereditarily. Zee explains to the narrator:

> So far as the nerve is concerned, that is not found in the hands of our earliest progenitors. . . . It has been slowly developed in the course of generations, commencing in the early achievements, and increasing with the continuous exercise, of the vril power; therefore, in course of one or two thousand years, such a nerve may possibly be engendered in those higher beings of your race who devote themselves to that paramount science through which is attained command over all the subtler forces of nature permeated by vril. (Bulwer-Lytton, 376)

The point is further illustrated in the narrator's hopeless attempts to manage the Vril-ya's artificial wings, on which they soar like eagles. Again Zee consoles the narrator for the inferiority of his race:

> Learn that the connection between the will and the agencies of that fluid which has been subjected to the control of the Vril-ya was never established by the first discoverers, never achieved by a single generation; it has gone on increasing, like other properties of race, in proportion as it has been uniformly transmitted from parent to child, so that, at last, it has become an instinct; and an infant An of our race wills to fly as intuitively and unconsciously as he wills to walk. He thus plies his invented or artificial wings with as much safety as a bird plies those with which it is born. (Bulwer-Lytton, 407)

This all sounds rather fanciful, at least to scoffers at Lamarck's assertion that the giraffe acquired its long neck by a similar willful striving, with each generation handing down its acquired fraction of an inch to its progeny, who added a further increment to the accumulated length, and so on, but Shaw argues for the idea so strenuously and with such ingenious analogies (along with some absurd ones) that one is forced to at least reconsider the possibility. Keeping in mind the example of the young Vril-ya born prepared to fly with artificial wings as we are now born prepared to walk, one can begin to understand what Shaw suggests in the following passage:

> We insisted that Evolution advanced more slowly than any snail ever crawled. . . . But when we have to consider the case of a man born not only as an accomplished metabolist, but with such an aptitude for shorthand and keyboard manipulation that he is a stenographer or pianist at least five sixths ready-made as soon as he can control his hands intelligently, we are forced to suspect either that keyboards and shorthand are older inventions than we suppose, or else that acquirements can be assimilated and stored as congenital qualifications in a shorter time than we think. (*Methuselah*, xxx–xxxi)

After pointing out the prodigies that already appear from time to time as apparently ready-made pianists or chess players, Shaw tried to explain the phenomenon in terms of what we already know does happen. He described "the miracle of condensed recapitulation"— that is, the discovery made by embryologists that a human fetus progresses from a speck of protoplasm, through several embryonic stages as a succession of primitive creatures, and finally becomes a human infant, thus condensing many eons of prehistoric development into only nine prenatal months. Shaw extrapolated this a bit further to suggest a very optimistic evolutionary scenario: "The time may come when the same force that compressed the development of millions of years into nine months may pack many more millions into even a shorter space; so that Raphaels may be born painters as they are now born breathers and blood circulators" (*Methuselah*, xxvii).

Although flying with artificial wings, playing the piano, and painting pictures are not the sort of evolutionary developments upon which the survival of our species depends, Shaw went on to identify what sort of willed evolutionary development would save us. He suggested that we should simply will ourselves to live long enough to learn wisdom—long enough to develop the political capacity necessary to establish a rational and humane civilization and to evolve morally into creatures who would be fit to live in such a society. In the last play of his "pentateuch," Shaw shows this goal achieved. The play begins thirty thousand years into the future on the morning of a wonderful birth, the result of a kind of "condensed recapitulation" that has become the norm. The newly born creature, apparently a fully formed teenage girl who is pulled from a huge egg, is told that the worst of her troubles are over:

> You have been growing for two years in the egg. You began by being several sorts of creatures that no longer exist, though we have fossils of them. Then you became human; and you passed in fifteen months through a development that once cost human beings twenty years of awkward stumbling immaturity after they were born. They had to spend fifty years more in the sort of childhood you will complete in four years. And then they died of decay. But you need not die until your accident comes. (*Methuselah*, 249)

As a creative extrapolation of early twentieth-century embryology, Shaw's utopian vision can be read as a delightful and intriguing metaphor. Yet Shaw doesn't seem to be speaking metaphorically in the preface; he seems, rather, to be claiming that we can actually change our physiology by thinking about it and *willing*. This demands a more strenuous leap of faith than even his fondest disciples can muster. For example he asserts that Lamarck's "fundamental proposition [is] that living organisms changed because they wanted to. . . . If you have no eyes, and want to see, and keep trying to see, you will finally get eyes." Shaw admitted that "this seems absurd to inconsiderate people at first blush," but he never really carried the point because none of his subsequent illustrations of this phenomenon "actually occurring" involve the acquisition of new organs, only the enhancement of existing ones (like the weight lifter's biceps) or the gaining of skills that involve training muscles already existing, such as learning to ride a bicycle. It seems more plausible that the Vril-ya could develop the ability to fly by continuous willing and practicing on artificial wings than that they should spontaneously sprout real wings for the same reason. Yet the idea of acquiring a bodily eye echoes an earlier use of the motif from Shaw's first "parable of Creative Evolution," *Man and Superman*, which might be a clearer expression of Shaw's concept. In the "Don Juan in Hell" scene, Don Juan, a devout believer in the religion of Creative Evolution, tries to explain its dynamics:

> To Life, the force behind the Man, intellect is a necessity, because without it he blunders into death. Just as Life, after ages of struggle, evolved that wonderful bodily organ the eye, so that the living organism could see where it was going . . . so it is evolving today a minds's eye that shall see, not the physical world, but the purpose of Life, and thereby enable the individual to work for that purpose instead of thwarting and baffling it by setting up shortsighted personal aims as at present. (*M&S*, 627–28)

It is a small step from this last remark about "short-sighted personal aims" back to the basic difference between those people who are morally capable of bringing about and then living in a socialist utopia and those who aren't. Here Heaven represents utopia, whereas Hell mirrors the world as it now stands. When the Commander expresses his revulsion at the idea that Don Juan wants to spend his eternity working to help the Life Force achieve its purpose, Don Juan responds "I do not blame your disgust: a picture gallery is a dull place for a blind man" (*M&S*, 617). Thus, if we recall the same "picture gallery" metaphor from the speech Shaw later made to the Fabians on this subject, we see Commander as the sort of person for whom it is useless to design Socialist utopias: he is an "unpolitical animal." Furthermore, the repeated use of the blindness metaphor indicates that Shaw connected spiritual enlightenment with public spiritedness. Once our "mind's eye" has evolved to the point at which it can see "the purpose of Life," we will no longer be interested in the "short-sighted personal aims" that are all we are now able to see.

Another key element in the world-bettering character that must be developed in humanity, Shaw believed, is the moral courage and energy to hope. Utopias are produced by *hopeful* people who long for a better world and better people to live in it, yet the Commander likes Hell precisely because one is told to leave all hope outside its gates. "Only think what a relief that is!" he tells a discouraged newcomer, "For what is hope? A form of moral responsibility. Here there is no hope, and consequently no duty, no work, nothing to be gained by praying, nothing to be lost by doing what you like. Hell, in short, is a place where you have nothing to do but amuse yourself" (*M&S*, 610). By reveling in a life of irresponsible idleness, the Commander identifies himself with the parasitic gentleman class that has no place in *any* socialist utopia. Bellamy and Morris took care of this problem through more enlightened social mores: when idleness is stigmatized as antisocial, it almost completely disappears. But Shaw saw it as a deeper problem requiring a more strenuous solution.

One of Shaw's critics identified the problem when he points out the principal drawback of the "religion" Don Juan serves: "it only meets the needs of a particular and rather rare type of man"—namely, the born world betterer. MacCarthy continues, "the instinct which makes us take to heart the welfare of mankind is only one of many, and it is the only one which the religion of Creative Evolution satisfies."[12] He is generous enough to add that in Shaw himself it is the strongest instinct, but he is not so generous in his assessment of human nature in general, and in this Shaw would sadly agree. But the point is, can this "instinct" (if it is an instinct) be instilled somehow, or, if it is a matter of intelligent self-interest ("self-interest" being seen by intelligent people to involve the interest of the race as a whole), will increasing the general level of intelligence in the race do the job? Don Juan describes his own zeal to serve the Life Force as a sort of instinct. He declares that "as long as I can conceive something better than myself I cannot be easy unless I am striving to bring it into existence or clearing the way for it. . . . That is the working within me of Life's incessant aspiration to . . . wider, deeper, intenser self-consciousness, and clearer self-understanding . . . the instinct in me that looked through my eyes at the world and saw that it could be improved." And, he adds, "It is the absence of this instinct in you that makes you that strange monster called a Devil" (*M&S*, 641–42). But as MacCarthy points out, the Devil's lack of this instinct is not at all unusual.

Shaw articulated the problem clearly here, but the solution is more elusive. In "The Revolutionist's Handbook," Tanner, drawing the discussion from the metaphysical to the practical sphere, asserts that "the need for the Superman is, in its most imperative aspect, a political one." He explains that because rule by the occasional Superman has failed, and we have therefore "been driven to Proletarian Democracy," it has become clear that "democracy cannot rise above the level of the human material of which its voters are made" (*M&S*, 704). Thus, because we have "now reached the stage of international organization [at which] Man's political capacity and magnanimity are clearly beaten by the vastness and complexity of the problems forced on him," the only possible solution is to somehow produce a nation of Supermen voters (*M&S*, 693). The difficulty of this task can be read in the two-part nature of the inadequacy in question: "political capacity and magnanimity." A lack of the former might be supplied by better education and perhaps by a eugenic effort to raise the level of intelligence in the species, but it is the moral dimension—which seems to correspond at least in part to the "instinct" for world bettering Don Juan describes—that makes a simple breeding program inadequate. Tanner enthusiastically endorses eugenics, yet he admits that it cannot be a systematic, controlled program, as is animal breeding, because the necessary qualities that constitute a Superman are too little understood. "What is really important in Man is the part of him that we do not yet understand," Tanner explains, but the Life Force knows what it wants, so the best we can do is to be sure our social institutions do not limit eugenic choices by class or culture barriers, then "trust to the guidance of fancy (alias the Voice of Nature) both in the breeders and the parents, for that superiority in the unconscious self which will be the true characteristic of the Superman" (*M&S*, 694).

Tanner expresses his proposal in curiously religious phraseology, describing the breeding of a Superman as improving the "Temple of the Holy Ghost," just as Don Juan identified those who make themselves bored and wretched pursuing individual happiness instead of serving the will of the Life Force as lost souls misled by the Devil (*M&S*, 694). Yet it is only a new way of looking at a very old idea. Shakespeare has his famous bastard Edmund express a similar belief that partners joined by the "Voice of Nature"—here called the "lusty stealth of nature"—are likely to produce offspring who "take more composition and fierce quality" than those engendered perfunctorily through the usual arranged marriages of the time (*King Lear*, I, ii, 11–12). Even Bellamy and Morris, who insisted that it is only the social and economic structures that need to be improved, rather than the human animal, endorse this idea of improving the race through freer selection of partners. With Morris the improvement is striking but principally aesthetic. One proud resident of this utopia asserts that:

> There are some people who think it not too fantastic to connect this increase of beauty directly with our freedom and good sense in the matters we have been speaking of: they believe that a child born from the natural and healthy love between a man and a woman, even if that be transient, is likely to turn out better in all ways, and especially in bodily

beauty, than the birth of the respectable commercial marriage bed, or of the dull despair of the drudge of that system. (Morris, 79)

Bellamy's utopians seem to be thinking more along Shavian lines, however, and to be gently but intentionally developing a sense of selective breeding. At first it is described as an automatic result of other reforms; now that economic equality has removed barriers of class and made people financially independent of their spouses, "there are nothing but love matches." Dr. Leete explains that "for the first time in human history the principle of sexual selection, with its tendency to preserve and transmit the better types of the race, and let the inferior types drop out, has unhindered operation" (Bellamy, 267). No longer the "lusty stealth of nature," this practice is sanctified as "one of the great laws of nature now freely working out the salvation of the race" (268). And Dr. Leete asserts that the results are not merely cosmetic: "I believe that when you have made a fuller study of our people you will find in them not only a physical, but a mental and moral improvement" (268). Interestingly it is the moral improvement—the "magnanimity factor"—that seems to be the most prized, and it is also the quality that is most deliberately bred to produce people who see beyond those short-sighted personal aims that misdirected their ancestors. As Dr. Leete explains, "Individualism, which in your day was the animating idea of society, not only was fatal to any vital sentiment of brotherhood and common interest among living men, but equally to any realization of the responsibility of the living for the generation to follow" (268). This sense of moral responsibility, not only for the entire race but for future generations, sounds very much like the Shavian "world-bettering instinct." In Bellamy's utopia it is deliberately sought in parents, and selection on these grounds has been sanctified by religious doctrine and enforced by social mores, just as Tanner suggests. Dr. Leete comments:

> Today this sense of responsibility, practically unrecognized in all previous ages, has become one of the great ethical ideas of the race, reinforcing, with an intense conviction of duty, the natural impulse to seek in marriage the best and noblest of the other sex. . . . Our women have risen to the full height of their responsibility as the wardens of the world to come. . . . Their feeling of duty in this respect amounts to a sense of religious consecration. (268–69)

In Shaw's first "parable of Creative Evolution," his idea of developing the Superman genetically sounds much like Bellamy's. Inspired by Don Juan's sermon about the service of the Life Force, Donna Ana dedicates herself to the mission of producing the Superman with a feeling of "religious consecration" such as Dr. Leete describes among his contemporaries. When she hears that the Superman is not yet created, she cries, "Then my work is not yet done. (*Crossing herself devoutly*) I believe in the Life to Come. . . . A father! a father for the Superman!" and she vanishes to seek him (*M&S*, 649).

In his first articulation of creative evolution, then, it is clear that Shaw was already taking the ideas common to Socialist utopians and working them up to a more metaphysical level. He was further inspired and motivated a few years later by a speech he had heard from Sir Francis Galton in 1904. Galton asserted that eugenics deserved "strong claims to become an orthodox religious tenet of the future, for Eugenics co-operates with the workings of nature by ensuring that humanity shall be represented by the fittest races. What Nature does blandly, slowly and ruthlessly, man may do providently, quickly and kindly."[13] If we substitute "Life Force" for "Nature" and "blindly" for "blandly," Galton seems to be harmonizing with the religious philosophy Don Juan describes, though Galton uses more secular terms. Shaw's response to Galton's speech was emphatic: "There is no reasonable excuse for refusing to face the fact that nothing but a eugenic religion can save our civilization from the fate which has overtaken all previous civilizations" (Armytage, 70–71). By the time Shaw wrote his second parable, the devastation of World War I had inspired him with an even greater sense of urgency. According to Stanley Weintraub, the war made Shaw realize that the human species faced two alternatives: establish Utopia or be overtaken by catastrophe.[14] So, in 1918, Shaw tried again, expanding the idea that originally filled one act into a cycle of five plays, this time dispensing with the embellishments of the romantic comedy that he believed distracted audiences from his real message the first time. "The effect [had been] so vertiginous, apparently, that nobody noticed the new religion in the centre of the intellectual whirlpool," he noted ruefully in the preface to this second parable. He also added that "the war has been a stern intimation that the matter is not one to be trifled with" (*Methuselah*, vcix-c). To assure that no one could miss the new religion being articulated here, Shaw began *In the Beginning*—back with Adam and Eve—and took it far beyond the suggestions of Bellamy, Morris, and even Bulwer-Lytton, though Shaw referred to the fantastically evolved "Ancients" he portrayed in the last play, *As Far as Thought Can Reach*, as his "coming race" (*EPWW*, 287).

Yet the message in the second parable had changed considerably from that of the first. For one thing, although Shaw had not abandoned Socialism personally and continued to wield his pen in its behalf elsewhere, this parable contains no Socialist reformers and no hint that political or economic changes will help matters; he turned his attention entirely to the idea of saving the world by radically refashioning the human animal itself—as before, through willed evolution. This time, however, the characteristic humans must develop is not a nebulous quality in the unconscious man that Don Juan seeks to describe; it is a single specific trait from which all else will follow: longevity—a few hundred year's worth. As an enlightened (and extremely long-lived) character explains, "It is not enough to know what is good: you must be able to do it. They [twentieth-century people] couldn't do it because they did not live long enough to find out how to do it, or to outlive the childish passions that prevented them from really wanting to do it" (*Methuselah*, 186–87). Again, this echoes Tanner in identifying the two-part inadequacy in the human species that makes it incapable of establishing the socialist utopia: lack of political capacity, which would point out "how to do it" and lack of "magnanimity," which would make us "really want" to live there.

J. Wisenthal asserted that by the time Shaw wrote his second parable of Creative Evolution he had changed his proposed solution (from eugenics to willed longevity) because he had reidentified the problem: "In *Man and Superman*, man's inadequacy is seen mainly in terms of a lack of intelligence; in *Back to Methuselah* it is seen mainly in terms of a lack of maturity."[15] This is a bit reductive, as both plays stress the need for everyone to accept the moral responsibility for the fate of the species that now only world-betterers take seriously, and surely both intelligence and maturity are essential in developing a character that will accept that responsibility, but the difference Wisenthal points out identifies Shaw's *emphasis* in each play. In *Man and Superman*, the difference between the vital, socially responsible Don Juan and the cheerfully complacent and self-centered Commander is presented as the result of an active "world-bettering instinct" in the former and an atrophied or absent one in the latter. In *Back to Methuselah*, the difference between the two types is a difference in maturity. Before the evolutionary leap to longevity is achieved, we see the same contrast between the rare "instinctive" world-betterers and the ordinary Commander type (most clearly, perhaps, in the parlor of the Barnabas brothers as they confront the hopelessly self-centered and dim-witted politicians, Burge and Lubin). Afterward, however, when the contrast is between long-livers and short-livers, Shaw insisted that maturity must effect the change from a race of complacent, self-absorbed, "unpolitical animals" like the Commander to the sort of person Don Juan represents—the zealous servant of the Life Force.

This distinction is emphatically illustrated in a confrontational discussion between the Elderly Gentleman, a short-liver, and Zoo, a long-liver, whose name and general superiority recall Bulwer-Lytton's Zee. In her blunt assessment of short-livers' mental habits, we are reminded not only of the distinction Shaw drew very early in his career between idealists and realists (*The Quintessence of Ibsenism*) but also between the self-centered pleasure-seekers drifting in Hell and Don Juan, who was desperately bored with their illusions. Zoo asks, "Why do you shortlivers persist in making up silly stories about the world and trying to act as if they were true? Contact with truth hurts and frightens you: you escape from it into an imaginary vacuum in which you can indulge your desires and hopes and loves and hates without any obstruction from the solid facts of life" (*Methuselah*, 177). Yet she answers the question herself: "It is not the number of years we have behind us, but the number we have before us that makes us careful and responsible and determined to find out the truth about everything. . . . If I knew I had to die in twenty years it would not be worth my while to educate myself: I should not bother about anything but having a little pleasure while I lasted" (183). And she finally decides, as does Bulwer-Lytton's "coming race," that it is the duty of the superior race to supplant the short-livers: "You only encourage the sin of pride in us," she tells the elderly gentleman, "and keep us looking down at you instead of up to something higher than ourselves" (249).

Here again one can apply metaphorically what may not be acceptable literally. If what Zoo says is true, that it is not longevity per se that produces wisdom and social responsibility but the different attitude toward the future, by which "we are made wise," then maybe three centuries are not necessary to acquire the same superiority the long-livers exhibit. If concern for personal well-being can be transferred to the well-being of the whole species, the same concern could be felt for the next three centuries that the long-livers feel for their lifetime. Shaw described the effects of this sort of enlarged self-interest in some of his fellow world-betterers. He explains that people

> with a developed sense of life—men like Ruskin and William Morris and Kropotkin—have enormous social appetites and very fastidious personal ones. They are not content with handsome houses: they want handsome cities. They are not content with bediamoned wives and blooming daughters: they complain because the charwoman is badly dressed, because the

laundress smells of gin, because the sempstress is anemic, because every man they meet is not a friend and every woman not a romance. . . . The very air is not good enough for them: there is too much factory smoke in it. They even demand abstract conditions: justice, honor, a noble moral atmosphere, a mystic nexus to replace the cash nexus.[16]

He seemed to recognize the same characteristic in himself, but he described it not as an instinct, exactly, as it is in Don Juan, nor as the effect of a provision of longevity (he couldn't have predicted his ninety-four years). He expressed it in terms of his religion—as the inexorable workings of the Life Force. In a speech about the implications of Darwin's theories, written in 1906 for the Fabians but never delivered, Shaw took his "we must make a religion of eugenics" response to Galton one step further, incorporating a reinterpretation of Nietzsche's Will to Power in the process:

> . . . We must make a religion of Socialism. We must fall back dogmatically on our will to Socialism, and resort to our reason only to find out the ways and means. And this we can do only if we conceive the will as a creative energy, as Lamarck did. . . . We have to conceive this will which inspires us with the purpose of establishing Socialism as being what everybody used to call the will of God, and what some of us now prefer to call the purpose of Life. . . . To attain and maintain such faith, you must attach yourself, not to the reasonableness of the miracle, but to the unquestionable fact that it actually does occur. (Smith, 46).

This sounds much like Shaw's later argument in *Back to Methuselah*'s preface for the physiological application of Lamarckian evolution, applied here to political-economic evolution. However, here he offered one example of Lamarckian evolution "actually occurring," which is much more plausible than those he later gives for the physiological process. He described the evolution of a world-betterer:

> Take my own case. . . . My life has been a miraculous transformation of a good-for-nothing boy into the writer of this paper and of several quite unaccountable uncommercial plays, through a mysterious will in me which has prevailed over environment, heredity, and every sort of external discouragement. What is more, that will is not me: it makes the merest instrument of me—often overworks and abuses me most unreasonably. It makes me perform the feats of a bold, energetic, resourceful man, though I am actually a timid, lazy, unready one. It makes me write things before I understand them; and I am conscious that my own subsequent attempts to explain them are sometimes lame and doubtful. There can be no doubt that all writers who are original or inspired—whichever you choose to call it—write down things which are seen by later generations to imply

a good deal that the writer himself would have vehemently denied. (Smith, 46–47)

With this admission from the pen of the author, it seems fair to interpret his second parable in a way that the creative or inspired author might not approve. And certainly critics have done so, although Eric Bentley reported that "a few staunch Shavians have taken the theme as it stands. It has become for them the religion of the twentieth century," most accept a view modified by their own prejudices and predilections (Bentley, 53). J. J. Peerboom, who believed Shaw is valuable to posterity only for the witty comic dialog his plays contain, asserted that "few people if any derive their ideas of what should be done with the world from his works"—particularly not from his "political reconstitution and his credible religion."[17] Some critics hold that not even Shaw really believed the theories he outlined in his parables and prefaces. Despite the apparently earnest and literal "metabiological" treatise in the preface, Wisenthal opines that the "principal function of the idea of longevity in the cycle . . . is not so much to say that we can and should extend our lives as to provide a basis for the related satirical point that we behave like children" (196–97). Max Beerbohm, who believed *Methuselah* to be Shaw's "best book," felt that Shaw had at last "come manfully forth, saying 'I G.B.S. *know* and in my own person *assure* you that there isn't a ray of hope for the improvement of man's lot on earth.'"[18] Yet in his *Everybody's Political What's What?*, Shaw referred to his pentateuch in a chapter about "Coercions and Sanctions"—(a practical consideration in any political discussion):

> When I contributed my Utopia in a batch of plays entitled *Back to Methuselah* . . . I also had to find such a check; but I could not be satisfied with an imaginary one, as that would have taken me no further towards possibility and credibility than the older Utopians. There is no real hope in impossible Utopias. . . . And so, without introducing any magic, I made it possible to accept a story in which by evolutionary development of purely natural forces wisdom had become awful to the extent of becoming lethal. (*EPWW*, 286–87)

Clearly Shaw's "hopeful" scenario is not as easy to accept as he claimed here, except perhaps metaphorically. Yet not all critics have denounced Shaw for this. Holroyd acknowledged that the "metabiological" treatise in the preface to *Methuselah* "is an example of that compound of Will and Hope called wishful thinking" (41). The historical context in which Shaw managed to maintain that wishful thinking seems, to this writer at least, to justify it as a courageous response to the situation, not one of weakness. Holroyd reminded us that Shaw lived in a time of "hideous fatalism," yet he wrote with the belief that, as Shaw himself put it, "our will to live depends on hope . . . for we die of despair, or, as I have called it in the Methuselah cycle, 'discouragement'" (36). On the larger scale, Holroyd added, "He believed that civilization needed a religion 'as a matter of life or death'"—and it had to be a credible, hopeful religion (36).

This is perhaps Shaw's greatest accomplishment. Unlike some of the other clear-sighted, socially aware, and morally committed philosophers who wrestled with the same problems, Shaw obstinately held to the belief that as a species we can will ourselves to evolve into more enlightened creatures and outgrow our follies and brutalities before—or even after—they bring about an atomic Armageddon. He portrayed this defiantly hopeful vision in the last play he completed, *Farfetched Fables* (1949). He was well aware of the cataclysmic dangers posed by modern arsenals, as he wrote with the demonstration of Hiroshima fresh in his mind, so it is not surprising that one of the fables shows humanity's near self-destruction. A later act has a Socratic sort of schoolmarm coolly reminding her students that the age of the world is no longer known because "we lost count in the dark ages that followed the twentieth century." Shaw also felt compelled to remind us of a danger that even Bulwer-Lytton found worrisome, so the schoolmarm adds that "we may be killed as idiots and savages if we meet a later and higher civilization."[19] However, instead of showing humanity supplanted by a fantastically evolved super race, he portrayed these far-future people as still recognizably human, yet more enlightened than we, and the last line of the fifth fable reechoes the dauntless hopefulness that informed Shaw's life work: "The pursuit of knowledge and power will never end" (511). Finally, with his *very* last comment on the subject, a remark in *Sixteen Self Sketches*, Shaw closed on this obstinately optimistic note: "Creative Evolution can replace us; but meanwhile we must work for our survival and development as if we were Creation's last word. Defeatism is the wretchedest of policies."[20] Ultimately, perhaps, this is the most valuable gift that a utopian can give us: not a panacea-program to cure all of our social ills but merely the hope we need to keep striving for something better.

Notes

1. Bernard Shaw, "Man and Superman," in *Bernard Shaw: Complete Plays with Prefaces*, 6 vols. (New York: Dodd, Mead and Company, 1963), 3: 708. Further references to this work will be noted as *M&S*.

2. Bernard Shaw, *Everybody's Political What's What?* (London: Constable, 1944), 1. Further references to this work will be noted as *EPWW*.

3. Edward Bellamy, *Looking Backward: 2000–1887* (Boston: Houghton, 1926), 203.

4. William Morris, *News from Nowhere* (New York: Vanguard, 1926), 108.

5. Warren Sylvester Smith, *Bishop of Everywhere: Bernard Shaw and the Life Force* (University Park, Pa.: Penn State University Press, 1982), 170–71.

6. Edward O. Wilson, "Is Humanity Suicidal?" *New York Times*, 30 May 1993, 24–29.

7. George Bernard Shaw, *Back to Methuselah* (New York: Brentano's, 1921), lxv–lxvii. Further references to this work will be noted as *Methuselah*.

8. Eric Bentley, *Bernard Shaw* (London: R. Hale, 1950), 56.

9. Lloyd J. Hubenka, *Bernard Shaw: Practical Politics: Twentieth-Century Views on Politics and Economics* (Lincoln: University of Nebraska Press, 1976), 239.

10. James L. Campbell, Sr., "Edward Bulwer Lytton's *The Coming Race* as a Condemnation of Advanced Ideas," *Essays in Arts and Sciences* (16 May 1987), 55–63.

11. Edward Bulwer-Lytton, *The Parisians: The Coming Race*, vol. 2 (Chicago: Rand, 1871), 449.

12. Desmond MacCarthy, *Shaw's Plays in Review* (New York: Thames, 1951), 135, 136.

13. W. H. G. Armytage, *Yesterday's Tomorrows: A Historical Survey of Future Societies* (Toronto: University of Toronto Press, 1968), 70.

14. Stanley Weintraub, *Journey to Heartbreak* (New York: Weybright and Talley, 1971), 295.

15. J. L. Wisenthal, *The Marriage of Contraries: Bernard Shaw's Middle Plays* (Cambridge: Harvard University Press, 1974), 196.

16. *Bernard Shaw: Complete Plays with Prefaces*, 1: 310.

17. J. J. Peerboom, "Shaw's Own Utopia," in *Between Dream and Nature: Essays on Utopia and Dystopia*, eds. Dominic Baker-Smith and C. C. Barfoot (Amsterdam: Rodopi, 1987), 207.

18. Michael Holroyd, *Bernard Shaw: Volume III 1918–1950: The Lure of Fantasy* (New York: Random House, 1991), 54.

19. *Bernard Shaw: Complete Plays with Prefaces*, 6: 518.

20. George Bernard Shaw, *Sixteen Self Sketches* (London: Constable, 1949), 236.

Heartbreak House and the Trojan War
Kay Li

In an interview with Leon Hugo, Stanley Weintraub commented that "for decades [*Heartbreak House*] was taken as vaguely allegorical, although it has many levels of meaning, including a *King Lear* dimension, a Trojan War dimension, and even the qualities of a dream. We are beginning to see them."[1] The *King Lear* dimension has been thoroughly covered in Weintraub's own essay, "Shaw's Lear."[2] The dream qualities have also been discussed by various scholars, such as John A. Bertolini, who considers the play a fragmentary dream world in which the dreamlike state implies a threatened and fragile order on the verge of collapse.[3] The Trojan War dimension remains a promising area for exploration.

Although *Heartbreak House* (1916–17) contains references to the Trojan War and other Greek myths, most obviously in the use of names such as Hector, Hesione, and Ariadne, the play does not merely mirror an ancient myth. There are various Shavian distortions as Shaw manipulates the interplay between ancient myth and modern reality for his own purposes. The characters, built mostly on archetypes, become Shavian archetypes from World War I.

In his speech "Troilus and Cressida" (1884), Shaw described the mythic Hector as "one of the many sons of Priam, King of Troy, . . . the chief Trojan warrior."[4] In *The Iliad*, which Shaw had read as a youngster,[5] Hector, fighting for a dying culture, takes his place in the forefront and spurs the Trojans. He reassures his wife, Andromache: "But if I hid myself like a coward and refused to fight, I could never face the Trojans and the Trojan ladies in their trailing gowns. . . . I have trained myself always, like a good soldier, to take my place in the front line and win glory for my father and myself."[6]

Shaw's Hector Hushabye also possesses physical courage. To prove his courage, he will deliberately court danger to convince himself that he is not a coward.[7] However, Shaw gives his Hector ironic twists. He falls asleep, spends his time dreaming, and tries to escape from his heroic identity. His first line in the play is an attempt to repudiate his name:

THE MAN. [*with a mixture of confusion and effrontery, depositing his hat and stick on the teak table*] My real name, Miss Dunn, is Hector Hushabye. I leave you to judge whether that is a name any sensitive man would care to confess to. I never use it when I can possibly help it. (5:83)

The first action of Hector on stage is "depositing his hat and stick on the teak table" (83). The hat and stick are comparable to a helmet and sword, an association that Shaw had made in *The Perfect Wagnerite* (1898), when he described Alberic's magic helmet: "This helmet is a very common article in our streets, where it generally takes the form of a tall hat."[8] Hector's stick later turns out to be a "sword-stick" in the daydream scene towards the end of act II. Thus by analogy, in taking off his helmet and sword, Shaw's Hector disarms himself. He is no longer a soldier, and will fight his antagonists only in daydreams. The playwright intends this Hector to be a "liar, boaster, hero, stylist, Athos and D'Artagnan rallied into a single passionate sincere humbug."[9] He is Hector Hushabye, a name that "suggests generational somnolence."[10] Being symbolic of the death of heroism and the demise of his country and civilization, he can only dream of heroism instead of acting out the heroic.

In some ways Shaw's Hector resembles Paris: their potentials are equally wasted and neither wants to fight. In *The Iliad*, Hector chastises Paris, "Sir, no reasonable man could make light of your achievements in battle: you have plenty of courage. But you are too ready to give up when it suits you, and refuse to fight" (Homer, 130–31). Similarly Shaw's Hector can recognize his enemies: the Mangans who use the universe to serve their own interest; the Randalls who spend their time in love and sentiment; and the Billy Dunns who are thieves. Yet this Hector will neither fight nor kill his enemies. Instead he will spare them "in simple magnanimous pity" (5:101).

In the midst of the war, Homer's Hector finds Paris in his bedroom attending to his beautiful armor, his shield and cuirass, and examining his curved bow while Argive Helen sits beside him with her ladies-in-waiting and superintends their fancy work (Homer, 125). In *Heartbreak House,* when the country is going into war, Hector attends to his dueling pistols while Hesione supervises the running of the house and the servants. Both evade their duty to save the country. In *The Iliad,* Hector reminds his brother of his duty:

Sir, you disgrace yourself by sulking like this, while our men are falling in action round the town and at the very walls. It is your fault that this city is invaded by the sounds of battle, and you would be the first to quarrel with anyone else whom you found shirking his duty in the field. (Homer, 126)

This rebuke applies to the inhabitants of Heartbreak House, whom Shaw described in the Preface:

> The same nice people, the same utter futility. The nice people . . . were the only repositories of culture who had social opportunities of contact with our politicians, administrators, and newspaper proprietors, or any chance of sharing or influencing their activities. But they shrank from that contact. They hated politics. They do not wish to realize Utopia for the common people. (5:12–13)

The facsimile edition of the revised typescript of *Heartbreak House* shows that Shaw originally intended a second mythic name from the Trojan myth, Hesione, to be called "Hecky" and "Hecuba":

> NURSE GUINNESS. She says Miss ~~Hecky~~ Hessy invited her, sir. . . .
> THE CAPTAIN. But how could he, with a daughter? I, madam, have two daughters. One of them is ~~Hecuba~~ Hesione Hushabye, who invited you here.[11]

In the Trojan myth, Hecuba is the second wife of King Priam and the mother, not the wife, of Hector. The reason that Shaw makes his Hecuba into a wife-mother figure may be found in an earlier record. Shaw began writing *Heartbreak House* on 4 March 1916.[12] In *I Wander*, A. Emil Davies recalls that in May 1914, while on an evening walk, Shaw said that he had long harbored the desire to write a fresh Oedipus, in which the hero, on ascertaining what he had done, would turn to the crowd and say: "Gentlemen, I am sorry to discover that the gentleman I have slain happens to be my father, and the further news that you tell me—namely that the lady who is my wife is also my mother—is most interesting, and, makes me regard that lady with redoubled affection."[13] Here Shaw inadvertently foreshadows the Hector-Hecuba marriage in *Heartbreak House*, in which Hector loves his wife with "redoubled affection."

There may be another explanation for the presence of Hecuba in *Heartbreak House*. In domesticating Hector, Hesione-Hecuba emasculates her husband and metaphorically destroys him. A mythic parallel is the emasculation and destruction of Pentheus by his mother in the Bacchic rites that Shaw discussed in his Fabian lecture "The Illusions of War" (26 October 1915, King's Hall, Convent Garden):

> You will remember how the women in that play, the Bacchants, under the influence of the god Dionysus, go mad, and roam the countryside in the darkness, seeking to tear the wild beasts of the mountain limb from limb, with hand and mouth. The king Pentheus tries to stop the orgy

and is himself torn in pieces: and his mother, also among the Bacchants, finds in the morning that she is holding not the head of a wild beast she has killed, but the head of her own son.

There are women in Britain today who have gone mad in the pursuits of wild beasts, who are killing Germans with their mouths. On the morrow when they awake after their frenzy they will find in their laps the heads of their slaughtered sons. (Gibbs, 232)

These sentiments are echoed in the Preface in the sections "War Delirium" and "The Sufferings of the Sane." Like the mother who kills her son Pentheus inadvertently, the parents of the young men from the East End of London were war-delirious as they sent their sons to the war. Shaw writes, "The young men were having their teeth set on edge because their parents had eaten their sour political grapes" (5:30). In the play Hector belongs to the upper class, and he shares only Hesione's "confounded madness" of love, not of war. He is nonetheless enervated by his "mother" Hesione-Hecuba, and his political apathy still drives the country to war, resulting in the loss of the country's "sons."

In the final version of the play, Hesione is Mrs. Hushabye. In classical mythology, Hesione, as Priam's sister and the Queen of Asia, was associated with both sackings of Troy. She was saved from a sea monster by Hercules, who then burned Troy when her father, Laomedon, cheated him of his pay. Hesione was also abducted by Telemon after the first sack of Troy, and the Trojans' demand for her return was a cause of the Trojan War. As a classical siren, Shaw's Hesione has the power to lure Mazzini and Mangan away from their professed aims by her "song," her coaxing, teasing, and laughing. Like her mythic counterpart, she lures the sailors of the Ship of State to their fates. As the Hesione Hushabye who has fallen asleep and tries to keep herself away from the real world, she tells Ellie, "But I warn you that when I am neither coaxing and kissing nor laughing, I am just wondering how much longer I can stand living in the cruel, damnable world" (5:123). In the Preface, Shaw warns that eventually "Nature" will "take her revenge" (5:17) and wreck the unattended Ship of State.

With their links to the Trojan War, Hector and Hesione are doomed. They are the inhabitants of "Heartbreak House," "cultured, leisured Europe before the war" (5:12). They indulge in music, art, literature, and the theater. The Heartbreakers dwell in dreams and "wish to realize their favorite fictions and poems in their own lives" (5:13). They leave everything to the capitalist and quicken the approach of the war. Although their archetypes are actively involved in the demise of the ancient civilization, Shaw's Hector and Hesione contribute to the modern catastrophe—World War I—in their moral paralysis.

A third mythic character is Ariadne, daughter of King Minos of Crete, who loved Theseus and helped him out of the Labyrinth, thus betraying her father. Shaw's Ariadne Utterword leaves her father to go away with her husband, Sir Hastings Utterword. Hastings, like Theseus, is "colonizing."[14] According to Weintraub, the real life models for Ariadne and her husband are Virginia and Leonard Woolf: "If the attractive but haughty and high-strung Virginia Woolf were transmuted into the handsome, imperious Lady Ariadne Utterword, wife to Sir Hastings Utterword, (who never appears in the play), 'governor of all the crown colonies in succession,' it may have been in part because of the occupation for Ariadne's unseen husband suggested by Leonard Woolf's more modest background."[15] Leonard Woolf had worked as an "extremely successful colonial servant" in Ceylon. According to Quentin Bell, Leonard Woolf "learnt to travel and to live alone, to undertake the duties of a policeman and to exert the authority of a magistrate, to send men to their deaths and watch them hang, to perform the endless and endless boring tasks of empire."[16] Lady Utterword echoes this when she comments that Hastings will save the country: "There is Hastings. Get rid of your ridiculous sham democracy; and give Hastings the necessary powers, and a good supply of bamboo to bring the British native to his senses: he will save the country with the greatest ease" (5:165).

As a colonial "savior," Hastings echoes Theseus, who represents Greek colonizing efforts. Hastings's "absent" role in *Heartbreak House* finds support in Shaw's address, "On Christian Economics," delivered at a meeting of the City Temple Library and Debating Society on 30 October 1913. Both Greek and modern colonizations start with an attempt at enlightenment and end in strife war:

> [The Greeks] established Democracy in Athens: and what was the result? Having by Democracy established the rule of all the people, and made Democracy practically a great mass of persons with equal political power, the people so enfranchised, the Democracy, destroyed enlightenment. They indulged in the most unjust and tyrannical wars. They engaged in the task of building up a great empire; which simply meant stealing other people's countries, and trying to add them to theirs. They plunged into wars; and when they got into trouble with their wars, when they provoked other people to repel them, then they said: If they were attacked by other people, their honour obliged them to go on fighting, and to subdue their enemies.[17]

The Greeks destroyed themselves in their imperialistic war: "Then they laid the whole thing in ruins. It was destroyed and smashed: and that wonderful thing, the empire which came out of Democracy, is now a dream of faded splendour" (Chappelow, 149). Just as the inhabitants of Heartbreak House indulge in their dreams of heroism, the inhabitants of Horseback Hall are obsessed with their dreams of empire building.

The Utterwords fit into the myth of the Trojan war in several ways. First in *The Iliad,* the Trojans are "horse-taming" Trojans (Homer, 73). Similarly Ariadne Utterword thinks that horses and stables are important and that Heartbreak House needs horses to make it a sensible, healthy, pleasant house. The Utterwords are the inhabitants of Horseback Hall, "a prison for horses with an annex for the ladies and gentlemen who made them, hunted them, talked about them and sold them, and gave nine-tenths of their lives to them, dividing the other tenth between charity, church-going as a substitute for religion, and conservative electioneering as a substitute for politics" (5:14).

After her desertion by Theseus, Ariadne married the god Dionysus. Shaw's Ariadne, however, is not associated with natural creation and extension of life. She rejects what is natural and original in herself, hating the strange, unconventional ways of the house. She "longs to be respectable, to be a lady, to live as others did, not to have to think of everything for [herself]" (5:347). Thinking about what one "ought" to do, she subjects herself to the social systems that suppress her potential. Shaw's Ariadne denies the working of the Life Force through herself.

The parallels to the Trojan myth for the most part give negative dimensions to Shaw's modern version of Troy. But *Heartbreak House* does not reflect the myth by providing only mirror opposites, for Shaw reinvents the myth positively in the characterizations of Captain Shotover and Ellie Dunn. Frederick P. W. McDowell has written about Shaw's association of his stylized characters with myth and legend.[18] The most stylized character, Captain Shotover, reincarnated as a puppet in *Shakes vs. Shav,* also derives in part from the Trojan myth. Although old, like King Priam, Shotover, more than a venerable king past his prime, has a positive archetype in Odysseus. In *The Iliad,* Odysseus is "nimble-witted," "a master of intrigue and stratagem" (Homer, 69). In Shaw's speech on *Troilus and Cressida,* he refers to "Ulysses, as a worldlywise chief, whose shrewdness makes him a man of considerable mark in the camp, where muscle is at a discount, and brain at an extravagant premium" (Dukore, 13). Similarly, Shotover, although able-bodied no longer, is intellectually active. The mythic Odysseus feigned madness to avoid going to the Trojan War. This feigned madness may be compared with Mrs. Hushabye's telling Mazzini, "You don't mind papa, do you? He is as mad as a hatter, but . . . extremely clever" (5:72), and Lady Utterword's saying to Ellie, "My father is a very clever man; . . . And I must warn you that it is sometimes very hard to feel quite sure that he really forgets" (5:69).

More important parallels are those of Odysseus's wanderings and Shotover's journey. Among Odysseus's adventures was his encounter with Circe, the witch who was skilled in all enchantments. The hero stayed in Aeaea with Circe until she had borne him three sons, Agris, Latinus, and Telejonus.[19] In an analogous way, Hector tells Randall at the end of act II, "You are under a spell, man. Old Shotover sold himself to the devil in Zanzibar. The devil gave him a black witch for a wife; and these two demon daughters are their mystical progeny (5:156).[20]

As a skilled navigator, Odysseus successfully steered his ship clear of Siren Land, between Scylla and Charybdis, and avoided the Wandering Rocks. Shotover stresses navigation in his response to Hector's uncertainty:

> HECTOR. Well, I dont mean to be drowned like a rat in a trap. I still have the will to live. What am I to do?
> CAPTAIN SHOTOVER. Do? Nothing simpler. Learn your business as an Englishman.
> HECTOR. And what may my business as an Englishman be, pray?
> CAPTAIN SHOTOVER. Navigation. Learn it and live, or leave it and be damned. (5:177)

Both Shotover and Odysseus represent the skilled navigator who will "lay his course and stand on his bridge and steer it" (5:176). The two navigators are heroic. As the Captain tells Ellie in act II, "At your age I looked for hardship, danger, horror, and death, that I might feel the life in me more intensely. I did not let the fear of death govern my life, and my reward was, I had my life" (5:146).

Like Odysseus's slaughter of the importunate suitors of Penelope to regain control of his household and kingdom, Captain Shotover runs his household as a kingdom, with himself setting the rules of the house and all his visitors defined according to his mariner terminology: Ellie is regarded as the daughter of the villainous pirate Billy Dunn, Mazzini is the pirate, and Mangan is "not able-bodied" (5:86). The Captain controls his house as if he were controlling his crew: he whistles for Mazzini, and he asks Mangan to help him in the garden. Finally, Ellie is the real mythic recreation of Helen of

Troy in *Heartbreak House*. She is Helen's namesake. Just as the mythic Helen occupies the central position of the Trojan myth, so Ellie dominates *Heartbreak House*. In the speech on *Troilus and Cressida*, Helen's youth, as well as her beauty, is emphasized even though she is "seven years nearer to forty" (Dukore, 12), for example, "those whose imaginations are filled and satiated by the beauty of Helen" (Dukore, 15). Similarly when Ellie first appears on stage, the Captain says, "Youth! beauty! novelty! They are badly wanted in this house" (5:68). Helen was involved in love pursuits, and Ellie is engaged in hers in her own way. The Greeks tried to take Helen away from an undesirable alliance to Paris, while Hesione and Shotover attempt to break the match between Ellie and Mangan. The interest in Helen's marriages is similar to the interest in Ellie's "marriages."

Ellie is central to Shaw's transformation of Trojan myth into Shavian myth. She is the one person who changes through the play. At first she is inside the rigid framework of the Trojan myth. Her dealings with Hector, who is disguised as "Marcus Darnley," reveal her worship of the valiant, brave, romantic figure in the Trojan myth who is successful in both love and war. She is enamoured of "Marcus Darnley," whose "life has been one long romance," and who "has done wonderful things" (5: 79, 81). But she soon frees herself from the romance and sentiment represented in Helen of Troy. Learning the true identity of "Marcus Darnley" is like discovering the impossibility of mythic heroism in modern times. She says, "Damn! . . . I am not damning him: I am damning myself for being such a fool. [*Rising*] How could I let myself be taken in so? [*She begins prowling to and fro, her bloom gone, looking curiously older and harder*"] (5:84). She sees neither heroism nor glory in the modern warrior hero.

Ellie progresses from "Marcus Darnley" to Mangan, the practical businessman, and eventually to Shotover. But Shaw's Helen does not run after dashing young men. She tells Shotover, "my dreams are dashed to pieces. I should like to marry a very old, very rich man" (5:148). The "marriage" she is looking for is one with a man who is a combination of Shotover and Mangan. Her heartbreak, however, implies her willingness to fight as she tells Captain Shotover:

> ELLIE. I feel now as if there was nothing I could not do, because I want nothing.
> CAPTAIN SHOTOVER. Thats the only real strength. Thats genius.
> (5:148–49)

When she becomes Captain Shotover's "white wife," the "marriage" is symbolic. She says: "I became Captain Shotover's white wife. . . .

I, Ellie Dunn, give my broken heart and my strong sound soul to its natural captain, my spiritual husband and second father" (5:168). The marriage is made "in heaven, where all true marriages are made" (5:168). The marriage of Ellie and the Captain is a mystical union of the strength of youth and wisdom of the old, of the impulse of life with the spiritual guidance toward an ultimate, salvational purpose.

Finally the Trojan myth may also throw light on this curious exchange toward the end of the play:

> HECTOR. [*returning from the house and striding across to his former place*] There is not half light enough. We should be blazing to the skies.
> ELLIE. [*tense with excitement*] Set fire to the house, Marcus. (5:179)

In *Journey to Heartbreak,* Weintraub has traced the origins of this ending to the Zeppelin attack on 1 October 1916. The Trojan myth may offer another explanation. Troy, burnt and blazing to the skies, is echoed in *Heartbreak House,* when Hector and Ellie wish the house to be burning. Yet Heartbreak House is not burnt by the Zeppelin. Instead, it is shining in the dark because its own inhabitants will it to be so, even though they may be inviting their own destruction.

Heartbreak House was once entitled "The House in the Clouds." To Weintraub's assertion that Shaw may be inspired by Aristophanes' play *The Clouds* and the Cloud Kingdom of Laputa in the third book of Swift's *Gulliver's Travels,*[21] the Trojan myth may add another source. In *The Iliad,* Zeus is the "Cloud-Compeller," the "Lord of the Clouds," the "Cloud-gatherer," or "the Marshaller of the Clouds" (Homer, 366, 372, 36). "The House in the Clouds" may then refer to the god's dwellings on Mount Olympus and the palace of Zeus. It may also stand for a house saved by the gods because when the gods want to save a mortal, they wrap that mortal up in clouds as a protection from danger. That Heartbreak House is "The House in the Clouds" shows that the gods may save the house now. Although the inhabitants of Heartbreak House are leaving their fate to Providence, Nature will strike back if man does not learn navigation. In the Preface, Shaw proclaims that "Nature . . . demoralizes us with long credits and reckless overdrafts, and then pulls up cruelly with catastrophic bankruptcies" (5:17).

Notes

1. Leon H. Hugo, "In Search of Shaw: An Interview with Stanley Weintraub," *SHAW: The Annual of Bernard Shaw Studies,* vol. 12, ed. Fred D. Crawford (University Park, Pa.: Penn State University Press, 1992), 103.

2. Stanley Weintraub, *The Unexpected Shaw: Biographical Approaches to G.B.S. and His Work* (New York: Frederick Ungar Publishing Co., 1982), 173–80.

3. John A. Bertolini, *The Playwrighting Self of Bernard Shaw* (Carbondale: Southern Illinois University Press, 1991), 124–25.

4. Bernard F. Dukore, ed., *Bernard Shaw: The Drama Observed*, vol. 1: 1880–95 (University Park, Pa.: Penn State University Press, 1993), 12. The speech was read in Shaw's absence to the New Shakespeare Society on 29 February 1884. References to this speech will be quoted in parentheses in the text.

5. Bernard Shaw, "The Best Books for Children," *SHAW: The Annual of Bernard Shaw Studies*, vol. 9, ed. Fred D. Crawford (University Park, Pa.: Penn State University Press, 1989), 25–28. In this article Shaw recommends *The Iliad* to children saying, "Lord Derby's translation of The Iliad was inexhaustible." He lists "Homer (not Pope's)" among those books he would recommend for boys.

6. Homer, *The Iliad*, trans. E. V. Rieu (London: Penguin, 1950), 128–29.

7. Bernard Shaw, *Collected Plays with Their Prefaces*, vol. 5, ed. Dan H. Laurence (London: Max Reinhardt, 1970–74), 84. Subsequent references to Shaw's plays and prefaces are to this edition, citing volume and page number parenthetically in the text.

8. Bernard Shaw, *Major Critical Essays* (London: Penguin Books, 1986), 205.

9. "Bernard Shaw on Heartbreak House," *Illustrated Sunday Herald*, 23 October 1921, 5.

10. Rodelle and Stanley Weintraub, intro. *Heartbreak House and Misalliance by George Bernard Shaw* (New York: Bantam, 1995), xix.

11. Stanley Weintraub and Anne Wright, *Heartbreak House: A Facsimile of the Revised Typescript by George Bernard Shaw* (New York: Garland, 1981), 7.

12. Stanley Weintraub, *Journey to Heartbreak: The Crucible Years of Bernard Shaw 1914–1918* (New York: Weybright and Talley, 1971), 155. Shaw wrote to Mrs. Campbell on 14 May 1916, "I never felt so morose in my life. I cant write: nothing comes off but screeds for the papers, mostly about this blasted war. I am old and finished. I, who once wrote whole plays *d'un seul trait*, am creeping through a new one (to prevent myself crying) at odd moments, two or three speeches at a time. I dont know what it is about. I began it on the 4th March: and I have hardly come to the beginning of the first scene yet."

13. A. M. Gibbs, ed., *Shaw: Interviews and Recollections* (Iowa City: University of Iowa Press, 1990), 420.

14. *Heartbreak House: A Facsimile*, xv.

15. *Journey to Heartbreak*, 165.

16. Quentin Bell, *Virginia Woolf: A Biography* (London: The Hogarth Press, 1990), 178.

17. Allan Chappelow, *Shaw: "The Chucker-Out"* (New York: AMS Press, Inc., 1969), 149.

18. Frederick P. W. McDowell, "Technique, Symbol and Theme in *Heartbreak House*," in *Critical Essays on George Bernard Shaw*, ed. Elsie B. Adams, (New York: G. K. Hall & Co., 1991), 89.

19. Robert Graves, The Greek Myths 2, (Harmondsworth, England: Penguin, 1981), 359.

20. Shotover has "a wife somewhere in Jamaica: a black one. [His] first wife" (5:148).

21. *Journey to Heartbreak*, 183.

On Shaw's Contemporaries

Family Dynamics in George Gissing's Novels
Melissa Witte Antinori

In George Gissing's *New Grub Street* (1891), Marian Yule, torn between following her own inclinations and submitting to her father's wishes, cries, "Is there a natural law, then, that a daughter must be sacrificed to her father?"[1] Many women in late–Victorian England were faced with this dilemma as the new woman, who challenged the Victorian ideal of domesticity and dependence, was battling to gain acceptance, and women's rights was an increasingly debated social issue. At the same time that opportunities for employment outside the home were opening up for women, there were still expectations that a woman remain obedient to the men in her family, and many fathers (and mothers, husbands, and brothers) would have answered Marian's question with a resounding "Yes!"

The debate over women's roles was a major theme of the fiction of the late nineteenth century, with novelists of both genders coming down on both sides. Some women writers spoke out against the new woman, proposing instead that traditional gender relationships be upheld. Eliza Lynn Linton, for example, published a volume titled *The Girl of the Period* (1883), a collection of *Saturday Review* essays that attacked feminism. In her novel, *The One Too Many* (1894), Linton portrays the new women as completely vulgar. Linton was joined by other novelists who were wary of the changing role of women. Walter Besant's *All in a Garden Fair* (1883) suggests that talented women should use their gifts in support of their husbands rather than for their own advancement. His 1882 novel, *The Revolt of Man*, fantasizes a future world where women rule, men are mere ornaments, and religion has been discarded. When the men revolt and regain their superiority, religion is returned and there are happy marriages.

On the other hand, the questions raised by the new woman sparked a whole subgenre of fiction. Grant Allen's wildly popular *The Woman Who Did* (1895) was one of the hallmarks of the new woman genre; it centers on a woman who decides to live without marriage, who toils to raise her daughter alone, and who is eventually driven to suicide by the oppressive nature of bourgeois morality. Thomas Hardy's *Jude the Obscure* (1895) is bitterly critical of marriage. Sarah Grand's novels, *The Heavenly Twins* (1892), which questions the sexual double-standard, and *The Beth Book* (1897), one of the most polemical new woman novels, were not only popular in their own day but are still considered important feminist works.

George Gissing entered the discussion through his major novels of the 1890s: *New Grub Street* (1891), *Born in Exile* (1892), *The Odd Women* (1893), *In the Year of Jubilee* (1894), and *The Whirlpool* (1897). In these novels, Gissing creates a series of female protagonists with varying degrees of independence from domestic situations and different stances on modern and traditional values. Although he is clearly sympathetic to his protagonists' plights and critical of the patriarchal system that entraps women, Gissing is never able to free them from that system, and he never poses a viable solution to their struggles.

Scholars have long disagreed about Gissing's view on women's roles: some argue convincingly for Gissing as a strong feminist; others see him as a staunch supporter of the traditional woman. Among those critics who classify him as a feminist are Robert Selig, who argues that Gissing was not pleased with Nancy Lord's decision to submit to Tarrant in *In the Year of Jubilee;* Irving Howe, who focuses on the heroine's fight for emancipation in his introduction to *New Grub Street;* and Jacob Korg, who writes that Gissing's views on the woman question were "clear, consistent, and uncompromising" and that Gissing, partially because of his own marital difficulties, hated the Victorian myth of the inferior woman.[2]

More recently, feminist critics have tended to read Gissing as somewhat ambiguous but essentially antifeminist. Alice B. Markow argues that Gissing did not look beyond Victorian feminist stereotypes and that he supported traditional female roles through his fiction. Deirdre David deals with the conflict between patriarchy and feminism in *The Odd Women* and holds that although the novel is about the conflict between the two, it is also about the conflicts within the feminist movement. She concludes that the novel does not completely embrace that movement although it is critical of the current system. Patricia Stubbs classes Gissing among the late nineteenth-century writers who led a counterattack against the women's movement. Pierre Coustillas, looking at the connection between Gissing's life and his fiction, posits that Gissing faced a real dilemma when it came to women and that he was "disgruntled at the mediocrity of the present . . . yet distrustful of progress."[3]

One aspect of this question that has not been examined is the role of family dynamics, especially as those family relationships affect Gissing's female protagonists. In five novels of the 1890s, a definite pattern emerges. Gissing depicts a series of tyrannical fathers and ineffective or uninterested mothers who primarily affect a daughter featured in each novel. These daughters want freedom but are so trapped by their upbringings that they are ultimately unable to break free, usually to their own detriment. In addition to the father/daughter relationships, Gissing explores women's roles through a series of mothers who are faulted on two sides. They are either unable or unwilling to question their husbands' power and are thus complicit in the system, or they are too interested in their own pursuits to devote themselves to their families and are, therefore, open to censure. In contrast, Gissing does present several "good" mothers whose maternal instincts are emphasized and who support themselves, because they have to, in traditionally female jobs. In Gissing's scheme no woman could have both a strong family relationship and fulfillment in another sphere. This can be seen in the family patterns outlined above and, finally, in a set of polar opposites: in *The Whirlpool*, Mrs. Morton raises a family in pastoral perfection; in *The Odd Women*, Rhoda Nunn is emphatically free from family ties.

It becomes clear that Gissing was never able to reach a conclusion on the proper social sphere for women. Although he is clearly critical of the patriarchal system and of the women who are complicit in it, he is equally critical of the women who ignore their family obligations in favor of independence and personal fulfillment. He never offers a median between the two extremes. In this way, Gissing is like the characters who populate his novels. Although he is painfully aware of the problems with Victorian patriarchy and the restricted role it prescribes for women, he is trapped within that system. Like the women he portrays, Gissing is too conditioned by the system he was born into to do more than criticize. He never provides a viable alternative and never wholeheartedly advocates change.

Many recent sociological studies of the Victorian family have not only increased knowledge of this aspect of Victorian culture but have also increased awareness of the relationship between fiction and the family, a relationship that is central to Gissing's narratives. The family was of primary importance in Victorian culture, especially in the middle classes featured in the novels I examine. In his study, *A Prison of Expectations,* Steven Mintz notes that the Victorian family was increasingly private and isolated and that children lived with their parents longer than they had in any previous period.[4] Paula M. Cohen explains this isolation: "Families were seen as retreats from a hostile external world and, hence, the definition of sex roles, the requirements of etiquette . . . evolved to enforce that separation."[5]

The middle-class family was especially difficult for a daughter to thrive in. Carol Dyhouse writes that although the privacy of the family was beneficial for men, who daily entered the larger world, "for women, it became a prison," and she notes that images and metaphors of confinement often appeared in women's writings about the family.[6] It seems to have been a widely accepted practice, one supported by many mothers, that brothers' needs and education took precedence over those of their sisters, and that sisters were expected to "dance attendance" on their brothers (Dyhouse, 16). Although boys were encouraged to have a variety of experiences as they entered their teens, girls of the same age were increasingly protected and cut off from the world, a concession to the social mores of the period. In addition, a daughter was expected to keep her father company, especially if he was a widower, and often one daughter in the family would remain unmarried to attend to her father—David Roberts uses the term "special servant"—as he grew old.[7]

The middle-class father was remote but sovereign. He may often have been absent from home, but his position of power was supported by tradition and by the mother, who seldom questioned his authority. The father could dictate the career of the son and could arrange the marriage of the daughter, who often passed from financial dependence on her father directly to financial dependence on her husband (Roberts, 62–71). Mintz writes that symbolically the father stood for "public and external conceptions of authority," as well as for authority in the home, and that "it is the father who provides the children with an example of instrumentality in contrast to the mother's affectivity" (Mintz, 61). Gissing understood that these family dynamics created many social problems—according to Jacob Korg, Gissing held this family structure responsible for his marital failures—but he was too much a product of the system to be able to promote its complete revision.

I. Fathers and Daughters: Patriarchy and Tyranny

Gissing does create some admirable fathers. Godwin Peak, who bears a distinct resemblance to Gissing, remembers his father with affection; Harvey Rolfe loves his son and takes great pains with his education; Arthur Peachey kidnaps his son so that he will not grow up under the pernicious influence of Ada; and Basil Morton is the picture of perfection.[8] The father/son relationship prospered under the established family system.

The problem arises when a father tries to dominate his daughter, to dictate her education, and to demand her intellectual and emotional allegiance. In the novels I examine, Gissing sets up a series of tyrannical fathers—Alfred Yule, Stephen Lord, Martin Warricombe, and Dr. Madden—who attempt to control their daughters either directly or through their wills. Gissing criticizes the patriarchal system that ruled the contemporary household, showing that it was neither viable nor desirable for the women forced to live under its strict rules. All the women affected by the Victorian patriarchal family are affected negatively.

The most tyrannical father, Alfred Yule of *New Grub Street*, also has the most interesting daughter. Yule himself is a pathetic figure, a writer of some talent whose chances for literary success were ruined by his marriage to a socially and intellectually inferior woman, and there are parallels between Yule and Gissing himself, who had lately embroiled himself in a similarly disastrous marriage. Gissing portrays Yule as such a coward and hypocrite, especially in relation to his wife and daughter, that it is impossible for the reader to sympathize with him. Yule managed Marian's education, training her to be a valuable literary assistant, and, until the period of the novel (she is twenty-three), Marian has been content with this life. When she develops a romantic interest in Jasper Milvain, she begins to crave independence. Yule is disturbed that his daughter is "occupied with something other than her old wish to aid and satisfy him, that she had a new life of her own alien to, and in some respects irreconcilable with, the existence in which he desired to confirm her" (*NGS*, 289). At the same time, Yule realizes that he cannot treat her with the "tyrannous usage" that marks his relationship with his wife. He does, however, still demand "an entire [intellectual] allegiance from his daughter; he could not bear to think that her zeal on his behalf was diminishing" (*NGS*, 290).

Yule sometimes conceals his attempts at control by tricking Marian into doing his bidding while still maintaining her respect. He realizes for instance, that Marian's writing has "merit of a kind quite distinct from anything of which he was capable," and the narrator makes it clear that "his" articles contain much of her writing. Still he will not allow her to sign her name to them until such an action can work to his own financial advantage (*NGS*, 81). His scheme to get Marian's money for his journal only wins him the scorn of both his daughter and the reader, as does his stubborn refusal to believe that Milvain did not write an article he found offensive in order to cause a rift between Marian and her suitor. The reader is assured that it really came from the pen of Fadge, Yule's nemesis, and that Yule knows this.

Marian herself is one of Gissing's strongest women, and Gissing uses her relationship with her father to highlight her power. Her father respects and fears her. In addition, her education has been both successful and useful. She is a talented writer, and at the end of the novel, the reader is given the satisfaction of learning that Marian was rumored to have done "all the work [her father] signed" (*NGS*, 541). Marian is very different from the women Gissing sometimes creates—shallow, cruel, status-conscious Amy Reardon and social-climbing Maud Milvain, for instance, who serve as Marian's foils in this novel. Unlike these women, she is level-headed and "not readily the victim of illusion; thinking much and speaking little." She knows what she can expect from life and is fully aware of the limitations placed on women of her education and social standing (*NGS*, 194).

Marian strongly protests the position that her father would dictate for her. Arguing with her mother about her right to refuse to give in to her father's magazine scheme, Marian asserts, "My patience is at an end when I am treated as if I had neither rights nor feelings. . . . Is there a natural law, then, that a daughter must be sacrificed to her father?" (*NGS*, 425). Later, on the verge of breaking up with Jasper, Marian uses similar language, stating that "there is no natural law that a child should surrender everything for her parents" (*NGS*, 530). It is unfortunate for Marian, but characteristic of her society, that on both occasions she would have Jasper be the beneficiary of her money, and that she would, in essence, transfer her loyalty from her father to her husband. However, she does not do this, and it is much to Marian's credit that she finally rejects Jasper, largely to maintain her own self-respect. The relationship ends with Jasper "suffering a severe humiliation" (*NGS*, 532).

The ending of *New Grub Street* illustrates Gissing's ambiguity about the woman question. Gissing clearly admires Marian. Adrian Poole goes so far as to postulate that "it was into Marian Yule that [Gissing] projected his deepest desires for emotional fulfillment, and his deepest fears about the value of . . . education and culture."[9] Yet for all her development, Gissing summarily dismisses Marian from the novel, telling the reader only that she took a job as an assistant librarian in a provincial town to support her mother and blind father, that "the name of Yule was no longer met with in periodical literature" (*NGS*, 534), and, later, that her father is dead. In deciding to accept the library job, Marian answers the question that plagued her:

there is, if not a natural law, then a social one, that asks her to sacrifice herself to her parents. By following this course, Marian does what is best for her father, but she also chooses the avenue of self-respect and the best alternative to a bad marriage that society can provide. At the same time, the reader knows that her talents would have been best used had the option to stay in London to write been open to her. However, Marian is still in an unusual position for a woman of her time in that she remains single and becomes the sole breadwinner for her family. For Gissing, perhaps, Marian represents the best of both worlds. She is educated, independent, and far above the Jasper Milvains of society, but she still ultimately accepts her place in the family hierarchy. Marian comes as close as any Gissing character to the mean between the traditional and the modern. It seems that Gissing does not know what to do with this modern woman after she accepts a more traditional, and perhaps incongruous, role, so he banishes her from London and from the novel.

In some ways, *In the Year of Jubilee*'s Nancy Lord is Marian's opposite. Although Marian's education taught her much, Nancy's has been a sham, although "Nancy deemed herself a highly educated young woman,—cultured was the word she would have used."[10] Marian at first struggles to get along with her father, but at the beginning of *In the Year of Jubilee*, Nancy rebels against the constraints her father sets for her, demanding that she be allowed to go about as she pleases and escaping from the escort he provides to guide her around the Jubilee. Where Marian is genuinely concerned with her father's business, Nancy is blissfully ignorant of her father's finances, thanks to his decision to keep her out of this sphere. Thus she is primarily concerned with her social status and with "experiencing" the world. To Nancy's credit, she is an intelligent woman, and at certain moments she feels the limitations of her education, although her inability to act on these feelings reinforces the uselessness of that education.

Nancy's father, Stephen Lord, is a somewhat more sympathetic figure than Alfred Yule. Lord had planned his daughter's life when she was a child. He confides to Mary Woodruff that he meant both of his children to be simple minded, that he wanted Nancy to marry "a plain countryman," and that he blames himself and his social status that his plan did not materialize (*Jubilee*, 80). Lord is not, like Yule, afraid of his daughter, but he is uncomfortable around her and feels some dismay that he cannot understand her. The narrator notes that Lord "never looked fixedly at his daughter, and even a glance at her face was unusual," and Nancy's sudden, uncharacteristic aggressiveness startles her father and makes him uneasy (*Jubilee*, 28).

Lord makes it quite plain to Nancy that he sets rules for her because she is a woman. When Nancy cites her age (like Marian Yule, she is twenty-three at the novel's outset) as a reason for independence, her father responds that "that would be something of an answer if you were a man." This remark angers Nancy, who fires back, "because I am a woman you despise me" (*Jubilee*, 28). She fails to realize, perhaps, that Lord does not despise her simply because she is a woman, but because he fears that she will become like her mother, who deserted her family to seek a more comfortable and more pleasurable life. That Nancy should be like her mother is unacceptable to Lord, who reveres domestic women like Mary Woodruff. Knowing that he is dying, he determines to leave a will forcing Nancy to remain single and live under Mary's care until she is twenty-six. If she marries before that time, she will lose her inheritance. Nancy, secretly married to Tarrant, must continue to keep her marriage and her child a secret, and out of financial necessity, she is forced to submit to Tarrant's neglect and an unfulfilling marriage.

Lord does seem motivated by unselfish impulses, and through the story of his own marriage, the reader is made to understand his concern for his daughter. However, this makes him no less a tyrant. Whatever the reader may feel about Nancy's choice of a husband—and Tarrant is considerably less attractive than the ambitious Crewe or the plodding Barmby—it is clear that Gissing uses her dependence on her father's money to criticize women's education.

Only because she is unfit for any gainful employment can Nancy's father have posthumous control over her actions. Unable to find a job and desperately lonely, Nancy begins to reject the notion of the modern woman and comes around to a more traditional point of view. "What right" [she muses] "had a mother to be searching abroad for tasks and duties? Task enough, duty obvious, in the tending of her child" (*Jubilee*, 297). In addition, she regrets that she chafed under her father's authority, lamenting the loss of "her friend in every best sense of the word, her guide and protector" (*Jubilee*, 325). Unlike Marian Yule, who even when deciding to support her parents never ceases to question the claims her father makes of her, Nancy concludes that her father's happiness should have been her highest concern and would have been her best education: "For long years it was in her power to make him happy, and, in doing so, to enrich her own life, to discipline her mind as no study of books, even had it been genuine, ever could" (*Jubilee*, 325). It is ironic that Nancy makes these rationalizations only when she has no other choice. She must submit to the conditions of her father's will or lose her money, and there is doubt that she would have reached the same conclusions had some other avenue been open to her. It is ironic, too, that the life she envisions had she been obedient to her father would have differed little from the life she is now living. She would have had little independence, she would have remained isolated from the intellectual society she craved, and she would have very likely been in an equally loveless marriage with her father's business partner. The traditional path is painful, but there is no viable alternative.

Sidwell Warricombe reaches a similar conclusion in *Born in Exile*. Faced with the choice of marrying Godwin Peak, whom she has come to love and respect, or remaining with her father, to whom she has become an increasingly important companion, she chooses not to darken her father's old age by deserting him. Sidwell, however, does not make this decision without much careful thought, and she realizes that her upbringing has "bound [her] to a certain sphere of life," ruefully acknowledging that "the fact that I have outgrown it counts for nothing" and admitting that she acts largely out of concern for her family's comfort.[11] In the eyes of society, Sidwell chooses "correctly," but this choice does not leave her to live the contented existence that many would imagine for her. Sidwell decides to stay with her father with full awareness of her reasons, acknowledging both that she has been conditioned by the expectations of her culture, which demands that she value her father's will above her own, and that she has been rendered unable to disregard those expectations, although her decision leads to her own unhappiness and Godwin Peak's death.

This father/daughter dynamic is also present in *The Odd Women*, although the only father, Dr. Madden, dies early in the novel and he is not, like Yule and Lord, overtly dominating. In one sense Madden is merely careless and unlucky. He has put off buying life insurance, and a strange twist of fate causes him to die in a freak accident on the eve of his decision to purchase a policy. However, the reader learns that Dr. Madden has very definite opinions about the role of women in society, opinions that are far-reaching in their effects. He tells Alice in the opening scene that girls should not be troubled with money matters. "Let men grapple with the world. . . 'tis their nature to" is his motto, and he admits that since her mother's death, he has turned to Alice for companionship.[12] Lounging on the lawn, surveying his offspring, Dr. Madden muses "what a delightful old age his would be, when some were married and had children of their own, and the others tended him—they whom he had tended" (*OW*, 4).

Dr. Madden directed his daughters' education, assuring himself that they have been given the knowledge necessary for ladies of leisure. Although it "never occurred [to him] that his daughters would do well to study with a professional object," he assumes that they will teach if they have to, but is unwilling to dwell on any unpleasant eventualities (*OW*, 3). One sister, Isabel, does become a teacher but is so overworked that she despairs and commits suicide at age twenty-two, and while Alice and Virginia dream of starting a school, their education has been so impractical that they are unable to earn the capital needed for their venture. Although physically absent, Dr. Madden's presence is felt throughout the novel, and Gissing uses Madden's influence on his daughters' education as a springboard for launching the criticisms of the male-dominated system and women's education that pervade the novel.

Like Madden, all these fathers misunderstand their daughters. Yule has given Marian a useful education, but in educating her he has failed to realize that this education would make her independent. Lord mistakenly equates independence with wantonness. Warricombe cannot recognize that his daughter has, in maturing, developed ideas incompatible with her former self. For their part, Gissing cannot allow the daughters—all strong women in other respects—to disavow their familial ties. Instead they end up sacrificing themselves to the traditional ideal, remaining in a system that clearly is not viable for them. This inconsistency is a result of Gissing's own equivocal stance on the woman question. Critical of the social traditions that require daughters to acquiesce to their father's wishes at the expense of their own, he cannot get beyond criticism and offer these daughters a way out of their quandaries.

II. Mothers: Modernity versus Domesticity

Gissing created few good fictional mothers, and the bad ones tend to fall into two categories. Mrs. Yule and Mrs. Warricombe are passive observers of the father/daughter relationships, whereas Ada Peachey, Amy Reardon, and Alma Rolfe are destructive mothers who could potentially ruin the lives not only of daughters but also of sons. The gender difference here is telling. When the mother is bad, the child is always a son and is given a supportive father. When the father is the destructive parent, the mother is complicit and cannot rescue her daughter. The admirable mothers are drawn to their daughters by instinct and, when they function outside the home, they are content to do so in traditionally female occupations.

Mrs. Yule's plight is pitiable. Having married outside her class, she lacks the education that would have made her an interesting companion for her husband or for Marian. This, however, is no excuse for the way she is treated. She is mentally abused by her husband, who vents his professional frustrations on her and who will not allow her to be close to her daughter. The narrator encourages the reader's sympathies, noting that "it can scarcely have been a light trial to the mother to know that contact with her was regarded as her child's greatest danger; but her humility and her love for Marian offered no resistance" (NGS, 96). Gissing suggests that both parents are dangerous to Marian. Mrs. Yule's fear of her husband makes her comply with his wishes, and she is unable to be Marian's advocate in her quest for independence.

Born in Exile's Mrs. Warricombe's inability to understand her daughter's plight is not merely the result of lack of opportunity. For her, social concerns are all-consuming, and none of her opinions is the result of profound thought. Mrs. Warricombe, for instance, is shocked at Buckland's graduation when an openly atheistic master speaks, not because of his ideas, but because of her social position. Like Mrs. Yule, Mrs. Warricombe could be dangerous to her daughter. Left to her own devices, she would have secured a match between Sidwell and the handsome and polite, but hypocritical, Bruno Chilvers. In addition, she has little sympathy with her daughter and is therefore unable to help her decide about Godwin Peak. To the end of the novel, Mrs. Warricombe remains blissfully unaware of the extent of Sidwell's relationship with Peak or of her pain in rejecting him.

Whether or not they are at fault, both of these mothers are nonetheless complicit in that system. Neither questions the authority of her husband—Mrs. Yule out of fear, Mrs. Warricombe because the idea never occurs to her—and neither offers her daughter any support in her struggle to become free. In both cases, the daughters choose their families over their own desires and bow to their fathers' wishes instead of pursuing their own.

Although Mrs. Yule and Mrs. Warricombe are passively menacing, a second group of mothers is actively dangerous to their children. Of his actively bad mothers, Ada Peachey of *In the Year of Jubilee* is unquestionably the worst. She enjoys the frivolities of fashion too much to take care of her child, she is slovenly, and she is well on the way to making her child like her. One of the first objects we see in the novel is "a broken toy, one of those elaborate and costly playthings which serve no purpose but to stunt a child's imagination" (*Jubilee*, 2). By the time her husband determines to leave her, Ada has become a "wild animal," revealing herself in her fight with her sisters as "the spawn of Whitechapel," seemingly the lowest form of humanity that Gissing could envisage (*Jubilee*, 253). Peachey does return to his wife for a brief period, and they have a second child, a daughter, whom Peachey is content to leave with his wife when he runs away for the last time. His son remains under his sister's expert care.

The Whirlpool's Alma Rolfe and *New Grub Street*'s Amy Reardon (Marian's cousin) both wreak havoc on their domestic tranquillity by seeking fame and admiration. Originally content to live quietly in the country with her husband and baby, Alma soon suffers from acute ennui and must return to the city to pursue a career in music. Alma admits that she has "no profound love of the art," and the narrator notes that there was "nothing more natural than her laying [her violin] completely aside when . . . she missed her sufficient audience."[13] Similarly, Amy openly admits to herself and her husband that "one of her strongest motives in marrying him was the belief that he would achieve distinction . . . [and] that no degree of distinction in her husband would be of much value to her unless she had the pleasure of witnessing its effect upon others; she must shine with reflected light before an admiring assembly" (*NGS*, 137).

Both women use their families to their best advantage. For Alma, it is most convenient to ignore her child, who never captures her attention or imagination, leaving his education to a hired nurse and his concerned father. Although she does not physically leave her husband, she emotionally detaches herself from him because he is unenthusiastic about her career, a feeling for which Gissing does not condemn him. This detachment causes Alma to turn to whoever will help her. Unfortunately, she puts herself into the wrong hands and becomes embroiled in the murder of Cyrus Redgrave, who years earlier had shocked Alma with his proposition that they live together without the inconvenience of marriage. Only total disgrace makes Alma see how much value her family really has, and realizing that she has lost her husband's love forever, she commits suicide.

Unlike Alma, Amy Reardon does take an active interest in her son. However, the depth of her attachment is suspect, and the narrator makes it clear that Amy's interest in her son is, in part, motivated by a desire to pique her husband. Tired of Reardon's lack of progress on his novel and tired of living in poverty and out of society, Amy "withheld as much as possible from the intercourse which might have been one of her chief pleasures . . . alleging that she devoted herself to a serious course of studies, that the care of house and child occupied all the time she could spare from her intellectual pursuits. The worst of it was, she had little faith in the efficacy of these fictions. . . . She grew angry with herself for being dishonest, and with her husband for making such dishonesty needful" (*NGS*, 138). Amy relishes the freedom she feels after leaving Edwin, and the narrator makes it clear that her decision to take him back will depend on his appearance and apparent financial status. Amy certainly has some feelings for her child and husband, and her despair when they die seems genuine. However, her attentions are primarily motivated by self-interest. She recovers from her bereavement quickly enough and is "rewarded" by becoming Jasper Milvain's wife, thereby obtaining the "reflected light" she so craved. Gissing condemns Amy for her choice. Although Jasper "triumphs," Amy, unlike Marian, does not see through the facade of his success.

In these five novels, there are four mothers whom Gissing does not criticize. Mary Woodruff, of *In the Year of Jubilee*, serves as a much better guide for Nancy than her own mother, who reappears, expressing concern for her long-abandoned children but ultimately hoping to gain some financial advantage from them. Mary is clearly Nancy's father's ideal, and he commits his daughter to Mary's care when he dies. The other three come from *The Whirlpool* and serve as foils to Alma Rolfe. Like Mary Woodruff, Mrs. Frothingham and Mrs. Abbott both assume the role of mother for children who are not their own. Both women have led questionable lives, especially Mrs. Abbott, who drove her husband to an early death through her desire for social advancement. Both reform themselves and become, in Gissing's scheme, admirable characters. Mrs. Frothingham attempts to make reparations to all those her husband's financial collapse hurt and takes an active interest in Alma's well-being, even though Alma is merely her stepdaughter. Mrs. Abbott becomes a teacher to support herself and her wards, the Wager children. All three women assume their roles out of a sense of duty and, Gissing suggests, natural instinct. All three earn their money through means that were widely accepted for women: Mary Woodruff is a housekeeper, Mrs. Abbott a teacher, and Mrs. Frothingham the beneficiary of her husband's will and, in a sense, the administrator of a charity.

The Whirlpool's third mother, the most "nearly perfect" mother of all, is Mrs. Morton, into whose "pure and healthy mind had never entered a thought at conflict with motherhood" (*Whirlpool*, 324). She manages the house efficiently and effortlessly and devotes herself with zeal and competence to her children's education. Mrs. Morton provides a contrast to Alma Rolfe and exists in a pastoral setting that has little in common with everyday reality. The other three women function in society and illustrate Gissing's approval of the woman who does so within traditional professional and domestic spheres.

In a society so dominated by the family, women without that encumbrance are remarkable. In the five novels I examine, there is only one woman who lacks family. Not surprisingly, she is found in *The Odd Women*. When Rhoda Nunn first appears in the novel, she has an invalid mother, presumably no father, and is "singled at a glance as no member of the Madden family" (*OW*, 3). Unlike the Madden girls, Rhoda knows that she will have to earn a living, and, at age fifteen, she is already preparing for her career. In most ways, Rhoda is lucky when compared with the Madden sisters. She has had no father to leave her unprepared, and whatever the Victorian reader may have thought of her politics and her social position, Rhoda is infinitely better off than the Maddens at the end of the novel, which leaves Monica dead, Virginia in the Victorian equivalent of Alcoholics Anonymous, and Alice bordering on religious fanaticism. However, Gissing depicts Rhoda as too ardent and uncompromising to be completely sympathetic and too abrasive to be a realistically successful advocate of change.

There seems to have been no real development across the novels in the period. The father/daughter relationship does not become progressively better. Women are never able to reconcile a nontraditional professional role with a traditional family one. All of Gissing's female characters remain trapped in the dominant family dynamic of late Victorian culture.

Adrian Poole observes that what Gissing most admired about Charles Dickens—apart from his literary and financial success—was Dickens's ability "simultaneously to share and criticize the central forces shaping contemporary society." This was Gissing's ideal image of the integrated, yet still independent, author (Poole, 110). However, Gissing felt this ideal was no longer possible in a literary world where, to be successful, a writer had to be like *New Grub Street*'s Jasper Milvain, pandering to public taste and telling the reading public exactly what it wanted to hear. Ironically, this ideal is an integral part of Gissing's own novels. He criticizes certain aspects of his society—the state of women's education, the stifling atmosphere of the family—but he is also immersed in that society, and one of its main components was the idealization of the traditional woman. Consequently, Gissing, like Marian Yule and Sidwell Warricombe, recognizes that a problem exists but is never able to advocate a complete revision of women's roles.

Notes

1. George Gissing, *New Grub Street* (London: Oxford University Press, 1958), 425. All future references to *New Grub Street* will be designated in the text as *NGS*.
2. Robert L. Selig, "A Sad Heart at the Late Victorian Culture Market: George

Gissing's *In the Year of Jubilee,*" *Studies in English Literature 1500–1900* 19 (1969): 703–20; Irving Howe, introduction to *New Grub Street,* by George Gissing (New York: Houghton Mifflin Co., 1962), v–xxi; Jacob Korg, *George Gissing: A Critical Biography* (Seattle: University of Washington Press, 1963), 185–86.

3. Alice B. Markow, "George Gissing: Advocate or Provocateur of the Women's Movement?" *English Literature in Transition* 25 (1982): 58–73; Deirdre David, "Ideologies of Patriarchy, Feminism, and Fiction in *The Odd Women,*" *Feminist Studies* 10 (1984): 117–39; Patricia Stubbs, *Women and Fiction: Feminism and the Novel 1880–1920* (New York: Barnes and Noble, 1979); Pierre Coustillas, "George Gissing's Feminine Portraiture," *George Gissing: Critical Essays,* ed. Jean-Pierre Michaux (New York: Barnes and Noble, 1981), 106.

4. Steven Mintz, *A Prison of Expectations: The Family in Victorian Culture* (New York: New York University Press, 1983), 11–17.

5. Paula M. Cohen, *The Daughter's Dilemma* (Ann Arbor: University of Michigan Press, 1991), 4.

6. Carol Dyhouse, *Feminism and the Family in England, 1880–1939* (Oxford: Basis Blackwell, Ltd., 1989), 14.

7. David Roberts, "The Paterfamilias of the Victorian Governing Classes," *The Victorian Family: Structure and Stresses,* ed. Anthony S. Wohl (New York: St. Martin's Press, 1978), 64.

8. For an extended discussion of the father/son theme in Gissing's fiction, see Pierre Coustillas, "Gissing's Reminiscences of His Father: An Unpublished Manuscript," *English Literature in Transition (1880–1920)* 32 (1989), 419–29.

9. Adrian Poole, *Gissing in Context* (London: MacMillan, 1975), 153.

10. George Gissing, *In the Year of Jubilee* (London: Sidgwick and Jackson, Ltd., 1911), 14. All future references to *In the Year of Jubilee* will be designated in the text as *Jubilee.*

11. George Gissing, *Born in Exile* (London: A. and C. Black, 1892), 3:244. All future references to this edition will be designated in the text as *BE.*

12. George Gissing, *The Odd Women* (New York: Stein and Day, 1968), 1. All future references to this novel will be designated in the text as *OW.*

13. George Gissing, *The Whirlpool* (London: Sidgwick and Jackson, Ltd., 1911), 245. All subsequent references to *The Whirlpool* will be found in the text and will be designated *Whirlpool.*

The Curious Affair of the Lady Venus
M. D. ALLEN

WHEN, as late as 1933, Lady Evelyn Cobbold became the first European woman to reach Mecca, she made less of a splash than she had hoped. The Foreign Office duly sent a copy of her *Pilgrimage to Mecca* (London: Murray, 1934) to the British Legation in Saudi Arabia, then located in Jedda, and the minister there permitted himself to wonder, in the privacy of a note back to the Foreign Office acknowledging receipt, whether Lady Evelyn's was a genuine first. In particular, Sir Andrew Ryan (1876–1949, minister at Jedda, 1930–36) was teased by memories of one possibly inconclusive case. On his behalf, Jedda's Chancery wrote,

> À propos of Lady Evelyn's claim to be the first European woman to get to the Holy Cities [of Mecca and Medina], we should much like to know whether any further light was ever thrown on the case of Zohra Begum, which formed the subject of Mr. Consul Zohrab's despatch to the Foreign Office No. 6 Consular of the 12th March 1879 and of the epilogue to "Six Months in Meccah" (London, 1881) by T. F. Keane, who records his meetings with her earlier in the same book. The Minister thinks it probable that other European women must have got to Mecca, but the only recorded case seems to have been that of Zohra Begum. . . . if indeed she was an European [spaced periods in original].[1]

It does indeed seem strange that the first thirteen or so centuries of Moslem/Christian confluence and conflict should have passed with no Western woman reaching Mecca and that the feat should have been left to this century and to a Scottish aristocratic convert to Islam. Was there no female equivalent of Joseph Pitts, an Englishman captured by pirates in 1678, forcibly converted to Islam and taken as a slave on the Pilgrimage? Did no Western wife of an African, Arab, or Asian Moslem—no other version of the Lady Jane Digby who married a Beduin sheikh in the nineteenth century—voluntarily accompany her husband on the *hajj*? And *was* Zohra Begum a European woman, despite her name?

Her story, as told by Keane in *Six Months in Meccah,* is affecting.

A "chatty old [Meccan] barber" once mentioned to him, "There is an Englishwoman in Meccah, 'The Lady Venus' by name."[2] Keane, posing as a Suni from Bombay who knows some English (but, in a double-blind, probably not as much as he claims), said, "I will speak English to her and find out who she is" (39). After some attention-getting comments about the incongruity ("I . . . once met a Cambridge B.A. before the mast in a whaler; but this seemed impossible even to me" [40]) and pitifulness of the woman's situation ("To have to spend a whole life . . . in such wretchedness and misery, buried alive in Meccah" [40]), the interview duly took place. Lady Venus (a literal translation of "Zohra Begum") was living in the house of an Indian Mutineer who had fled to Mecca to escape British vengeance. She was

> sitting on the floor in the costume of the country—a figure squatted down with a sheet thrown over it and the edges well tucked under, two slits somewhere near the eyes with pieces of gauze sewn over them for looking through. Give the whole a convulsive subdued shaking, and you have the "Lady Venus" as I first saw her. . . .
> She evidently understood my real character, and it seemed a painful interview to her. We sat silently for some minutes, the motion of her hand to her eyes under the veil showing she was in tears. . . .
> I found that she had been amongst Mohammedans since 1858; and satisfied myself, in the half hour's conversation, that she was a real, educated Englishwoman. . . . She told me the part of the Haram in which she prayed, where I could meet her any day at noon. (43-44)

Subsequent meetings did take place. Keane reports that Lady Venus beckoned to him from under her garments at the Haram (the part of the mosque reserved for women), that he followed her at a distance, and that they talked together. "How we let loose our English tongues! Sometimes we laughed loudly, sometimes she cried. . . . Before parting she raised her veil and showed me her face, which was as English as my own" (55). Some weeks later, Lady Venus, by prearrangement, walked back and forth under Keane's window. He met and learned more about her:

> As well as my memory serves me, she told me that her name was "Macintosh," her father a doctor, and that she had lived in Devonshire in her youth, that she was at Lucknow at the time of the siege, and had been taken from there by a leading rebel. She avoided going into particulars, so that I did not ascertain whether she went willingly or as a captive. She said she had lived a year or so in India with this man, and that he had been hunted out of the country by the English, who set a price on his head, and had found refuge in Meccah, taking her with him; that he

had died eight years before, leaving her in poverty, and that she now made a living by embroidering skull-caps, which she sold to the dealers in the bazaars. . . .

She mentioned the names of a number of men living in Meccah who she said had been rebels or mutineers, also telling me the prices set on their heads by the English Government, and appeared perfectly set up in everything connected with the siege and relief of Lucknow. (171–72)

On a later occasion, she showed him what Keane calls her "much-thumbed treasure"—five pages of an almanac, with Coronation Day and the anniversary of Waterloo marked (188), and on yet another she became "slightly hysterical" and endangered them both (189). On their last meeting, they walked two miles outside Mecca. Keane asked, "'If I come back for you will you go to England with me?' to which she replied 'Yes,' much in the same tone as the little boy answered the lady who asked him, 'Could you eat a bun?'" (200). Again she behaved "foolishly."

Three times I said "With you be peace" and left her, but she followed me to the gate of the Haram, and I had to go back and speak to her and tell her that people were noticing her strange conduct. The last time I went back I led her to the opposite side of the Haram, and then said "good-bye" and ran out of one of the near gates. As I passed out I looked out and saw her sitting down against one of the pillars and a number of children standing round looking at her. This was the last time I saw the "Lady Venus." (210)

The story figures occasionally in standard accounts of travelers in the Middle East. Augustus Ralli devoted a chapter to Keane and three pages to Lady Venus in his *Christians at Mecca*,[3] and R. H. Kiernan (*The Unveiling of Arabia*) gives him a paragraph, including the observation that "his story . . . aroused considerable incredulity when it appeared in print, especially that part which dealt with the Englishwoman in Mecca."[4] Keane rates a couple of pages in Robin Bidwell's *Travellers in Arabia*, in which he is said to have "wandered around happily . . . chattering with a Muslim lady who, as Miss McIntosh [sic], had been taken prisoner during the Indian Mutiny."[5] For Richard Trench in *Arabian Travellers*, Keane's *only* importance is his meeting "that most extraordinary of Meccan residents, the redoubtable Miss Macintosh." Trench's two paragraphs about her, influenced by the stereotypical indomitable English spinster abroad, contain details (for example, the claim that she was "sent to India as a governess") that can only have arisen in his imagination.[6]

John Fryer Thomas Keane, the man without whom there would

be nothing known of the allegedly English Zohra Begum, was born in Whitby, Yorkshire, the eldest son of the highly respected Rector there in 1854. Both the Rector and his wife had Anglo-Indian connections: in 1846 the Rev. William Keane (1818–73) had become Senior Canon of St. Paul's Cathedral, Calcutta. Giedon Smales reports that "he [W. Keane] early learnt one of the numerous languages of India, and preached to the natives in their own tongue."[7] His son described his father more extravagantly as "perhaps one the best speakers of native dialects in India."[8] William Keane was obliged to return to England, apparently for health reasons, in 1852. In the following year, he married Elizabeth, "the daughter of the Honourable J. F. Thomas, a Member of the Council of Madras" (Smales, 190). It seems that Keane owes his three forenames to his distinguished maternal grandfather. Perhaps this highly respectable background was a little too respectable for the young Keane. He ran away to sea at the age of twelve. The rest of his life was, in a word taken from one of his book titles, a "wanderer's." Before performing the *hajj* in 1877–78, he had, at the age of eighteen, obtained a second-mate's certificate and "served in that capacity in many seas."[9] After the Pilgrimage, he worked as a journalist in London (1879–83), was a correspondent in French China (1884–85), worked as a journalist again (1887–90), and then began the long association with Australia, where he spent the rest of his life. He includes in his *Who's Who* entry that he "spent 1890–99 in the far interior, mostly in unexplored country" and that in 1903 he "worked for 95 days of 12 hours each as a cane-cutter in the northern cane-brakes of Queensland, to prove that the work could be done by white men." He died in the Eventide Home in Charters Towers, Queensland, on 1 September 1937. His burial record, under the heading "REMARKS," reads "SENILE DECAY."[10] Born in a confident and expansive age, Keane was almost unkillable and, in his own words, sought fulfillment in "a life of the wildest adventure . . . in every quarter of the globe."[11]

The most memorable of his exploits was his performance in disguise of the *hajj*. The most memorable part of Keane's hajj—distinguishing it from the experiences of other Europeans in Mecca, including the Englishman Herman Bicknell, his immediate predecessor (1862), and the Dutchman Snouk Hurgronje, who followed him (1885)—is his encountering Zohra Begum. If his cheerful and unprofound narrative is enlivened by other adventures, including a schoolboy's crying, for some unfathomable reason, the dread word "Christian!" and its almost fatal aftermath, and a fellow pilgrim's avenging of an insult by the infliction of a wound that again almost has fatal consequences, then it is still the passages about Lady Venus that remain in the mind.

In the "Conclusion" to *Six Months in Meccah*, entitled "Lady Venus," Keane writes that he has been "withholding [his] MS. from the publisher for the last eight months in the hope of being able to add, in conclusion, the [complete] story of the 'Lady Venus'; or, at least, to be able to assure the reader of her release" (205). On his return to England, Keane had spoken to "gentlemen who had been either long residents in India or were well-known travellers in the East" (206). These gentlemen brought the existence of an Englishwoman in Mecca to the attention of the government, which asked the Foreign Office to instruct its Consul at Jedda to send a Moslem agent to the Holy City. (It is the consequent report of Mr. Consul Zohrab that Sir Andrew Ryan recollects half a century later.) "The inquiry," writes Keane, "found my statements of her existence and locality correct, but she had left Meccah a short time previously for India, accompanying the family with whom she had been living in Meccah. As she was now no longer within the range of the Foreign Office (Consular), the India Office was moved to go on with the necessary inquiry, and with some difficulty the lady was traced in India and at last found" (206).

So far, so accurate. But Keane's next sentence—"Whether she is really an English lady, now unwilling under her sad and painful circumstances to disclose her real identity, is open to doubt"—indirectly confesses that although subsequent investigations had indeed confirmed "my statements of her existence and locality," they had not confirmed Lady Venus's alleged Englishness, nor her status as a captive. The semiofficial report of the English magistrate in India whose wife was eventually allowed to speak to Lady Venus is quoted at length, including its author's considered judgment that "in the face of her repeated and unreserved statement it is difficult if not impossible to believe that she is an Englishwoman, although fair enough to pass for one. . . . My own impression is that her father (of whom she says she knows nothing, and about whom her mother would never disclose anything to her) may have been an Englishman, and her mother, as she says, a Kashmirin" (209–10). Keane quotes the magistrate's finding that "she . . . denies . . . that she is an Englishwoman who was ravished from her friends during the Mutiny, forced to turn Mohammedan and marry her ravisher" (208). In his last paragraph, he does what he can to buttress his book's main selling point, the mingled romance and horror of an *Englishwoman*'s spending two decades in Mecca against her will: "Either her present statement is true, or, as some think, after her sad and painful captivity and degradation of more than twenty years, and the uncertainty she may feel about finding a home and maintenance open to her, she prefers to remain in her present obscurity and seclusion" (212).

By the time the Foreign and India Offices had concluded their investigations, nobody thought that Zohra Begum was an English captive, and Keane probably never had.

The Public Record Office papers, F.O. 370/461, documenting the search for and eventual interview with Lady Venus, not only flesh out Keane's eight-page "Conclusion," but also clarify what he recorded truthfully and what he elaborated. What they do not do, however, is determine who Zohra Begum really was.

According to Augustus Ralli, only thirteen Westerners had performed the hazardous exploit before Keane, and only three of these—the enslaved Pitts (in 1680), the celebrated Sir Richard Burton (1853), and Keane's immediate predecessor, Herman Bicknell (1862)—were Britons. However, some of Keane's forerunners had provided detailed accounts of the Moslem Holy Cities, their buildings, and the rites practiced therein and thereabout. Even the inquisitive Burton, writing nearly thirty years previously, had found nothing new to say about Mecca. D. G. Hogarth's magisterial *The Penetration of Arabia* (1904) notes, "In a place already so well described as Mecca there was nothing for him to discover, and nothing for his successors, Von Maltzan and Keane, who likewise saw it only during the brief sojourn of the pilgrims."[12] Although some publisher would find a book on the *hajj* acceptable, and it might even sell well, a new angle was needed. Keane saw in the figure of Zohra Begum, suitably embroidered, that new angle.

We have no way of knowing whether Keane consciously planned to arouse interest in the book he had projected by telling his "story to a number of gentlemen who had been either long residents in India or were well-known travellers in the Middle East" (206), or whether he spoke irrepressibly and soon found himself in deeper waters than he had anticipated. A letter of 23 January [1879] from E. B. Thomas (here is one of Keane's Anglo-Indian uncles) discusses possible rescue missions with an unnamed Foreign Office official and reveals that Captain Richard Burton, the author of *A Personal Narrative of a Pilgrimage to El-Medinah and Mecca* (1855), had been consulted: "It will be done best (Capt: Burton thinks) by private effort, disguise & reward for rescue. The favour I might have to ask from the F:O: is only an intimation to your consul at Jedda, to 'afford such aid as he safely and properly could.' . . . I am appealing to the 'Indian Mutiny Fund' Office, for the necessary aid which I am in hopes they will grant—they have just called a special meeting on the case" (P.R.O.). As a postscript Keane's uncle adds that "the matter is not unknown to Ld: Salisbury [the Foreign Secretary]—thro' Capt. B."

Things moved quickly after that. The Foreign Office letter to the consul in Jedda, James Zohrab (8 February 1879), contains a note of skepticism but takes the allegation seriously:

> The woman in question is stated to be educated and intelligent, but now in misery and poverty and desirous of escaping from Arabia.
> Mr. Keane's account, improbable as it is, may possibly be true, and if so every exertion shld: be made to find out this woman and to get her away in safety from Mecca. (P.R.O.)

But it was too late. Zohrab was able to confirm (12 March 1879) that an Englishwoman had been "brought to Mecca about 22 years ago by some Indian fugitives from the mutiny." She had entered the harèm (i.e., the quarters reserved for women—there is no question of sexual servitude) of an Indian after the death of her husband (nationality not stated) the previous year. After her protector died, she had been taken to India by his son a mere nine days before the date of Zohrab's letter. "She is tall & thin between 40 & 45 years of age and when she left Mecca was concealed under a white cloak" (P.R.O.).

The next letter of significance in the file is again from E. B. Thomas, addressed to a Lt. Col. Burne, Political Secretary in the India Office. Keane was now receiving more attention than he had probably expected. The anger and desire for vengeance for the events of 1857 and 1858 in Thomas's letter could well have made his nephew uncomfortable. After noting that Keane was about to leave once more for Mecca to attempt the rescue of Lady Venus, with whatever feelings of reluctance or resignation, Thomas describes himself as "having from the first, taken much interest in the case, and used my best effort to bring it to notice, and induce action in the matter." He supposes Lady Venus to have been taken to India in part "to prevent her ... disclosing the knowledge she had of Indian Mutineers, still hiding in Mecca, their last refuge." Then in the third of his numbered paragraphs, rage and contempt manifest themselves:

> 3. If she has ever been, as is conjectured, a *lady*, or even any respectable European female, it is impossible to suppose that she *can* desire to *remain* in her present degraded and painful position or be *really*, (as may be pretended), a *willing* captive, and convert to the Mahomedan faith. . . .
> 4. . . . It would surely be a duty, both public and private, to rescue her from a position of such unparalleled misery and degradation.

5. The known facts of the Indian Mutiny, comprise many dark and sad tales of suffering and death, undergone by English officers and ladies; *their* sufferings were great, but are almost out done [sic], by the prolonged captivity and mental misery of the captive now sought to be rescued—

Whether the Indian Government see fit to act on it or not, it might be interesting to learn from the captive, what she *knows* of the escaped Mutineers yet harbouring in Mecca.

It is possible the Nana himself may be amongst them. (P.R.O. Emphasis in original.)

Nana Sahib, the "demon of Cawnpore," had ordered or permitted the massacre of British officers, women, and children after having offered them safe-conduct. This incident outraged British public opinion. Nana Sahib escaped the gallows, probably dying of fever in Nepal in 1859, but British officers were arresting men resembling him as late as 1895.[13]

The son of Zohra Begum's Indian protector had brought only two widows of his father from Mecca, neither of whom was likely to be Zohra Begum, and British officials could not ignore the sanctities of the harem. Then W. T. Martin, the officiating magistrate of Aligarh, discovered "that there was another widow and that she was actually an 'Angrezin' [i.e., Englishwoman or foreigner] without children" (P.R.O.). Martin's wife was deputed to speak to her, and on 26 June 1879, "Magistrate, Aligarh" was able to telegraph, "INTERVIEW with lady in question took place last night. She is not English—perhaps Eurasian. Mr. Keane's description answers generally, but is not confirmed on material points" (P.R.O.).

Keane had included in his "Conclusion" the finding that "she . . . denies that she is an Englishwoman, who was ravished from her friends during the mutiny, forced to turn Muhammadan and marry her ravisher." The one-and-a-half page account of Zohra Begum's life included in Martin's full report denies the truth of other of Keane's stories.

> While at Mecca I was known as an Englishwoman, and four Europeans at different times came out of curiosity to have an interview with me. I never saw their faces, but always conversed with them from behind a purdah. I never made any signs, overt or covert, to any European in a mosque, nor did any European follow me for a long way after I left the mosque and then have an interview with me. I do not recollect having had an interview with a young Englishman so recently as only a few months ago. . . . I positively deny that I was carried away by force

during the mutiny, nor did I ever complain of oppression. I never expressed any desire for escape from Mecca. What was there to escape for? (P.R.O)

It is no surprise that Keane chose not to quote from or refer to the document embodying Zohra Begum's comments made during the interview. His final "Note" to the book in which he narrates the second half of his Pilgrimage (*My Journey to Medinah*, published later in the same year as the Mecca volume, 1881) is somewhat testy:

> Throughout the whole of the enquiry, instituted by the Government, to ascertain the truth of my statements concerning her, she has been extremely reticent as to her antecedents. But she has admitted that she is English [this contradicts both the truth and concessions made at the end of the earlier volume], and it has been discovered with tolerable certainty who she really is [an exaggeration, at best].
> She is now amply provided for in India, and has expressed a desire that she be left unmolested in that country, in her present retirement, and the obscurity of a native home.
> Every possible inducement has been held out to her to return to Christianity; but as she remains obdurate, nothing can be done for her, and I unquestionably can give no more publicity to her case, or divulge anything further concerning her. (*My Journey to Medinah*, 211–12)

His claim in the same place that he now possessed a private letter written to him "by the English lady whom I met at Mecca," from which he does not quote, seems dubious at best.

It is likely that Keane never met nor even saw Zohra Begum. He probably heard about her during his half-year stay in Mecca in some detail and recognized a good thing when he heard it. The "painful" first interview with Lady Venus in tears, her walking about under Keane's window, and her repeated exclamations of "Ah, child! You don't know what it is to me to see you" (189) probably never happened.

Keane's fabrications were no doubt suggested by the famous story of the Mutiny's Miss Wheeler, the Eurasian daughter of General Wheeler. She, according to a version widely propagated by melodramas, books, and magazines, killed her Indian abductor and his family and then threw herself down a well as the only way of expunging the shame she had suffered. Keane is less likely to have heard the story of Amelia Horne, another Eurasian woman whose manuscript account is to be found in the British Library. "She was, she claimed, forcibly converted to Mohammedanism and married to a mutineer who eventually allowed her to escape to Allahabad after she had signed a paper exculpating him" (Hibbert, 194–95).

Just as Miss Wheeler's real history is so much more poignant than the crude cartoon version of British myth, so is the known history of Zohra Begum more touching than Keane's vulgar playing to the gallery. She was a Eurasian, not an Englishwoman, the widow of a shop-keeper and glassware-merchant, not a Mutineer, the object of Indian kindness and hospitality, not of violence and sexual outrage. Martin, who was not allowed to see her, writes of the mysteries still surrounding her, including the "vicissitude of fortune over which a veil still hangs (her own story to the contrary not withstanding)" that took her to Mecca, and including the high quality of her English, as manifested in a letter she wrote to him, now almost certainly lost:

> It will be observed that the letter has but few mistakes either in spelling or in idiom; and it is all but impossible to believe that she would have been brought up otherwise than as an English-speaking person, and therefore the mystery about her is only enhanced. (P.R.O.)

At least this should increase the reputation of Lady Evelyn Cobbold. On 3 September 1934, the Foreign Office Library, having done its homework, was able to write to the Jedda Chancery, "Zohra Begum was at best a Eurasian, and therefore provides no counterblast to Lady Evelyn Cobbold's claim to be the first European woman to visit Mecca.

"We cannot find any mention of any other European woman having reached Mecca."

Notes

Public Record Office file F.O. 370/461 is British Crown copyright and is reproduced with permission of the Controller of Her Britannic Majesty's Stationary Office.

I am grateful to Professor Virendra Sharma of the University of Wisconsin -Fox Valley for help in the elucidation of certain foreign words and phrases in F.O. 370/461.

1. Public Record Office. F.O. 370/461.
2. J. F. T. Keane, *Six Months in Meccah: An Account of the Mohammedan Pilgrimage to Meccah. Recently Accomplished by an Englishman Professing Mohammedanism* (London: Tinsley, 1881), 38.
3. Augustus Ralli, *Christians at Mecca* (London: Heinemann, 1909).
4. R. H. Kiernan, *The Unveiling of Arabia: The Story of Arabian Travel and Discovery* (London: Harrap, 1937), 191.
5. Robin Bidwell, *Travellers in Arabia* (London: Hamlyn, 1976), 128.
6. Richard Trench, *Arabian Travellers*, (Topsfield, Mass.: Salem House, 1986), 93.

7. Giedon Smales, *Whitby Authors and Their Publications with the Titles of All the Books Printed in Whitby, A.D. 670 to A.D. 1867* (Whitby: Horne, 1867), 190.

8. J. F. T. Keane, *My Journey to Medinah: Describing a Pilgrimage to Medinah, Performed by the Author Disguised as a Mohammedan* (London: Tinsley, 1881), 211.

9. *Who Was Who, 1929–1940* (London: A. & C. Black, 1941).

10. John Wehlow (town clerk), Charters Towers, Queensland. Copy of burial record in letter to the author, 22 October 1992.

11. J. F. T. Keane, *Three Years of a Wanderer's Life* (London: Ward and Downey, 1887), 204.

12. D. G. Hogarth, *The Penetration of Arabia: A Record of the Development of Western Knowledge Concerning the Arabian Peninsula* (London: Lawrence and Bullen, 1904), 188.

13. Christopher Hibbert, *The Great Mutiny: India 1857* (New York: Viking, 1978), 207, 387.

Additional Verse by Hilaire Belloc: An Edition

MIKE MARKEL

IN an article in *The Chesterton Review,* I described the Boston College Belloc collection, consisting of some one hundred boxes of the writer's papers and books, including his manuscripts, library, correspondence, diaries, and notebooks.[1] And in *English Literature in Transition 1880–1920,* I presented and analyzed some of Belloc's published but uncollected political verse, mostly dating from the period of the Marconi scandal.[2] The Estate of Hilaire Belloc has granted permission to publish the manuscript verse from the Boston College collection.

Presented here is a brief sampling of those manuscript verses, with editorial notes covering provenance and selected topical references. All the poems are copyright 1997 The Estate of H. Belloc and printed by permission of Peters Fraser & Dunlop. I have tried to follow the principle of final authorial intention, that is, to reproduce the version of the poem that Belloc would have considered final. The minute stages of Belloc's composition process are not recorded. For example, I have not indicated whether a passage was a superscript insertion or an emendation. I have recorded, however, those passages in which Belloc had not yet decided on which of two alternative phrases to use. Standard editorial symbols have been used: [?word] for an uncertain reading, and [word] for an editorial insertion.

One cautionary note is necessary immediately. I cannot with complete certainty say that a manuscript poem has never been published, for Belloc did not keep detailed records. In fact, his personal diary contains a disconcerting entry for 5 November 1920: "Found at Maurice's [Maurice Baring] house a good deal of original verse of my own which has not been published. Did not know it existed." Although I have searched the available indexes, it is possible that one of several of these poems might have been published.

You will notice that most of the poems printed here are undated. In many cases, I cannot place a poem even within a particular decade, for Belloc's style, working methods, and, to a large extent, his subjects and opinions, remained unchanged throughout his adult life. In other cases, references to external events indicate that a poem must have been written after a certain date. However, because Belloc was the consummate grudge carrier it would be risky to say that a poem was written soon after a certain date; in his correspondence, for example, he frequently railed against rival politicians years after their deaths.

[On what known hills?]

I
On what known hills? In what remembered skies?	a
Or over what familiar following seas	b
Or in what bower of morning did you rise	a
West Wind of the contented? That to these	b
Dull shores of ageing—an appalling breeze	b

Quick with the Drums of Life you bear the power
To stir the buried Dead and wake th'accomplish't hour?

II
Why will you vex me? I have paid the Debt	a
Which all to the Inexorable pay:	b
The Soul's long dues of Hardening and Decay	b
That should redeem me from this Olivet	a
Of purposeless but passionate regret	a

For Paz del mar[1] and that strong Youth of Mine
When I was nursed in light and kissed of lips divine.

III
The Californian Mountains come at night
They come at night and rob me of my rest.
They lift in peace along the stainless west
And call me till the beckoning of that sight
Resolves the world of darkness and a light
Is shining in the wraith that laughs and stands
⎧ a ghost within me stands.
A captain-hearted boy ⎨ of new discovered lands.
⎩

Source: Appears on a plain sheet of paper approximately 20 x 25.5 cm. A second sheet of the same size contains a different but less complete version: the first two stanzas are virtually the same, but stanza III contains only three and one half lines. Also appearing on this second sheet are seven uncompleted lines (some containing accent marks in place of words) of stanza IV.

Commentary: A third sheet of paper, titled "Schema," throws additional light on this fragment. "Schema," essentially a listing of first lines (or portions of first lines) of stanzas, indicates that Belloc planned a poem of twelve stanzas, the first three of which begin as in the fragment printed above. The ten complete first lines are as follows:

1) From what known hills, in what remembered skies
2) Why will you vex me, I have paid the debt
3) The Californian mountains come at night
4) There lies the lake
5) [Indecipherable]
6) You are more terrible than Sleep and Death
7) But you bear that which died and will not die
8) And in the places I no longer know
9) Feed me with beauty as the flowers are fed
10) For now the night completed tells her tale
11) Till all resolves to silence—Olivet!
12) So nightly to his lamp alone he sang.

In the essay "On Coming to an End" (collected in *On Nothing & Kindred Subjects* [London: Methuen, 1908]), Belloc quotes from his own uncompleted poem. Curiously, he does not identify himself as the poet. He merely writes:

> . . . that gloomy modern *Ode to the West Wind*,
> unfinished and touched with despair, though it will
> speak of____
>   . . . that outer place forlorn
> Which, like an infinite grey sea, surrounds
> With everlasting calm the land of human sounds;

yet also returns to the sacramental earth of one's childhood where it says:

> For now the Night completed tells her tale
> Of rest and dissolution: gathering round
> Her mist in such persuasion that the ground
> Of Home consents to falter and grow pale.
> And the stars are put out and the trees fail.
> Nor anything remains but that which drones
> Enormous through the dark . . .

And again, in another place, where it prays that one may at the last be fed with beauty—

> . . . as the flowers are fed
> That fill their falling-time with generous breath:
> Let me attain a natural end of death,
> And on the mighty breast, as on a bed,
> Lay decently at last a drowsy head,
> Content to lapse in somnolence and fade
> In dreaming once again the dream of all things made.

In a letter to Mrs. Raymond Asquith dated 23 September 1932, Belloc writes, "I hesitate about publishing the West Wind while I am alive—it is so intimate. We'll see." (*Letters from Hilaire Belloc*, ed. Robert Speaight [London: Hollis and Carter, 1958], 230).

Ballade of the Mr[']s

> Though Mr Lucas[1] is with Methuen's now
> And Mr Douglas[2] in Southampton Street
> And Mr Baring[3] must be wondering how
> To make his income and expenses meet
> And Mr Nuttall[4] cannot sell his wheat
> And Mr Churchill[5] has a swollen head
> Yet all are happy and their lives a treat:
> But Mr Belloc wishes he was dead.
>
> The gifted author of "The Golden Bough"
> A Mr Frazer[6] whom I often meet
> At Cambridge has [?consented] to endow
> The Union with his writings, all complete.
> Moreover I am hardly indiscreet
> In letting it be known that Mr Stead[7]
> Is not contented with the British fleet
> But Mr Belloc wishes he was dead.
>
> I hear that Mr Archer[8] will allow
> That he regrets the violence and heat
> With which [he] wrote on Ferrer[9] and his [?row]
> And has [?apologized] to Mr Skeat.[10]
> And Mr Miles,[11] who doesn't care for meat:
> Is willing to allow us eggs instead
> They all are most amenable and sweet
> But Mr Belloc wishes he was dead.
>
> Prince, Mr Montague[12] [sic] has got the gleet[13]
> And Mr Lyttleton[14] [sic] is ill in bed
> And Mr Masterman[15] has frozen feet.
> But Mr Belloc wishes he was dead.

Source: Appears on the reverse of a letter written to Belloc by James E. Lyons, Manager of the Northern Newspaper Syndicate, on 13 January 1911. The text of the letter is as follows:

Dear Sir,

Many thanks for yours of yesterday's date. We are pleased to hear that you are agreeable to write for us and as to title, we think if the article is called "What can be done with a Million" it would serve our purpose. As to terms, for the short article we require we do not see our way to pay more than £7.7s.

Hoping to hear that you agree to write on these terms, we remain,

Yours Faithfully,

Commentary: In a letter dated 2 December 1935, to Evan Charteris, Balliol alumnus and Chairman of the National Portrait Gallery, Belloc writes: "no incantations, no, nor pious prayers / Restore the even current of affairs. / Was ever thus. No further shall I strive. / I do not even want to keep alive" (*Letters*, 252). These lines echo "Thou shalt not kill; but need'st not strive / Officiously to keep alive," from Arthur Hugh Clough's "The Latest Decalogue."

The Sucking Pig.

The Pig, The Pig, the Sucking Pig
This little beast will not grow Big.
The Calf will grow to be a Cow
But not the little Pig—as how?

The Kitten Cattens by and by
But not the little Pig—and why?

The kid will grow to be a goat—
But not the Pig—they cut his throat.

Source: Appears on a sheet of drawing paper, approximately 11.5 x 17.5 cm., that seems to have been torn from a notebook. Following this extract is "The Whale" in its published form (cf. Belloc's *Complete Verse*, ed. W. N. Roughead [London: Duckworth, 1970], 237).

The Brave Sportsman (Triolets)

I
When I hunt the Wild Hare
I go boldly to meet him.
It's a splendid affair
When I hunt the Wild Hare,
He makes off at a tear
But I always defeat him.
When I hunt the Wild Hare
I go boldly to meet him.

II
When I sniggle for Eels
They are doomed to disaster.
You can't think how it feels
When I sniggle for Eels:
They all take to their heels
And admit me their master.
When I sniggle for Eels
They are doomed to disaster.

III
When I go for the Trout
It is perfectly glorious!
I give one hearty shout
When I go for the Trout,
And they scatter in rout
And they leave me victorious.
When I go for the Trout
It is perfectly glorious!

IV
When I shoot with a gun,
Which I do on occasion,
I have wonderful fun.
When I shoot with a gun
People start on the run
Without any persuasion;
When I shoot with a gun,
Which I do on occasion.

Source: This poem, written in ink and signed "H Belloc," appears on a blank sheet of funereal stationery approximately 20.5 x 25 cm.

Commentary: This poem consists of triolets, which are a French verse form of eight lines in which the first two lines are repeated as the last two, and the first line is repeated as the fourth.

[There was a young woman of Rhyl]

> There was a young woman of Rhyl
> Who was feeling exceedingly ill
> But she took, on Advice
> Beeton's[1] Oxygen Rice
> And felt very much better, Until.

Source: Appears on a blank sheet approximately 20.5 x 25 cm.

Commentary: Rhyl is a small town on the northern coast of Wales.

[To see how much Petrol remained in the tank]

> To see how much Petrol remained in the tank
> A Match was ignited by Timothy Ball,
> And but for the balance that stands at the bank
> His unfortunate widow has nothing at all.

Source: Appears on a torn sheet (torn dimensions approximately 20.5 x 18 cm.) that also contains a fragment of another unpublished poem ("Mr Bebel saw the Devil"), as well as some arithmetic jottings.

Notes

I would like to express my appreciation to the staff of the Boston College Libraries, and of the University of Edinburgh; the National Endowment of the Humanities; Beth Bauer, Bernard Bergonzi, Richard Binder, Raymond Brebach, Jay Corrin, Fred Crawford, Owen Dudley Edwards, Mark Greenberg, John P. McCarthy, and A. N. Wilson (Belloc's biographer) for their valuable assistance. My greatest professional debt is to Stanley Weintraub.

1. Michael H. Markel, "The Manuscript Poetry of Hilaire Belloc," *The Chesterton Review* 12, no. 2 (May 1986), 221–29.
2. Michael H. Markel, "Hilaire Belloc's Uncollected Political Verse," *English Literature in Transition 1880–1920* 32, no. 2 (1989): 143–56.

Notes to poem: [On what known hills?]

1. I cannot identify "Paz del mar." Perhaps it is an original phrase, "peace of the sea," which would be consistent with Belloc's typical attitude toward the sea.

Alternatively, the reference in stanza III to California suggests that Belloc might have been referring to Del Mar, a coastal town near San Diego, but there is no evidence that he ever visited there.

Notes to poem: Ballade of the Mr[']s

1. Edward Verrall Lucas (1868–1938), English essayist, journalist, and critic. Lucas was a literary adviser at Methuen's publishing house. In 1906, Lucas published *A Wanderer in London*.

2. James Douglas, English journalist. Southampton Street is the address of the *London Opinion*, for which Douglas wrote a weekly column. He also contributed regularly to several other journals. In 1909, Douglas published *Adventures in London*.

3. Maurice Baring (1874–1945), English diplomat, novelist, and poet. A close friend of Belloc, Baring was one of the few contemporary writers Belloc read. An authority on Russia, Baring published *The Russian People* in 1911.

4. Probably Harry Nuttall (1849–1924), English statesman. Nuttall was a Liberal member of Parliament for Stretford, Lancashire, from 1906 to 1918. The president of the Manchester Chamber of Commerce, Nuttall was an import-export businessman. The reference to wheat probably concerns the trade reciprocity agreement between the United States and Canada enacted in early 1911. This agreement raised the price of Canadian wheat imported by England and thus hurt traders such as Nuttall. The agreement was soon revoked by the next Canadian government.

5. Churchill's ardent imperialism angered his Liberal colleague Belloc. (As Prime Minister in 1943, Churchill offered Belloc the Companionship of Honour, but he refused it.) In January 1911, Churchill became embroiled in the "Stepney Siege." A group of bank robbers, later associated with Bolshevist causes, was holed up in a London house after an unsuccessful robbery in which three policemen were killed. Although Churchill, as Home Secretary, protested that his role was simply to provide "covering authority," he was roundly accused of overreacting: he brought in the Scots Guards and even an artillery piece. The firefight lasted for hours; eventually the house burst into flames, killing several of the robbers.

6. Sir James George Frazer (1854–1941), Scottish classicist and anthropologist. In 1911, Frazer gave a series of seven lectures at Cambridge on "The Fear and Worship of the Dead," especially in the various South Pacific islands. Belloc's point is presumably that Frazer has agreed to give a public recital of his published works. In a letter to his friend E. S. P. Haynes dated 3 June 1907, Belloc wrote,

> I have often noticed that people who write books which are interesting and yet show a lack of intellectual grip, turn out when one meets them in private life to be mad. . . . This chap Frazer goes on precisely as I have seen lunatics go on in Asylums. He sits in a corner muttering and mumbling to himself with a terrified and surly look in his eye. . . . (Quoted in Robert Speaight, *The Life of Hilaire Belloc* [London: Hollis and Carter, 1957], 431)

7. William Thomas Stead (1849–1912), British journalist. As editor of the *Pall Mall Gazette*, he wrote a series of articles, "The Truth about the Navy," advocating massive appropriations to rebuild the British navy, largely in response to German naval expenditures. During the period 1908–11, he argued in another journal, the *Review of Reviews*, for the "two keels to one" policy: that England should maintain twice the German naval expenditures.

8. William Archer (1856–1924), English playwright and critic, best known as a translator of Ibsen. See note 9.

9. Francisco Ferrer y Guardia (1859–1909), radical Spanish anticlerical, antimonarchist educator. Acquitted of involvement in the 1906 attempt to murder Spanish King Alfonso XIII, he was convicted in 1909 of complicity in the violent uprising that followed a general strike in Barcelona. His execution was condemned worldwide as a miscarriage of justice. William Archer was sent to Spain by *McClure's Magazine* to investigate the Ferrer case. His investigation led to two articles in the magazine (November and December 1910). These articles were later reprinted as a book, *The Life, Trial, and Death of Francisco Ferrer*, which was harshly critical of the Spanish government's action. Among the commentators he attacked in this book was Belloc, who had written two pamphlets defending the execution. The following passage from Archer's book (New York: Moffat, Yard, 1911, 90–91) suggests something of the tone and substance of the dispute. Archer quotes from one of Belloc's pamphlets:

"He gambled with success on the Stock Exchange, greatly increased his wealth, but consistently applied what could be spared from the private consumption of his mistress and himself to a well-organized anti-Christian propaganda."

Now it is perfectly true that Ferrer, in his dealings with money, showed considerable business capacity: a form of worldly vision which is not reckoned criminal, one understands, even in the Society of Jesus.

10. Rev. Walter William Skeat (1835–1912), English philologist. A pioneering scholar of early English literature, Skeat was the first president of the English Simplified Spelling Society, of which William Archer was the first secretary. I cannot identify Archer's "apology" to Skeat.

11. Eustace Hamilton Miles (1868–1948), English athlete, food writer, and restauranteur. A tennis champion from 1898–1912, having won many English, American, and international championships, Miles wrote numerous books on food and sport. He was an enthusiastic food reformer, claiming that only "proteids" offered good health. His cookbooks offered several egg recipes. Miles also wrote on the transmigration of souls.

12. Probably Samuel Montagu, first Baron Swaythling (1832–1911), British financier and member of Parliament. Lord Swaythling was the head of the family that produced Edwin Montagu, Herbert Samuel, and other political and financial figures whom Belloc despised, largely because of their involvement in the Marconi scandal.

13. "A morbid discharge of thin liquid from a wound, ulcer, etc.," (*OED*). Lord Swaythling died on 12 January 1911.

14. Alfred Lyttelton (1857–1913), British statesman. He served as a Liberal Unionist member of Parliament 1895–1905. As Secretary of State for the Colonies (1903–5), Lyttelton reluctantly approved the introduction of Chinese laborers into the Rand, a move that Belloc opposed strongly. Lyttelton joined the Conservative party and served again, 1906–13.

15. C. F. G. Masterman (1874–1927), British statesman. Masterman was a good friend of Belloc when they both entered Parliament in 1906. Unlike Belloc, however, Masterman rose rapidly in the party ranks and became more conservative. Belloc and Cecil Chesterton attacked him in the *New Witness* and in their book, *The Party System*, as a politician who sacrificed his ideals for political power. Belloc's statement that "Mr Masterman has frozen feet" perhaps suggests that he became incapable of

taking constructive action. Masterman's December 1910 election to Parliament from West Ham was contested and he was unseated in June 1911.

NOTES TO POEM: [THERE WAS A YOUNG WOMAN OF RHYL]

1. Isabella Beeton (1836–1865) was the best-selling author of several cookbooks and other works such as *The Book of Household Management*. Nancy Spain, in *The Beeton Story* (London: Collins, 1956), writes,

> With the Boer War and the food shortage of the two world wars, Isabella Beeton was suddenly read as "escape" literature. Men on Scott's Antarctic expedition, prisoners in Singapore prison camps, announced that she was their favourite reading. By 1947 this compliment was debased. The name "Beeton" in a musical hall, on the radio, is now good for a hearty roar of laughter. Usually it is accompanied by the beginning of the sentence "Take ninety eggs. . . ." (183)

On Speculative Fiction

The Golem-Robot Intersection
Milton T. Wolf

Machina sapiens has been anticipated through the centuries, prefigured in the mechanical contrivances of scientists and inventors and in myth, fantasy and fiction. As Isaac Asimov has so cogently stated:

> The creation of robots was looked upon as the prime example of the overweening arrogance of humanity, of its attempt to take on, through misdirected science, the mantle of the divine. The creation of human life, with a soul, was the sole prerogative of God. For a human being to attempt such a creation was to produce a soulless travesty that inevitably became as dangerous as the golem and as the Monster. The fashioning of a robot was, therefore, its own eventual punishment, and the lesson, "there are some things that humanity is not meant to know," was preached over and over again.[1]

What appears to be a dichotomy between technology and mysticism is no more than different modes of knowing. The scientific Weltanschauung, based in reductionist reasoning, derives from the theory that to know something one must be separated from it in order to analyze it and to understand its difference from the observer. On the other hand, in mysticism—for example, Oriental epistemology—the degree to which one becomes the thing is the degree to which one understands it. Outside the natural sciences, man has recognized not only different ways of knowing but even different orders of "reality"—poetic, musical, mystical—that present different symbolical representations of experience.

The golem and robot share a similar ancestry, rooted in what is, perhaps, an innate desire to obviate the natural birth process, to re-create life, especially intelligent life, and to customize it to our purposes. Archaeologists have discovered a plethora of pictures, totems, and graven images that testify to the panhuman attempt to call forth the mystery of the life process. From prerecorded times it is evident that man, the toolmaker-artist, has been interested in creating life on both the symbolic and artificial level (i.e., what didn't exist before in Nature). From this "fabril" tradition has arisen the man-made artifact, the extension of the human body and the abiding dream of producing its ultimate copy that cheats death of its due. The ancients, lacking sophisticated technology, had to fabricate some other way of instilling quasi-human abilities into artificial objects, so they made use of vague supernatural forces and depended on mystical abilities beyond the reach of most men. Daedalus supposedly built statues that could speak and move. Homer relates in the *Iliad* that Hephaistos, the Greek god of the forge, manufactured several maid-helpers out of gold who could speak, spin, weave, and do other domestic chores. (This desire for labor-saving devices without the opprobrium of slavery appears almost coterminous with humanity's hope to escape death.) The possibility of breathing life into an artifact and creating human-like creatures has provoked heated debate about whether the mimicking of life is the proper function of mankind. Some have argued that to imitate the prerogative of the divine is an act of derangement or hubris. Even the religious prohibition against making "graven images" was rooted in the fear that God would not be pleased with competitors. St. Augustine railed against the magical statues and talking contrivances of late-classical paganism, castigating them as empty idols created by self-deluded men and as wicked projections of selfish human fantasy. St. Thomas supposedly destroyed an automaton constructed by Albertus Magnus because he thought it could only be the work of the devil.

Nevertheless, almost all peoples of the world have worshipped images, particularly those resembling the human physique (though often combined with animal characteristics, like wings, claws, or horns). These simulacra often took the form of pictorial glyphs, totems, dolls, or statues and were often worshiped in the belief that these objects were "alive" with the represented god's spirit.

The ancient Egyptians, for example, devised wax or clay figures called *ushabti*, which they placed in coffins to "answer" for the dead person with whom they resided. When these images were then combined with the appropriate litanies or chants, gods could be "animated" to act on the behalf of the supplicant(s). Reciting the right "words" ultimately became the basis of many religious holy orders. Egyptian scribes were considered a "priestly" class who could mediate between life and death, when certain magical words were combined with "graven images." The creation of the Jewish golem harkens back to this tradition.

This awesome reverence for the "Word" combined with "graven images" and a natural philosophical preoccupation with "Death" and its meanings produced not only organized religions, but, among an always adventurous few, the search for more empirical ways of crossing over into that "undiscover'd country from whose bourn / No traveler returns." Such curiosity in the medieval era fostered a search by more profane scholastics into the realm of homunculi, golems, and automata. Later, this same inquiry would produce robots and cyborgs.

The mystical creation of the golem has a "reality" that even today permeates our continued attempts at "artificial life." The medieval alchemist's search for homunculi and the Jewish rabbi's attempts to create a golem were parallel excursions into new life forms. The alchemists' search for the truth was just more secular than that of the rabbis, although both kept a close watch on the "research" of the other.

According to the *Encyclopedia Judaica*, the "golem" was:

> a creature, particularly a human being, made in an artificial way by virtue of a magic act, through the use of holy names. The idea that it is possible to create living beings in this manner is widespread in the magic of many peoples. Especially well known are the idols and images to which the ancients claimed to have given the power of speech. Among the Greeks and the Arabs these activities are sometimes connected with astrological speculations related to the possibility of "drawing the spirituality of the stars" to lower beings. The development of the idea of the *golem* in Judaism, however, is remote from astrology: it is connected, rather, with the magical exegesis of the *Sefer Yezirah* ("Book of Creation") and with the ideas of the creative power of speech and of the letters.[2]

Golem generally means something that is "unformed and imperfect." The biblical Adam was first made into a golem (without a soul) so that he might witness God's creation of the world, and in this unformed state he was shown all the future. During the Middle Ages, those Jewish rabbis who were adept in the knowledge and creation of a golem were often called "kabbalists," and it was the belief of many of these scholars that the high point in one's studies was reached when one could produce a "golem." This "ritual" act of creation was seen not only as a mark of one's erudition and purity but also as a way of communing with God. Among its early practitioners, there was never any practical benefit to be gained from this ceremony. It was perceived as a festive rite that hopefully led to an ecstatic, mystical experience in which a golem was "felt" to be created. While the formula for this creation is extant, suffice it to say that a mixing of "virgin" soil with water and the recitation of certain Hebrew letters and numbers, said in a very specific order, could bring about the desired "golem."

One of the leading scholars of Jewish mysticism and the symbolism of the Kabbalah, Gershom Scholem, in dedicating a newly built Israeli computer (which he dubbed Golem No. 1), told his audience that the Kabbalists felt the universe was:

> built essentially on the prime elements of numbers and letters, because the letters of God's language reflected in human language are nothing but concentrations of His creative energy. Thus, by assembling these elements in all their possible combinations and permutations, the Kabbalist who contemplates the mysteries of Creation radiates some of this elementary power in the Golem. The creation of a Golem is then in some way an affirmation of the productive and creative power of Man. It repeats, on however small a scale, the work of creation.[3]

Later, this basic formula was elaborated and encrusted with numerous and diverse interpretations. One such was that the golem would serve his creator by performing certain, mostly menial tasks. Like the fabled "Sorcerer's Apprentice," the golem ultimately runs amok, displays willful behavior, acts destructively, and, unfortunately, must be returned to the earth from which he (there are few references to female golems) was concocted. (The most popular of the golem legends, of course, is associated with Judah Loew b. Bezalel of Prague [ca. 1512–1609].)

While the Kabbalists were refining their mystical incantations with the golem, clock makers and other mechanical artists were building automata that used the state of technology to imitate the movements of lifelike figures. During the fourteenth century, one of the favorite automata seen in the streets of Europe was the clockwork creature announcing the time of day from its perch in the monumental cathedrals.

Building on the developments of the weight-driven, pendulum controlled clocks invented in the Middle Ages, later artisans and craftsmen created mechanical, spring-driven replicas of man (called androids) that seemed, indeed, to demonstrate lifelike behavior. The French clockmaker, Pierre Jacquet-Droz (1721), and his son, Henri-Louis (1752), crafted several of these mechanical men that could write letters, draw, and even play musical instruments. And Jacques de Vaucanson, a member of the French Academy of Sciences, was known to have constructed a mechanically animated duck that flapped its wings, pecked at corn, drank water, and "expelled" its intake.

Most historians regard these mechanical "automata" as being the forerunners of robots, and "golems and homunculi" as the literary, imaginative equivalent. Fiction, and art in general, not constrained by the necessity of waiting for theories to be proven, can speculate and, sometimes, lead the way in projecting the destiny of mankind. This interchange of ideas between fiction/art and science/technology has been an extremely valuable cross-fertilization in man's attempt to make an intelligent lifeform in its own image.

From the nineteenth century on, especially in German literature, extrapolations of the golem legend became common. By the twentieth century, such literary accretions as the golem's sexual attraction to women or the symbolic association of the golem with the politically repressed (particularly the enslavement of the working class) circulated widely in Europe. Gustav Meyrink's novel, *Der Golem* (1915), presented the golem motif as an allegory about how man was being "automated" by modern society. In 1920, Meyrink's novel was made into a classic silent film, and in 1921, the Czech dramatist, Karel Capek (who lived many years in Prague, home of the most famous golem), brought the golem symbolism to an apotheosis with his internationally celebrated play *R.U.R.* (*Rossum's Universal Robots*) in which the word "robot" was first used.

Even as the age of the mage/wizard gave way to that of the scientist/technician, the golem/homunculus found new life in ever more sophisticated automatons.

> The art and occult science of creating a manlike creature has passed from the alchemists and intuitively gifted individuals of the Middle Ages to the mathematicians, physicists, and engineers in the twentieth century. There is an almost mythic bond between the two, the continuing fascination with robotics, the challenge of man making man.[4]

As technology evolved, the human imagination relied less and less on magic to make its dreams and adventures possible. The machine, especially robots, replaced the magic carpet. But the ambivalence about a magic carpet only bespeaks a fear of ourselves displaced onto our technological creations, a fear of uncontrolled, inner monsters—of golems and Frankensteins.

This alienation and fear of displacement ebb and flow. Like the golem the robots are regarded as useful or clever so long as they remain docile and obedient. However, when they cease to be dependent on man and ape him with a terrible insolence, they lose their precociousness and are no longer amusing. In fact, like his reaction to Mary Shelley's "reanimated dead matter," man is appalled that things have gotten so out of control. Some have gone so far as to suggest that God, in fashioning Adam and Eve, created the first robots and gave them their programs in the forms of genes. Others have felt that robots have an advantage over mankind, because their programs can be changed periodically, whereas a human is condemned to a single program for an entire lifetime.

This ambivalence about the fruits of science has its roots deep in the English literary tradition. Jonathan Swift's *Gulliver's Travels* (1721–25) is only one of the many satires on scientists and their inventions. Samuel Butler's classic *Erewhon* (1872) speculates about a future utopia in which the inhabitants decide to ban all complex machines, because of fear that they will eventually develop a consciousness of their own and control man. In his forebodingly titled "The Machine Stops" (1909), E. M. Forster portrays a future in which man is totally reliant on machines.

Most of the early fictive robots were clanking monsters, bent on revenging themselves on their creators and on mankind in general. This "Frankenstein complex," as Asimov has dubbed it, continued, with permutations, not much abated since its inception with Mary Shelley's eponymous work. During the 1950s and early 1960s, automation was a dirty buzzword embodying all the neo-Luddite fears of humans being made redundant or forced to become subservient to machines. And much modern fiction about man and machine intelligence, like the golem legend, reiterates this reversal of the master-servant relationship between man and the robot he creates.

Human relationships with computerized robots are evident in the numerous ways in which we routinely attach ourselves to them: hearing aids, artificial hearts, livers, limbs, pacemakers, and an increasing panoply of biosensors to monitor our bodily activities. In fact, human bodies are modified with so many computerized robotics that many could be considered to be in the initial stages of cyborg growth. (A "cyborg" is a human modified by robotic technology and is short for "cybernetic organism.") The TV character who starred in *The Six Million Dollar Man* was essentially a cyborg. Although most of us are only the "couple hundred dollar" version, it is only a matter of time before many of us will become more expensive cyborgs.

Hans Moravec, the world renowned roboticist, has remarked that "we are very near to the time when virtually no essential human function, physical or mental, will lack an artificial counterpart."[5] This symbiosis between man and machine has become so close that for a vast array of activities, "pulling the plug" would be the equivalent of social suicide. Frank Herbert, in *Destination: Void*, suggests that machine intelligence married to human intelligence leads to survival in the future. Cyborgs may pave the way to this survival.

The symbiosis between man and machine goes back to the earliest animation fantasies. Golems provide mirrors for those fantasies and the human flaws they attempt to remedy. From golems and homunculi to Frankenstein's monster, from clockwork automatons to robots, cyborgs have evolved as metaphor for human tools and technology. *Machina sapiens* remains the irresistible force that impels the human drive in successive intersections like that of the golem and the robot.

Notes

1. Isaac Asimov, *Robot Visions* (New York: ROC, 1990), 5–6.
2. Gershom G. Scholem, "Golem," *Encyclopedia Judaica*, (New York: Macmillan, 1971), vol. 7, 753.
3. Arnold O. Goldsmith, "Introduction," *The Golem Remembered, 1909–1980* (Detroit: Wayne State University Press, 1981), 19.
4. Marvin Minsky, ed., *Robotics* (Garden City, N.Y.: Anchor Press/Doubleday, 1985), 29.
5. Hans Moravec, *Mind Children: The Future of Robot and Human Intelligence* (Cambridge: Harvard University Press, 1988), 2.

Octavia Butler Writes the Bible
John R. Pfeiffer

The author of ten novels and five short stories, Octavia Butler has received critical commentary as a writer of science fiction, a feminist writer, and an African-American storyteller. Yet, largely ignored in that commentary, the single most pervasive reference in her writing has been the Judeo-Christian Bible.

In fact, the protagonist (possibly Butler's fictional persona) Lauren Oya Olamina in Butler's *Parable of the Sower* (1993) explains the nature of the influence of the Bible on *Earthseed*, a religious book she is writing:

> "A lot of it isn't very poetical.... But it's what I believe, and I've written it as well as I could." I showed him four verses in all—gentle, brief verses that might take hold of him without his realizing it and live in his memory without his intending that they should. Bits of the Bible had done that to me, staying with me even after I stopped believing.[1]

The sentiments of Olamina are directly repeated by Butler in the "Afterward" of her short story, "Near of Kin" (1979), collected in *Bloodchild and Other Stories* (1995). Here Butler comments not only on the significance of her debt to the Bible and to her Baptist upbringing but also on the paradoxical nature of the debt:

> As a good Baptist kid, I read the Bible first as a series of instructions as to how I should believe and behave, then as bits of verse that I was required to memorize, then as a series of interesting interconnected stories.
> The stories got me: stories of conflict, betrayal, torture, murder, exile, and incest. I read them avidly. This was, of course, not exactly what my mother had in mind when she encouraged me to read the Bible. Nevertheless, I found these things fascinating, and when I began writing, I explored these themes in my own stories.[2]

In her fiction Butler has transformed religious training and belief into literary myth. Remarkably her novels successively exhibit an increasing incidence of biblical references, even though, like her fictional counterpart, Olamina, Butler "stopped believing." Meanwhile, she is predictably hostile where she might be expected to be, considering that traditional interpretations of the Bible have rationalized male chauvinism, justified slavery, and supported fraudulent secular and religious institutional agendas. Although she asserts that she has set belief in Judeo-Christian theology aside and is keenly aware of the terrible suffering the Bible has been made to sponsor in the world, she uses it in her stories as a touchstone. She says she was weaned on the Bible and loved its stories, especially their violence. Her reference to the Bible is therefore not surprising. It is clear, too, that she is taken with the epic conception of time and human personality, as well as the evangelical voice, of the Bible. Her stories exhibit these elements. Ultimately Butler's appropriation of the Bible is meant to subvert it where it is perverse, embrace it where it is cogent, and finally to substitute for it a personal scripture, indeed, a theology, of her own. Beyond this her agenda must be the gnomic one of storyteller.

Biblical influence is present in Butler's first novel *Patternmaster* (1976)—one of five Patternist novels that also include *Mind of My Mind* (1977), *Survivor* (1978), *Wild Seed* (1980), and *Clay's Ark* (1984)—even though the novel presents no explicit reference to the Bible.[3] In *Patternmaster*, the biblical elements consist of references to fertility and genealogy, even as the story of the emergence of a successor-leader of the superhuman patternists progresses. The Southern California climate and terrain of the story are not unlike the Middle East where Old Testament Hebrews struggled and longed for a messiah to lead them to a land where they could settle in security. The familial houses in *Patternmaster* are patriarchal, and characters have biblical names such as Joachim, Michael, and Jason. Still, this biblical tone might be accidental or subconscious were it not corroborated by the increasing explicitness in all of Butler's later novels. Furthermore, her imagination is provoked by history, and her stories are in search of epic meanings. The epic multiplicity of "books" of the Bible seems to be the inspiration moving Butler to write groups of novels, the extraordinary *Kindred* (1979) being the only book she has written that is not part of a series.

An explicit allusion to the Bible appears for the first time in Butler's second novel, *Mind of My Mind*, in the characterization of Rachel Davidson, one of the parapsychological superperson protagonists of the novel. Her parents were ministers, and Rachel has assumed the identity of a Christian preacher faith-healer as a way to use her psychokinetic healing powers. More than merely healing cancer and psychological illnesses, she could regrow limbs for her flock. However, she stops short because "she would have had to show herself to be more than a faith healer. She was afraid of what people might decide she was. Whether or not she accepted the story of Christ as fact, she realized that anyone with abilities like his—and hers—could get into trouble if he really put them to work" (71). Set in a late twentieth-century America, *Mind* makes this reference to the Bible as if its importance in culture were vestigial and marginal.

Like *Patternmaster*, *Mind* is also preoccupied with fertility and genealogy. *Mind* includes the death of the demonic parapsychological patriarch Doro, whose four thousand-year life is a calendric analogue for the age of Hebrew culture, with its concomitant emphasis on preserving a special race/species of people who mate within the tribe, often within the family, incestuously. Doro is like an Old Testament patriarch with his fabulous longevity, autocratic personality, and power. He is displaced and killed by Mary, who is more powerful than he and who represents a new parapsychological dispensation, the beginning of the Patternist web. In *Mind*, the killing of Doro by Mary replays the Judeo/Christian biblical tension in the advent of Christianity as a threat to end the Jewish history that fostered it.

In *Survivor*, Butler's debt to the Bible is more explicit and extensive. Jules Verrick is a Christian minister who has adopted an Asian-African woman child and called her Alanna, saving her from summary extermination by members of his congregation, as was the usual fate of feral children on the unhappy future earth of Butler's story. Alanna's salvation recalls the escape of the child Jesus from Herod's decree that all infant male children under two years of age be killed. Verrick takes Alanna with his wife and congregation to a colony on the planet of the Kohns. Alanna's identity is symbolically messianic, while Verrick's community of Christians seems Hebraic in the tyranny imposed by the Kohn planet's indigenous Garkohn. The Garkohn force the humans to use meklah, a drug to which they have been addicted for generations. Alanna's role is to be captured by another Kohn people, the Tehkohn, who force her to withdraw from her addiction to meklah, the first human to do so. Eventually she leads the Tehkohn to defeat the Garkohn, enabling Verrick's people to begin a migration, Hebrew-like, to find their own land on the new planet. Alanna remains behind with the Tehkohn to breed with their leader in an interspecies miscegenation, an analogue to Jesus' eventual embrace of gentiles.

Butler's incorporation of other explicit biblical references in *Survivor* is not facilely allegorical. Verrick's community is unequivocally a Christian splinter sect. The biblical references are a means to present

Alanna's character. Pregnant with a Tehkohn-fathered child, Alanna is fearful, and "for the first time in her life, she longed to be the wife of some ordinary Bible-quoting Missionary man" (164). Earlier, Verrick and Alanna discuss whether Alanna could bring herself to kill an enemy in battle (she can) and refer to the Bible for support: "'Thou shalt not kill,' quoted Jules. 'Not that,' she said. ' . . . He that smiteth a man, so that he die, shall surely be put to death'" (30). Earlier still, in considering her preference for practical clothing, usually men's styles, Alanna remembers that her foster mother Neila Verrick quoted Deut. 22:5, "The woman shall not wear that which pertaineth unto a man, . . . for all that do so are abominations unto the Lord thy God" (19). Alanna disregards her mother's admonition without qualm. In these references the Bible is a nuisance or irrelevant to a self-respecting person.

Butler removes any doubt of the importance of the Bible in her stories in *Wild Seed*, the genesis myth of her Patternist saga. A chronicle of the Patternist people, the novel consists of three books with biblically extracted titles: "Book I, Covenant, 1690" (six chapters); "Book II, Lot's Children, 1741" (chapters 7 to 10); and "Book III, Canaan, 1840" (chapters 11 to 14, plus Epilogue). Beyond the biblical section titles, there are no direct references to the Bible in the stories themselves. Even so, the story in each section is a combination of biblical tale analogues. "Covenant" clearly substitutes the Doro/Anyanwu relationship for the God/Abraham relationship of Genesis. The female Anyanwu replaces the spurious patriarchal maleness of the Hebraic Abraham in Butler's reinvention of the biblical fable. *Seed* sets up a matriarchal genealogy, and Anyanwu is assigned the fabulous longevity and fertility of a biblical patriarch. Moreover, the capricious treatment of Anyanwu by Doro as he tries to bend her to his will by threatening her children is a transmutation of the Old Testament God's cruel test of Abraham, ordering him to sacrifice his son Isaac. That Doro and God are cruel because the inexorable events of nature are cruel, Anyanwu must accept. Butler invites the reader to contemplate such implacable forces.

Butler's conversion of the Genesis myth in *Seed* continues in the marriage of Anyanwu, at first the consort of Doro, to one of Doro's sons, Isaac. With Isaac she has children. Her marriage to Isaac also insinuates incest between mother and son. The tincture of blasphemy and moral abomination of this is very likely Butler's intent. Aware that the Bible itself acquiesces in the confounding of tradition and morality, she has deliberately written her own violation of tradition. Such is Butler's alteration of the Old Testament story of Lot. Thus *Seed*'s second section, "Lot's Children," recalls the daughters of Lot,

Abraham's nephew, who had children in incest with their father. These children founded the tribes of Moab and Ammon. The incest notwithstanding, God intervened to preserve lands so that the Moabites and Ammonites would prosper. At worst the Old Testament God did not punish the incest. In fact God clearly blessed its issue. Butler uses the suggestion of incest in *Seed* to depict the conflict between Doro and Anyanwu that arises when he wants to breed her with her children, or her children with her children. Optimistically considering the possibility of offspring with new and different parapsychological powers from his eugenic program, Doro reflects, "They were a pleasant mystery that careful inbreeding would solve" (146).

In *Seed*'s final chapter, "Canaan," Butler has the shape-shifting Anyanwu transform herself into a male plantation owner, Edward Warrick. Hermaphroditic, she can bear children as a woman and sire them as a man, but as a man she can sire only female children. Her longevity and parapsychological power enable her to secure the plantation and make it an oasis of safety in a history of slavery. It is not Canaan, a "promised land," but it encourages the hope of one. More like an actual land of milk and honey in *Seed*, California is named in the Epilogue as the place to which Anyanwu will eventually migrate to help establish the Patternists there, where they will establish a thriving culture.

The latest written of the Patternist novels, *Clay's Ark*, is set in the southwestern United States desert country of the early twenty-first century. Biblical allusions pervade it. The "Ark" of the title invokes Noah's Ark of Genesis, as it names the spaceship that brings back to earth from a Proxima Centauri planet the colonizing microorganism that will extinguish homo sapiens and repopulate Earth with a new species. The "Clay" of the title is for Clay Dana, the instigator of the star expedition, who had feared that the expedition would be stopped by "turn-of-the-century irrationality—religious overzealousness on one side, destructive hedonism on the other, with both heated by ideological intolerance and corporate greed. The Dana faction feared humanity would extinguish itself on Earth, the only world in the solar system that could support human life" (154). In the overview of the Patternist novels, original humanity is, if not extinguished, at best a zoological antique. Three of *Ark*'s five chapters bear biblically associated titles: "Part 1: Physician," "Part 3: Manna," and "Part 5: Jacob." The black, principal protagonist of *Ark* is Asa Elias Doyle ("Eli"). Asa is the biblical name for physician. Though Eli was the expedition geologist, he assimilates a physician's identity because his wife, Disa, was a doctor. He had also been "a minister for a while, . . . [a] boy minister at the turn of the century when the country was full of ministers" (36). Eli follows in the footsteps of his maternal grandfather, Jacob Moore (Jake), "a good man, an old-style shouting Baptist preacher who had stepped in and taken the place of his father when his father died" (29). More biblical reference appears when Blake Maslin's daughter Keira asks Eli if he is part of a religious cult:

> "Cultists?" Eli said smiling a real smile. "No, we didn't come up here to worship anybody, girl. There were some religious people up here once, though. Not cultists, just . . . What do you call them? People who never saw sweet reason around the turn of the century, and who decided to make a decent, moral, God-fearing place of their own to raise their kids and wait for the Second Coming." (21)

The events of the novel and the Second Coming are again connected when the perverted "family" of "car rats" that has kidnapped Blake and his daughters are observed

> . . . watching a movie from the ranch family's library—a 1998 classic about the Second Coming of Christ. There had been a whole genre of such films just before the turn of the century. Some were religious, some antireligious, some merely exploitive—Sodom-and-Gomorrah films. Some were cause oriented—God arrives as a woman or a dolphin or a throwaway kid. And some were science fiction. God arrives from Eighty-two Eridani Seven.
> Well, maybe God had arrived a few years late from Proxima Centauri Two. God in the form of a deadly little microbe that for its own procreation made a father try to rape his dying daughter—and made the daughter not mind. (168)

In these passages *Ark* explicitly associates the biblical apocalypse of the Second Coming with its own story of pestilence, catastrophe, and apocalypse. The degraded late twentieth-century humanity of Butler's earth is in a process of self-annihilation. The Proxima Centauri Two organism is one of the means by which a staggering humanity will be transformed into a new species—"converted" (39, 50, 85, 92, 125, 145, 196) is the term Butler uses. Conversion causes biologically invaded humans literally to be "born again," that is, be genetically altered, and thereafter not human any longer. Their muscles and senses are stronger and keener than human. Significantly, their morality is prospectively more noble. The children of the converted are even stranger than their once-human parents. Genetic transformation through breeding as well as parapsychologically manipulated DNA are processes under way in the other Patternist novels as well as in the Xenogenesis Trilogy novels discussed below.

The narrative report of the disposition of the microorganism to "survive and multiply" (30) echoes the Genesis "increase and multiply." Biblical personality appears in the person of Gabriel Boyd, the "white-haired patriarch of the household—a stern man who believed in an outdated, angry God and who knew how to use a shotgun" (41). He thinks "heaven is only for God and his chosen" (56). He is the puritanically protective father of the caucasian Meda with whom Eli would have twin boy "clayarks" named Jacob and Joseph—only a minor liberty by Butler with the biblical twin-son issue of Isaac in Esau and Jacob. Eli gets along with Gabriel because Eli

> . . . knew his Bible. This in particular impressed both the old man and his wife. Few people read the Bible now, except as literature. Religion was about as far out of fashion as it had ever been in the United States—a reaction against the intense religious feeling at the turn of the century. But Eli had been a boy preacher during that strange, not entirely sane time. He had been precocious and sincere, had read the Bible from Genesis to Revelation, and could still talk about it knowledgeably. (55)

Eventually infected by the organism and experiencing the compulsion to "multiply," Gabriel ". . . felt he had gone from Patriarch and man of God to criminally depraved pervert unable to keep his hands off his own daughter. Nor could he accept these feelings as his own. They must be signs of either demonic possession or God's punishment for some terrible sin" (69). Gabriel, however, rises about his puritanical delusion before he dies, and blesses the Eli/Meda union, which has produced Joseph and Jacob. Jacob in particular is the vangard "clayark" offspring, a herald of the arrival of one of the new species (the other species is of evolved humans with parapsychological powers) of the Patternist earth.

Butler's persistent theme in the Patternist novels is that humanity as it is is not sufficient. She replaces mankind in her stories with species that are potentially morally superior. The overarching biblical themes of migration and aspiration to moral transcendence are epic enough and popular enough to be a founding metaphor for *Clay Ark*.

In *Kindred* (1979), published one year after *Survivor*, Dana, the protagonist, has been brought up by an aunt and an uncle, the latter a minister.[4] Her ancestors go back to slavery times, and their names are written in a family Bible. Thereafter, plunged by time travel into the maelstrom of slavery in the antebellum South, Dana/Butler make only a few explicit references to the Bible and Christianity. The Methodist minister quotes the Bible to rationalize the keeping of slaves: He "dispensed candy and 'safe' Bible verses ('Servants, be obedient to them that are your masters'). The kids got candy for repeating the verses" (183). The same minister also pronounces that education is bad for slaves (237). When Hagar, Dana's great-grandmother, whose birth and survival Dana must assure, is born, Alice reflects, "If Hagar had been a boy, I would have called her Ishmael. In the Bible, people might be slaves for awhile, but they didn't have to stay slaves" (234). This remark transforms the biblical story of the concubine Hagar and her son Ishmael who are banished from Abraham's household. Subsequently God blessed Ishmael and his children by allowing them to have destinies as free people. In response Dana thinks, "I . . . congratulated myself that the Bible wasn't the only place where slaves broke free. Her names were only symbolic, but I had more than symbols to remind me that freedom was possible—probably—and for me, very near" (234). After Hagar is safely born, Alice dies and is buried by a "coal-black deep-voiced freedman" minister who reads from Job and Ecclesiastes until Dana "could hardly stand to listen. I had shrugged off my aunt and uncle's strict Baptist teachings years before. But even now, especially now, the bitter melancholy words of Job could still reach me. 'Man that is born of a woman is of few days, and full of trouble. He cometh forth like a flower, and is cut down: he fleeth also as a shadow, and continueth not" (252).

With just six explicit references to the Bible, *Kindred* also contains numerous implicit references. The novel re-creates the historic slavery of Africans, like that of the Old Testament Hebrews, a subjugated nation/people/race that somehow kept its integrity. Dana, thrust from the 1970s into antebellum American history, resembles a would-be messiah transported from New Testament to Old Testament times. In *Kindred*, as in her other novels, the biblical reference is mostly to the Old Testament. It is often a history and an anthropology of people who, despite their lives of helplessness and pain, chose to live them.

The Old Testament describes slavery in Hebrew families as if it were moral, even natural, with slaves instructed to keep their places and accept their condition. As a people, African-Americans felt a powerful kinship with Old Testament Hebrews who were enslaved in Egypt before wandering landless and homeless. Permitted opportunities to worship, even to have their own ministers, they used biblical materials in their work songs but were allowed to profess openly only themes of resignation, patience, grieving, and hope for rest in a "promised land." These elements are all easy to find in the

African-American slave narratives, the primary models and sources for *Kindred.*

In 1987, Butler published the first novel of her Xenogenesis Trilogy. The invitation to read the trilogy as a biblical analogue is immediate. *Dawn,* subtitled *Xenogenesis,* immediately elicits an association with Genesis.[5] The protagonist of all three novels is prebiblical Lilith, the name in rabbinical literature of Adam's first wife, not mentioned in Genesis. Her dispensation is primordial, wilder than Eve's and wonderfully maverick in possibility of offspring, and Butler revels in the latitude that she allows Lilith. Galactic traders in genes, the alien Oankali arrive on earth after mankind's nuclear war. Their spaceship is a Noah's ark of new genetic material that they will barter in exchange for human material, and in the process they will vitalize and improve surviving human DNA. They rescue Lilith, nursing her to health and changing her genetically so that she, now alien in DNA, can become the instrument of a repopulation of earth. Like Anyanwu in *Seed,* she, as healer, can alter genetic codes. "Xenogenesis" is literally an "alien beginning." The Oankali use genetic material just as the Old Testament God made Eve from Adam's rib. "If they've got one of you, they can use it to make another you even if you've been dead for a hundred years and they haven't got anything at all left of your body. And that's just the start. They can make people in ways I don't even know how to talk about" (93). There are other Genesis echoes as well. Lilith is told that she has been made pregnant, and will bear a daughter: "I mixed a girl to be a companion for you. You've been very lonely" (246). Later the reader learns the Oankali plan to "reseed Earth with human communities" (143). The pervasive concern with seminal seed in the Old Testament so passionately inspires Butler that she uses as titles *Wild Seed, Parable of the Sower,* and *Earthseed: The Books of the Living.* The God analogue, the Oankali, recreate Lilith genetically to give her great strength and longevity.

In *Adulthood Rites* (1988), the second novel of the Xenogenesis series, the "genesis" enterprise proceeds.[6] The process of putting genetically improved humans back in communities on earth is ongoing. On the very first page, there is another Genesis echo: "There was light!" (3). Later the reader learns that "the books most likely to be desired by other villages" are "Bibles—using the memories of every village they could reach, Phoenix researchers had put together the most complete Bible available" (124). The only other major biblical reference in *Adulthood* is a symbolically complex passage describing the artifacts in a museum at the first of the new villages planted on the postholocaust earth:

> There were crosses like the one on Gabe's coin—crosses of metal, each with a metal man hanging from them. Christ on the cross, Akin remembered. There were also a picture of Christ rapping his knuckles on a wooden door and another of him pulling open his clothing to reveal a red shape that contained a torch. There was a picture of Christ sitting at a table with a lot of other men. Some of the pictures seemed to move as Akin viewed them from different angles.
>   Tate, who had reached the house before him, took one of the moving pictures—a small one of Christ standing on a hill and talking to people—and handed it to Akin. He moved it slightly in his hand, watching the apparent movement of Christ, whose mouth opened and closed and whose arm moved up and down. The picture, though scratched, was hard and flat—made of a material Akin did not understand. He tasted it—then threw it away from him, disgusted, nauseated. (142)

With Butler's relegation of artifacts of the Christian myth to a museum in the new land, she begins her regeneration of the human race. Her description of the museum's contents evokes the Sermon on the Mount, the Last Supper, Christ's crucifixion, and a perverse communion rite in the form of Akin's tasting of the plastic picture. Cast in the role of matriarch-as-the-new-messiah, Lilith, in her bearing of new DNA to humanity, is equivalent to Jesus' bringing in a new moral order to mankind.

In *Imago* (1989), the third Xenogenesis novel, two remarkable references stand out.[7] In the first, the woman Jesusa and her man Tomás are troubled about their physical and emotional dependence on the mutant human Jodahs. Jesusa is obviously a female substitute for the biblical Jesus. Tomás's role, in imitation of the biblical doubting Thomas, is to question Jesusa's doubt about the new order. Ultimately they will accept this symbiosis but not without profound fear. Jesusa remarks: "This is an alien thing Jodahs wants of us. Certainly it's an un-Christian thing, an un-Human thing. *It's the thing we've been taught against all our lives.* How can we be accepting it or even considering it so easily?" (124). The two eventually accept the ménage à trois analogic relationship with Jodahs. In so doing, they consecrate a new dispensation. For Butler the new era represents a healing of the diseased human genetic code, despite its being a permutation of bestiality and sodomy. The healed humans must now adopt new behavior that will fulfill their destiny as altered beings. The analogy with Jesus as a transformer of the rigidly genetic Hebraic law is apparent. At one point, the narrative of the genetic reconstruction of humanity, a "First Mother," story is retold. She is reported to have had a number of daughters and a son, all of whom were human and properly formed. The details of this account are vintage Genesis analogues. They illustrate Butler's title, *Imago*, in their suggestion of the Genesis pronouncement that man is made in the image of God, even though Butler ironically asserts that the Old Testament image is flawed and that the transhuman new species is, perhaps, a healed image of God.

Parable of the Sower (1993) as a novel is baldly proselytizing and explicit in its definition of the human condition and what to do about it. Written entirely as a personal journal, it is captioned with excerpts from a book of spiritual guidance that the protagonist journal writer published sometime after the journal's events had transpired. It is titled *Earthseed: The Books of the Living* by Lauren Oya Olamina. It is carefully dated, beginning on Lauren's fifteenth birthday, 20 July 2024, and includes entries for seventy-three days before ending on 10 October 2027.

Biblical reference in *Parable* is especially important to this novel's meaning. Lauren's favorite book of the Bible is Job (14). She is challenged by the inscrutability of human experience, where justice and happiness are chimeras more often than reality. Later Lauren remembers words from Ecclesiastes, "To everything there is a season" from which she draws the center of the belief system that she is forming: "Change is part of life" (25). The quotation from Ecclesiastes is very near the verse that includes the words "earth abides," which are used as a title for George R. Stewart's celebrated postcatastrophe novel of 1949. The setting of *Parable* is fittingly postcatastrophic. Lauren later quotes a long passage from Genesis:

> Today, Dad preached from Genesis six, Noah and the ark: "And God saw that the wickedness of man was great in the earth, and that every imagination of the thoughts and of his heart was only evil continually. And it repented the Lord that he had made man on the earth, and it grieved him at his heart. And the Lord said, I will destroy man whom I have created from the face of the earth; both man, and beast, and the creeping thing and the fowls of the air; for it repenteth me that I have made them. But Noah found grace in the eyes of the Lord."
>
> And then, of course, later God says to Noah, "make thee an ark of gopher wood; rooms shalt thou make in the ark, and shalt pitch it within and without with pitch."
>
> Dad focused on the two-part nature of this situation. God decides to destroy everything except Noah, his family, and some animals. *But* if Noah is going to be saved, he has plenty of hard work to do. (63)

Butler uses this Old Testament excerpt to define the conditions of humanity as self-mutilating, self-destructive, and self-defeating for the most part. But there is a hope to which Lauren clings.

Later when her minister father is murdered outside the Robledo enclave, Lauren takes his place as preacher, an identity she adopts with increasing deliberateness as she writes and expounds more of her *Earthseed* scripture. On one occasion she preaches from Luke 18:1–8:

> The parable of the importunate widow. It's one I've always liked. A widow is so persistent, [sic] in her demands for justice that she overcomes the resistance of a judge who fears neither God nor man. She wears him down.
> Moral: The weak can overcome the strong if the weak persist. Persisting isn't always safe, but it's often necessary. . . .
> "We have God and we have each other. We have our island community, fragile, and yet a fortress. Sometimes it seems too small and too weak to survive. And like the widow in Christ's parable, its enemies fear neither God nor man. But also like the widow, it persists. *We persist.* This is our place, no matter what." (124–25)

Lauren's family will be driven from their home in Robledo and killed, but Lauren does not give up her resolve to survive. Meanwhile, as conditions in Robledo deteriorate and drug-driven pyromaniacs begin burning the homes in the enclave, Cory Olimina, Lauren's foster mother, declares, "'My God,' . . . in a small whispery voice, . . . from the Book of Revelation: 'Babylon the great is fallen, is fallen, and is become the habitation of devils'" (133). Deep into the narrative, the reader learns that Lauren has heard the commandments "Honor thy father and mother" and "Thou shalt not kill" (169), but she must violate the one against killing to survive. Other references occur as fifty-seven-year-old Taylor Franklin Bankole, whom eighteen-year-old Lauren will eventually marry, remembers, "When my wife was alive, we went to a Methodist church. Her religion was important to her, so I went along. I saw how it comforted her, and I wanted to believe, but I never could." Lauren answers, "We were Baptists. . . . I couldn't make myself believe either" (239). Still, Lauren does believe in the religion that she is creating in Earthseed, about the future of which Bankole is doubtful:

> "It sounds too simple. . . . If you get people to accept it they'll make it more complicated, more open to interpretation, more mystical, and more comforting." . . . "With you or without you, they will. All religions change. Think about the big ones. What do you think Christ would be these days? A Baptist? A Methodist? A Catholic? And the Buddha—do you think he'd be a Buddhist now? What kind of Buddhism would he practice?" (240)

The book ends with the excerpt from Luke 8:5-8 that has inspired the novel:

> A sower went out to sow his seed; and as he sowed, some fell by the way side; and it was trodden down, and the fowls of the air devoured it. And some fell upon a rock; and as soon as it was sprung up, it withered away because it lacked moisture. And some fell among thorns; and the thorns sprang up with it and choked it. And other fell on good ground, and sprang up, and bare fruit an hundredfold. (299)

In this context of biblical reference, Butler builds the story of Lauren's creation of Earthseed. People are Earthseed. Some will live and prosper. The mood and content of Earthseed are biblical without embarrassment: "Bits of the Bible had done that to me, staying with me even after I stopped believing" (183). Although Lauren insists that she does not believe in the *Bible* or in "that kind of God" (72), her actual personal beliefs are catechetical and biblical in procedure, if not in substance. She concludes, "*Why is the universe? / To shape God. Why is God? / To shape the universe. . . . God / is Change*" (72-73). Out of her biblical rehearsal, Lauren (and Butler herself perhaps) seems to evolve a dynamic pantheism and a Bible of her own.

The importance of biblical reference to Butler's inspiration continues. In a 1995 interview reporting details of a $295,000 MacArthur grant she was awarded, Butler announced that she was at work on a new novel tentatively entitled *Parable of the Talents*.[8]

Notes

1. Octavia Butler, *Parable of the Sower* (New York and London: Four Walls Eight Windows, 1993), 183. Further page references to this and the other Butler works mentioned in this article are expressed parenthetically in the text.
2. Octavia Butler, *Bloodchild and Other Stories* (New York and London: Four Walls Eight Windows, 1995), 85.
3. Octavia Butler, *Patternmaster* (New York: Avon Books, 1979); *Survivor* (Garden City, N.Y.: Doubleday & Company, Inc., 1978); *Mind of My Mind* (New York: Warner Books, 1994); *Wild Seed* (New York: Warner Books, 1988); and *Clay's Ark* (New York: St. Martin's Press, 1984).
4. Octavia Butler, *Kindred* (Boston: Beacon Press, 1988).
5. Octavia Butler, *Dawn* (New York: Warner Books, 1987).
6. Octavia Butler, *Adulthood Rites* (New York: Warner Books, 1988).
7. Octavia Butler, *Imago* (New York: Warner Books, 1989).
8. "Octavia E. Butler Gets $295,000 MacArthur Grant," *Locus* (July 1995), 8.

On Modern Drama

Joe Orton's Bookends: *Head to Toe* and *Up Against It*

SUSAN RUSINKO

In an unnaturally shortened playwriting career that included only three long stage plays—*Entertaining Mr. Sloane, Loot,* and *What the Butler Saw*—and four short pieces originally intended for radio or television—*The Ruffian on the Stair, The Erpingham Camp, The Good and Faithful Servant,* and *Funeral Games*—Joe Orton has found a niche in modern drama, alongside Harold Pinter and Tom Stoppard, as a major language innovator on the English stage. His name has earned adjectival status for an idiosyncratic brand of black farce that is heavily dependent on turning the epigrammatic nature of language on its heels with a controlled abandon that brought strong encouragement from both long-established writers such as Terence Rattigan and revolutionary playwrights such as Harold Pinter.

Two of his nonstage works, a novel and a screenplay, neither published nor produced in his lifetime, deserve attention as markers between which a lifelong endeavor to become "somebody" was finally realized. *Head to Toe*, a novel written before his successes on the English stage, and *Up Against It*, a screenplay written after those successes, take shape as a curious pair of bookends to his career. Completed in 1961 and published posthumously in 1971, *Head to Toe* is a work he had hoped to rewrite some day. He was given that opportunity when in 1967 Walter Shenstone, a producer of Beatles' films, asked him to write a film for the famous four singers. When Orton reread the novel, he was aware of its faults but felt that "as a basis for a film it was more than adequate."[1] He looked forward to doing "all my box of tricks—Sloane and Hal [characters from earlier plays]—on them. After all, if I repeat myself in this film, it doesn't matter. No one who sees the film will have seen *Sloane* or *Loot*" (*Diaries*, 66).

Orton's return to the novel for the plot of the screenplay involved a considerable narrowing of scope, from the mock-epic style of the earlier work to that of mock-romance in the play. Both main characters, Gombold and McTurk, nonetheless, share similar experiences. Both are Orton's spokesmen for themes that are central to his life and career. Yet they are vastly different in the author's purpose in writing about them and, consequently, in the seriousness of their respective portrayals. Gombold is a fully developed character, whereas McTurk and his three companions are created to provide roles for the four Beatles. Gombold's epic journey, resulting in his being educated into becoming a writer, makes of the novel a bildungsroman, a fictional allegory of sorts for Orton's own life. Renamed McTurk in the screenplay, the hero is reduced to a caricatured Don Juan who, in pursuit of his ideal love, Rowena, is the author's spokesman for the destruction of romantic myths of love and war even as Orton uses those myths to accomplish his purpose. Having already waged war in his novels and stage plays on conventional attitudes toward marriage and sexual identity, he extended his attack in *Up Against It*, most aggressively in the ending in which McTurk, Low, and young Ramsay happily marry one woman—Orton's sexual-sharing "trick" that he proudly and frequently pointed to in regard to his first long play, *Entertaining Mr. Sloane*.

The two works enjoy a symbiotic relationship in their history as well as their content. They suffered similar fates during Orton's life, the posthumously published novel rejected by two publishers and the screenplay returned to Orton by the Beatles. The latter was subsequently purchased by Oscar Lewenstein. On 9 August 1967, Orton's appointment with Richard Lester to discuss its production was aborted by Kenneth Halliwell's murder-suicide in the one-room London flat that the two men shared.

Head to Toe: Seismic Disturbances

The novel clearly marks the end of Orton's unsuccessful fiction-writing career, and he, like its main character, would soon find himself serving a prison term. In a further irony, he claimed that it was in prison that he, again like his fictional counterpart, had acquired the detachment necessary to his writing for the stage. Charles Monteith, an editor at Faber and Faber, turned the novel down in 1961 because it was "several degrees too odd."[2] With Monteith, readers may well question the merits of the novel and agree with John Lahr that *Head to Toe* was Orton's first crude attempt at using farce as an act of literary aggression (Lahr, 125). The target of his aggression, authority in its varied forms, is central to his stage plays as it is in earlier novels written in collaboration with Kenneth Halliwell.

The novel begins with Gombold's straying onto the head of a giant and concludes with the giant's death. Hundreds of feet tall, the giant is symbolic of a world whose hypocritical systems its main character learns to disturb by creating panic with the use of verbs and nouns in the right hands. Innocently drawn into adventures, such as the assassination of a prime minister and a war between the Left Buttocks and the Right Buttocks, he begins his long journey with a fall into a hole, after which he travels down one side of the giant and up the other. In one of his later adventures, he meets a wise man who educates him into the belief that the pen is mightier than the sword and can create seismic eruptions. It is hardly a secret that Gombold is Orton's fictional double in this respect. With their peculiarly Ortonesque blend of humor and violence, the events of the novel are packed with what Orton has frequently referred to as his "box of tricks," tricks of both language and action that have delighted some members of his audience even as they have outraged others. Experimenting with a fanciful mixture of anarchic ideas and literary images, Orton in the novel gives definition to both the content and style that he sharpened to a razor's edge in his plays.

With an epic structure that is essentially Dantean but that blends the dream style of Alice's adventures in Wonderland, the satiric savagery of a Swift and a Voltaire, the hyperbolic optimism of a Rabelais, and the Joycean autobiographical portrayal of the artist as a young man, the novel's literary evocations may seem haphazard but are appropriate to the nightmarish nature of Gombold's experiences. At one point Gombold and his friends take refuge in the Trojan Horse. At another, he meets Doktor von Pregnant, a Tiresias-like figure who looks about two thousand years old and whose knowledge of the history of the world is imparted to the attentive student. The Doktor's influence on Gombold is similar to that of Halliwell on Orton. Halliwell's classical education was a strong contrast with Orton's abysmal ignorance of the classics. During their more than fifteen years of living together, Halliwell was responsible for introducing Orton to the major Western classics.

The allegorical journey as structure for the novel becomes a parody of Dante's famous journey when Gombold finds himself alone, frightened, and beset by a variety of dangers. He escapes from captors and prisons by swimming through sewers and into an ocean, a parody of the underground rivers in the Dantean universe. He travels downward through his hell and then perversely upward toward his purgatory and paradise, the last taking the form of learning how to "rage correctly." His physical journey ends, however, not in paradise, but in the execution of his friends—Pill, O'Scullion, and Squall.

Shortly thereafter, Gombold discovers the death of the giant, and, depressed about the prospect of living on a corpse, he enters the wood (the hair) for the last time and climbs down.

Early on he is drawn into a revolution in which he kills a woman prime minister. From that point on, he finds himself in military struggles that culminate in the war in which one side is eventually indistinguishable from the other. Like Voltaire's Candide, he keeps running into former acquaintances who may have been hanged, drawn, and quartered but who miraculously reappear. There are Swiftian characters who embody the varying characteristics of Lilliputians, Brobdingnabians, and Yahoos. Hints of Rabelais's Gargantua can be seen in Gombold's huge appetite for learning, his lengthy itemizations, and exaggerations such as a ball at the country house of Lord and Lady Beersheba, with their three million guests. If Candide's education consists of the opposing theories of optimism and pessimism and Gargantua's the Renaissance world's knowledge, Gombold's is that of instruction by Doktor von Pregnant, whose phenomenal memory enables him to recall in Joycean style the whole of "Shoxbear, Arrispittle, Grubben, Taciturn, . . . and Kneetchur."[3]

But it is Dante whose influence is most evident from the start. Finding himself in his "wood," the hair of the giant, Gombold encounters two combatants. For helping them, he is deserted by them, one the fattest man on earth, and the other, Vulp, a mock-Virgil to Dante's guide. Alone once more he is frightened by three animals—an eagle, a cock, and a lion—a parody of Dante's leopard, lion, and she-wolf. References to a woman, supposedly Gombold's mistress, Beatrice, are parodic suggestions of Dante's ideal love. No moral Virgil or Beatrice these, Orton's Vulp and Beatrice have but one purpose: to survive. Dante's influence continued into Orton's stage plays, as, for instance, in one of his most famous mock-epigrammatic lines spoken by Eddie to his sister to whom he has just proposed sharing a lover: "You showed him the gate of hell every night. He abandoned Hope when he entered there."[4]

In a perverse tribute to his father whose life was spent as gardener to the city of Leicester, Orton adds to the humans and animals Gombold meets a curious third group of creatures from the plant world—truffles, pumpkins, carrots, daisies, melons, loganberries, weeds, leaves, thistles, and the rose—the elder John Orton's favorite flower. These war with each other no less than do their counterparts in the human and animal worlds. Gombold endures their rebuffs and hesitates to make requests of them. One floral voice illustrates Orton's famous use of freshly turned clichés: "I wouldn't be closeted with a carrot for all the tea in China" (*Head*, 14). Claude, a loganberry, gloating over having scratched a picker whose fingers were "five hideous things plunging down," complains that "it's enough to turn a raspberry pale" (*Head*, 13). In this wonderland, Orton's talking plants even discuss books on plants, recalling for the reader Orton's criminal defacing of the gardening books he had borrowed from the public library.

Gombold recurringly confronts holes in the giant's body, each hole propelling him into a new adventure and emphasizing the topsy-turvy nature of the world—much as the rabbit hole did for Alice. Near one hole, he is beaten for his attempts to help a fat man who turns into the prosecutor at the trial of Gombold's three friends at the end. Alice's tea party is rendered as the hospitality that he is offered at some times but denied at others. There is, as in Alice's land, the continued aura of the dream. Gombold dreams frequently, with one of his more disturbing nightmares involving a "goat, father of Fornicationists, preaching chastity, a big-bellied virgin, a pair of pink combinations. He saw twelve figures armed with sickles hacking away his testicles," his castration "the seed of God" giving "form to the formless" (*Head*, 82). The nightmare ends with one of Orton's stylistic hallmarks, the undercutting of nightmarish violence with a return to daylight reality. Gombold awoke from his dream crying and "continued to moan to himself until the warder entered with breakfast" (*Head*, 82). Gombold's prison experience has its moments of isolation, eerily foreshadowing Orton's, in which the only "communicants were men of his imagination . . . who peopled the silence and told him of their lives" (*Head*, 70).

Orton's aggression against authority is treated farcically in the anarchic sexual identities he assigns his characters. Enraged by Gombold's break-in and his interruption of a bedroom episode, Vulp and his wife call for help. A fat policewoman appears, and, embracing Gombold, provides him with his first bit of comfort. Her transsexual humanity is as natural as is his assumed role as her wife. The blurring of sexual identity—a recurring theme that involves transvestism—is at the heart of the plot of his last stage play, *What the Butler Saw*. Gombold even promises never to wear "Daddy's clothes," for a time contentedly wearing a frilly apron. But soon he is tempted by the idea of the power in the male clothes that she wears, and he dons them elatedly as he begins a new series of adventures.

Among Gombold's many adventures, the most important is his meeting in prison with Doktor von Pregnant, a rebel like himself who, although his side had won, had been thrown into prison. The Doktor has concocted elaborate plans for escape and has written his life's work, *A Concise History of the World and Its Interests*, on paper he has made from several shirts. Like Gargantua, Gombold is tutored by the Doktor, patterned after Kenneth Halliwell, Orton's lover, who broadened Orton's literary horizons. Gombold wonders "if the Doktor were not one of his waking visions" (*Head*, 76). In a parody of Ben Jonson's tribute to Shakespeare, Gombold confesses to "little Litthom and less Glook" (*Head*, 77). The two sketch out a plan of education that includes, "Glook, Litthom and Hoobray, Trukkish and the many dialect forms of Greerman" (*Head*, 79). They also discuss Sir Thomas Browne, Petrarch and Laura, and Achilles. As the Doktor talks, Gombold dreams. The Doktor is the intellectual and Gombold the artist. When they finally escape, having swum sewers and an ocean, the old Doktor dies peacefully, in markedly ironic contrast to Halliwell's violent murder/suicide of himself and Orton.

With the Doktor's death, Gombold "had broken from his chrysalis and emerged whole" (*Head*, 86). Orton's own chrysalis had broken in prison during his and Halliwell's six-month separation. His education by Halliwell completed, he spoke often of the detachment he developed during those six months. His wholeness was like that of his fictional hero who evoked a Joycean elation at being "part and parcel of the world, of the ocean, of the universe," yet conscious of the "great waves determined to dash him to pieces on the rocks, to smash his freedom before he had tasted it" (*Head*, 86). In the grip of an eagle, he was flown over the giant's body, and they fell "towards the city situated between the navel and the groin" (*Head*, 88). Gombold's dream resembles the experience of Joyce's Stephen Dedalus who heard the maiden along the shore calling him to his vocation.

Not until the end of a series of harrowing experiences does the subject of Gombold's writing emerge. He realizes then that "words were more effective than actions; in the right hands verbs and nouns could create panic" (*Head*, 174). Gombold then bought a dictionary to study the construction of a sentence. He "studied the chemistry and behaviour of words, phrase design, the forging, casting and milling, the theories of paraphrase and periphrase, the fusing and the aiming" (*Head*, 175). His study included "the propagation of idiom . . . and came up with a preliminary theoretical answer. A sentence no more than six words long, with no adjectives and in the second person plural, should result in the complete collapse of the enemy power" (*Head*, 175). Lahr notes in his biography of Orton that Orton had made a practice of compiling long lists of words, probably like those described by Gombold.

In 1964, three years after the completion of *Head to Toe* (originally titled *The Vision of Gombold Proval*), Orton's first play, *The Ruffian on the Stair*, was broadcast on BBC Third Programme. This first success brought with it the force of Gombold's words—that "to be destructive words had to be irrefutable" and that spoken rather than printed words, if one could "lock the enemy into a room somewhere," would "create some sort of seismic disturbances" (*Head*, 175). Successive performances of Orton's plays produced his long-hoped-for disturbances in management impresarios and in the middle-class Edna Welthorpes (one of Orton's several epistolary aliases), but from admirers like Terence Rattigan and Harold Pinter, Orton received only accolades. Had Orton lived to see the publication of the novel in 1971, he would have read Auberon Waugh's proclamation of it as "worthy of Swift" (*Head*, book jacket).

Up Against It: Anarchy in Full Bloom

Having already aimed his farcical gun at sexual mores in *Ruffian on the Stair* and in *Entertaining Mr. Sloane*, at the law in *Loot*, at organized holiday camps in *The Erpingham Camp*, at corporate impersonality in *The Good and Faithful Servant*, at religion in *Funeral Games*, and at psychiatry in *What the Butler Saw*, Orton's parting shot, this one at literary traditions of love and war, took the form of a musical screenplay commissioned and then rejected by the Beatles. The purity of its farcical style bears resemblance to that of *What the Butler Saw*, which he was still polishing at the time of his death.

Love, politics, revolution, and financial greed fuel the plot, beginning with the exile of McTurk and Low by Father Brodie and Mayor Terence O'Scallion and ending with a most unconventional marriage ceremony performed by the very same Brodie in the presence of O'Scallion.

With exile as their lot, McTurk and Low are led to the outskirts of the city in a ritual procession headed by Brodie, O'Scallion, and an assortment of civic dignitaries. McTurk's crime was sex with Rowena who was seen entering his room nude, and Low's was the blowing up of the War Memorial, an allegorical statue of the figure of Peace. Low's remonstrance that he was only placing a wreath at the monument at the request of a World War II veteran had met with no success. (Orton also used the bombing of a statue of Winston Churchill in *What the Butler Saw* as one of several climaxes in that play.)

With his undying love for Rowena, McTurk sets off with Low on a series of adventures resembling some of Gombold's in the earlier work. The two exiles are joined eventually by a father-and-son duo, the Ramsays, the father dedicated only to the *idea* of revolution, regardless of its nature. As in the novel, all four are drawn into revolutions and counterrevolutions, to the point, as in the novel, that no one seems to know who is on which side or what the fighting is about, except for the elder Ramsay who enlists them for his current project, the assassination of Lillian Corbett, a female prime minister. At a political convention in Royal Albert Hall, he proclaims his aim to "undermine people's confidence in the government of the day."[5] To do so, he advocates tactics of "the smear, the lie, and, in extreme cases, even the truth" (*Against*, 21). In McTurk and Low, Orton recreated the characters of Hal in *Loot* and Nick in *What the Butler Saw*, both compulsive truth tellers whose problems only increase with each truth they relate.

Set in the context of a bloody uprising, *Up Against It* is Orton's tribute to the id-releasing anarchy that by 1967 had become his recognized metaphor for the demolition of authoritarianism. In a wicked lampooning of Shakespeare's balcony scene in *Romeo and Juliet*, McTurk attempts to declare his undying love for Rowena. He is the lightest of lightweight Romeos to Rowena's Juliet, who is the most modern woman in the world. As such, she rejects McTurk in favor of the rich Coates, the screenplay's version of the novel's Vulp. Because he is rich, Coates can afford to have bad teeth and to possess Rowena as his wife. The lovers manage to meet clandestinely in settings ripe with romantic clichés—moonlight, roses, nightingale, and waltz—which are continuously undercut by realities such as war and prison. In Orton's parodic heaven, Rowena responds impatiently to McTurk's assertion that she has been constantly in his thoughts: "I must go. Love seems out of place in a garden in the moonlight" (*Against*, 64). Though McTurk endures blow after blow, he is rewarded finally with the requisite happy ending. Perverse in its Ortonesque nature, the wedding ceremony features three bridegrooms marrying, not Rowena, but Patricia Drumgoole who, as Orton's parody of Shakespeare's nurse, had earlier served as pander to Rowena and McTurk.

At a low ebb in his fortunes, McTurk escapes from a yacht and, washed ashore, awakens to find himself taken care of by none other than Connie, the policewoman who coincidentally appears whenever nourishment of any sort is needed, her only price being sexual favors. The incident here evokes the Haidee episode in Byron's *Don Juan*, in which nature, uncomplicated by social civilities, is allowed to take her course freely. Far from the purity of Haidee, however, Connie is a rising politician who exerts her influence at will.

During one of several prison terms, McTurk complains of conditions, only to find himself moved to yet a worse cell. Like Gombold, he escapes by digging into a sewer and swimming to the open sea. Washed ashore he is consoled once more by Connie who enlists him on her side. Asked whom they are fighting, Connie replies, "The rebels, of course." She ignores his confession of sympathy with the rebels and gives him an alcohol rub as a parting present.

Again as with Gombold earlier, Voltaire is parodied in McTurk's meeting up with the people who have been thought dead, among these Patricia Drumgoole, who reintroduces herself as a graduate of Father Brodie's pantry. As with Voltaire's Candide in his undying love for Cunegonde, however ugly she has become over the years, McTurk remains constant in his love for Rowena. But unlike Candide's philosopher-tutor, Pangloss, and Orton's Doktor von Pregnant, the elder Ramsay functions more as a cog in the plot machinery than as an important philosopher-tutor.

Good and evil, at the heart of wars in romance literature, here take the form of modern ideologies. These involve a series of revolutions in which the current matriarchy is being threatened by the males. Both the Prime Minister and Archbishop of Canterbury are women, and the men fall into three groups: those drawn in for financial gain (Coates and O'Scallion), those who want only to survive (McTurk and Low), and those for whom rebellion is its own excuse for being (the Ramsays). At one point, the bedraggled elder Ramsay acknowledges the muddle he has made of the fighting. When McTurk promises to have him "safe and sound in a well-run all-male hospital," Ramsay, in yet another of his anarchical turnabouts, will have nothing to do with the rebels and proclaims: "Back to the women! Our only hope" (*Against*, 58).

The big battle is not strategically planned but, rather, accidentally begun by the crashing of an ambulance into a lorry, its violence involving even the stretcher bearers who have to be fought off. Everyone is a potential enemy. The scene is another of Orton's farcical "tricks," resembling the bloody crash in the funeral procession in *Loot* and the climactic piling up of bodies in all states of dress and mistaken identities in *What the Butler Saw*.

The play ends with the carrying of the bride over the threshold by her three bridegrooms in a perfection of the theme of sexual sharing that Orton had begun in *Entertaining Mr. Sloane*. His original plans included four bridegrooms to be played by the Beatles as a composite character and one bride, providing "lots of opportunities for sexual ambiguities" (*Diaries*, 64). He later changed the composite to three separate young men and the elder Ramsay. In his *Diaries*, Orton relishes the idea that Harold Pinter's sexual sharing in *The Homecoming* owed something to his own treatment of the subject in *Entertaining Mr. Sloane*.

As Orton's only original filmscript, the play is interesting for the ironic circumstances surrounding its two unsuccessful attempts at production. In the midst of his most successful year, 1967—*Loot*'s success in the West End; the sale of *Loot* for a movie production; a revision of *Erpingham Camp* for a new production with *Ruffian on the Stair*, with the new combined title, *Crimes of Passion;* and finishing what was to be his last stage play, *What the Butler Saw*—Orton eventually sold his rejected screenplay to another producer for £10,000 and 10 percent of the producer's profits. As his last unproduced legacy to the world, the screenplay resisted posthumous changes by writers brought in for that purpose: Charles Wood, James Saunders, Roger McGough, and Christopher Logue. To date it has not been produced, and it remains "a tantalizing remnant of what might have been, the last comic fragment of a voluptuary of fiasco" (*Against*, xix).

Up Against It however, underwent yet a third attempt at production, this time on stage at the Public Theater in New York on 4 December 1989. Misguided admirers, according to Mel Gussow, managed to "obliterate whatever charm existed in the screenplay."[6] The effort to create a stage musical from a film musical ran into all kinds of production difficulties, with disastrous results similar to those that plagued the first productions of Orton's plays.

As posthumous publications, *Head to Toe* and *Up Against It* remain ironic, albeit minor, witnesses to Orton's unfinished career and life, the one an early fictional autobiography of the making of an artist and the other a late example of the seasoned style of the somebody Orton had always intended to become.

Notes

This article is an adaptation of a chapter in Susan Rusinko's book, *Joe Orton* (Twayne Publishers, 1995).

1. Joe Orton, *The Orton Diaries*, ed. John Lahr (London: Methuen-Minerva, 1989), 76; hereinafter cited in text as *Diaries*.
2. John Lahr, *Prick Up Your Ears*, 2d ed. (New York: Alfred A. Knopf, 1991), 125; hereinafter cited in text as Lahr.
3. Joe Orton, *Head to Toe* (London: Anthony Blond, 1971; Methuen, 1986; New York: St. Martin's Press, 1987), 76; hereinafter cited in text as *Head*.

4. Joe Orton, *The Complete Plays* (London: Eyre Methuen, 1976; reprint, 1991), 143.

5. Joe Orton, *Up Against It* (New York: Grove Press, 1979), 21; hereinafter cited in text as *Against*.

6. Mel Gussow, review, *New York Times,* 5 December 1989, 17.

More Than Noises Off:
Marsha Norman's Offstage Characters
Tracy Simmons Bitonti

In a 1983 *New York Times* article, drama critic Mel Gussow celebrated the increasing numbers of new women dramatists emerging in a theater that had previously been "a male preserve."[1] Among the women gaining recognition for their playwriting talents were Beth Henley, Tina Howe, and, especially, Marsha Norman. Norman's drama career began in 1977 with *Getting Out*, and in 1983, she won a Pulitzer Prize for *'night, Mother*. A 1988 volume, *Four Plays*, made more easily available not only *Getting Out* but also the two one acts that make up *Third and Oak* (1978); *The Holdup* (1980-83); and *Traveler in the Dark* (1984).[2]

Much of the critical attention to Norman's plays thus far has taken a feminist approach, since much of her work deals with women's experiences and concerns. A few scholars have focused on particular elements of Norman's dramatic technique. Lisa J. McDonnell compares and contrasts the work of Norman and Beth Henley, focusing on their most distinctive narrative methods.[3]

Leslie Kane traces "an impressive development of thought and technique" in Norman's plays, discussing hallmarks such as a confined setting, bonding of mother and child, and uses of humor. One element Kane touches on that could be explored further is Norman's use of "absent characters dramatically realized."[4] There have been many notable examples in theater history of characters who never appear, yet who influence a play's action—e.g., Captain Alving in Ibsen's *Ghosts* and Tom and Laura Wingfield's father in Tennessee Williams's *The Glass Menagerie*. But there have been few playwrights who use this technique as consistently as does Norman.

The offstage character is an important device in drama because of the necessary economies of the stage. In fact, the main reason Norman's 1987 novel, *The Fortune Teller*, became a novel instead of a play was that Norman "realized that she would not have enough room onstage for all the characters."[5] In a novel there is more room for memory and flashback, and Norman could show scenes with characters such as protagonist Fay's ex-husband Ed, or Colleen Masters, a catalyst of the novel's action. The offstage character is a way to compensate for the lack of such room in drama. Esther Harriot has praised Norman's ability to make the most of the theater's limitations, pointing out her use of confined space, tight structure, and economy of language.[6] Norman's uses of offstage characters are another element of this skill. The technique has another practical advantage: fewer onstage characters means fewer actors who must be paid, and production costs must be taken into consideration.

Offstage characters can serve the same kinds of functions that McDonnell attributes to the narrative technique of characters' storytelling: they can influence or reveal something about onstage characters or serve as foils, affect the plot, provide comic relief or moments of pathos, or reflect the play's themes (McDonnell, 96, 98). Norman incorporates each of these uses to varying degrees. *The Holdup* relies the least upon offstage characters, who are simply onstage character enhancers. In *Getting Out* and *'night, Mother,* they are influences and foils, with touches of humor in the latter play. In *Third and Oak* and *Traveler in the Dark,* the offstage characters are the primary plot catalysts.

Norman was using this technique from the start of her career. *Getting Out* simultaneously depicts Arlene Holsclaw's efforts to adjust to life after prison and dramatizes the process that had led her there. Norman uses the experimental technique of having two actresses play the same character at different points in her career; on one part of the stage, Arlene struggles to establish her independence and maturity, while on another part of the stage, Arlie, her younger and wilder self, reenacts important scenes from her life. Although these scenes do feature a few of the people who influenced Arlie, such as a school principal and generic prison guards, some of the most important characters remain unseen.

One of these offstage characters is Arlie's father, who has sexually abused her. She lies to her mother ("Daddy didn't do nuthin' to me," 16), indicates that abuse has occurred more than once ("don't touch it. It'll git well. It git well before," 15), and screams in terror ("No, Daddy! I didn't tell her nuthin'. I didn't! I didn't!" 17). The school principal catches her with money, which Arlie claims she earned "doin' things" for her daddy (17), yet she is later enraged by (and beats up) a fellow juvenile hall inmate who accuses her of sleeping with her father for money (23). This combination of sex and money helped lead her into prostitution, and the combined negative sexual experiences most likely contributed to her worst crime: she shot a cab driver who apparently was sexually harassing her after she told him not to touch her.

The characterization of the offstage father is continued in Arlene's mother's denial of the abuse. She says, "He weren't a mean man, though, your daddy" (15), and remembers Arlie's "tellin' them lies about that campin' trip we took, sayin' your daddy made you watch while he an me . . . you know. I'd have killed you then if them social workers hadn't been watchin" (21). She tells Arlene that he claims to be dying and that he has not worked for six or seven years, making her drive the cab that supports them instead. She also recalls an incident in which little Arlie tried to kill her drunken father by bringing him a sandwich of bologna and toothpaste—and the stage directions indicate that for the first time Arlene is "finally enjoying a memory" (19), as she does at the end of the play remembering the time she was locked in the closet and peed in every one of her mother's shoes (56).

Another offstage character who is important in the development of Arlene's character is the prison chaplain. As Esther Harriot points out, he was the first person to call Arlie by her full name and to treat her as a human being, thus beginning the process of the transformation from Arlie to Arlene (Harriot, 131). Bennie, the former guard who has driven Arlene home to Kentucky in the hopes of continuing and advancing his voyeuristic relationship with her, is envious of the chaplain. Arlene quotes the chaplain, indicating his influence: "Animals is wild, not people. That's what he said." Bennie responds, "Now what could that four-eyes chaplain know about wild?" (9). When she unpacks the picture of Jesus the chaplain had given her, Bennie snidely remarks, "He got it for free, I bet" (10). Bennie, like the other men in the play, wants to exploit Arlene sexually, whereas the chaplain had shown her nothing but kindness.

Arlie initially resists the chaplain's visit, but soon is anxiously inquiring whether it is his day to visit. She is later devastated when he is transferred. He gives her a Bible with her name "right in the front of it," and her reading from it is an important part of her rehabilitation (46). Moreover, he had told her that Arlie was her evil self which God would take away so that she could be good. When he left, she became hysterical and stabbed herself repeatedly with a fork in an attempt to kill "Arlie" (53). This incident was the key to her transformation. Recalling it to her new friend, Ruby, helps Arlene to complete the process, to grieve for and finally recognize the lost part of herself (Harriot, 134).

A third key offstage character is Arlene's son, Joey, named for the yellow "Joey-bear" that was her security as a child. Arlie had wanted to be pregnant; she falsely told the doctor at a juvenile institution that she was, saying that "kids need somebody to bring 'em up right" (22). When she did become pregnant with Joey, she resisted institutional pressures to have an abortion. Pregnant Arlie's touching speech to her baby as she imagines him reveals both the defeatist attitude her experiences have given her and her desire to protect him:

> Best thing you to be is stay a baby 'cause nobody beats up on babies or puts them. . . . (*Much more quiet*) that ain't true, baby. People is mean to babies, so you stay right here with me so nobody kin git you an make you cry an they lay one finger on you (*Hostile*) an I'll beat the screamin' shit right out of 'em. They even blow on you an I'll kill 'em. (30)

Joey was the reason she had broken out: "I guess I just went crazy after [they took him away]. Thought if I could jus' git out an find him . . ." (30).

Arlene's main goal now that she is out of prison is to have Joey with her; she repeats this hope to her mother and to Carl, her former pimp. Her mother scoffs and does her best to puncture this hope. Arlene practically has to beg her mother for details of the glimpse that the latter had of Joey two years previously. When her mother callously says that Joey "got your stringy hair" (16), Arlene clings to this bit of information, returning to it in their conversation and transforming it when she later says to Bennie, "[Mother] says Joey's a real good-lookin' kid" (29).

Carl reacts to Arlene's hopes in a different way: he uses Joey as a tool for manipulation and emotional blackmail. He tries to persuade her to come to New York with him and take up prostitution again by telling her what she could give Joey:

> If you was a kid, would you want your mom to git so dragged out washin' dishes she don't have no time for you an no money to spend on you? You come with me, you kin send him big orange bears an Sting-Ray bikes with his name wrote on the fenders. He'll like that. . . . Joey be tellin' all his friends 'bout his mom livin' up in New York City an bein' so rich an sendin' him stuff all the time. (49)

Lisa McDonnell calls this "the strongest temptation of all," indicating that Arlene's resistance to it helps her regain her dignity (McDonnell, 102). Although Joey never appears, his existence reveals something about the characters of Arlene, her mother, and Carl.

Whereas the male offstage characters all have some kind of influence on Arlie/Arlene, the females—Arlene's sisters, Candy and June—are foils for Arlene, representing alternative paths she could have chosen. Like the male characters, they also add to the depiction of onstage characters. Candy is the previous tenant of the dirty, cramped apartment Arlene is moving into. Her upstairs neighbor, Ruby, reveals that Candy left owing her needed money and that she was slovenly, using an empty can of Raid to hit the bugs. Arlene's mother says that Candy has been "screwin' since day one" (20), and Ruby confirms that Candy has returned to a pimp. Arlene responds angrily: "No, it ain't okay. Guys got their dirty fingernails all over her. Some pimp's out buyin' green pants while she . . . Goddamn her" (41). Arlene rejects this lifestyle, just as she has rejected the option represented by June, who is not only married to a jailbird and constantly pregnant like her mother but also a dope dealer.

Discussion of Candy and June also illustrates the callousness of Arlene's family's relationships. When Arlene first asks her mother where Candy is, her mother responds, "You got her place so what do you care? I got her outta my house so whatta I care?" (15). Esther Harriot points out that when Ruby says to Arlene, "Candy said you was in Arkansas," and Arlene responds, "Alabama" (41), it is a good "illustration of her family's indifference," because "all that Candy can remember of her sister's whereabouts is the first letter of the state" (Harriot, 134).

In Norman's next plays, the one-acts *The Laundromat* and *The Pool Hall*, which combine to form *Third and Oak*, the offstage characters are the main catalysts for the onstage action (or, more accurately, discussion). Two lonely women who define themselves in relation to their offstage husbands[7] come together at a very late hour in *The Laundromat*. Deedee, a talkative young woman, is upset about her husband, Joe, who is cheating on her. Alberta's husband, Herb, is dead, and she is finally bringing herself to do the laundry he left behind. Through the women's conversation, their husbands are extensively characterized. Joe is lazy and has a cruel streak. Deedee says he does not laugh when she makes a joke but would if she tripped over the coffee table (61). Deedee also admits that "Joe hates black people. He says even when they're dancin' or playin' ball, they're thinkin' about killin'" (74); and this comes just after she has chastised Alberta for being prejudiced.

Herb, by contrast, appears as a gentle man. He called his wife "Bertie, my girl" and enjoyed watching her cook Thanksgiving dinners (although this made her nervous). He liked to garden and would fetch and wipe off a lawn chair so that Alberta could come out and watch him in the sunshine. He had a sense of humor, putting out an "Herb Garden" sign and joking, "Can't we wait until it's old enough to walk?" to Alberta's request to take out the garbage (78). Norman's wealth of vivid details makes these characters almost as interesting and "real" as the ones onstage.

Both of the men have a great deal of power over their wives. Joe does not want Deedee to work, so she has to hide the menial job she has taken. Joe is not ready for children, so Deedee cannot have any yet. Most importantly, Deedee is well aware that Joe is "mean and stupid" and that he is unfaithful, but she does not want a divorce (76–77). Even though Herb is dead, he influences Alberta: she tells Deedee, "I found our beachball when I cleaned out the basement. I can't let the air out of it. It's his breath in there" (79). She continues to match his black socks even though she realizes she no longer has to, and she has kept his clothes, even the shirt he died in. Although the source of Herb's continued power is love, unlike Joe's, both men have left their wives facing loneliness. Alberta is learning to deal with it—she is at least able to wash most of the laundry—and she encourages Deedee to do the same.

Two minor offstage characters are worth noting in this play. One is Deedee's mother—as Leslie Kane points out, "Repeating the paradigm employed in *Getting Out* [with Arlene's mother and Ruby], Norman provides us with two mothers: an indifferent, critical mother and a mother surrogate" (Kane, 262). Deedee usually takes her laundry to her mother's house: "She got matching Maytags. She buys giant-sized Cheer and we sit around and watch the soaps till the clothes come out" (61). But the detergent is the only "cheer" in the house; Deedee reports that her mother does not want to talk to Deedee, saying, "Just leave 'em, I'll do 'em" (61), because she does not believe Deedee is capable of setting the dryer heat properly. Deedee tells Alberta that her (Deedee's) mother is the last person she would talk to about her troubles, but Deedee can confide in Alberta.

The other minor offstage character is Alberta's Aunt Dora. Alberta tells Deedee that she has not cried since Aunt Dora's rabbit Puffer died. When he died, Aunt Dora admonished her not to cry: "He didn't mean to go and leave us all alone and he'd feel bad if he knew he made us so miserable" (75). Aunt Dora did not follow her own advice, eventually lapsing into silence and dying in a nursing home. Norman implies that Alberta will not follow in Aunt Dora's footsteps.

The Pool Hall also revolves around offstage characters. Like Deedee, Shooter Stevens, a black DJ, is in a troubled marriage. He has come to talk things out with Willie, the owner of the pool hall and the best friend of Shooter's father (the original Shooter Stevens, a pool hustler). Shooter's wife Sondra, his father-in-law George (his father's and Willie's other best friend), and his father not only are the catalysts for the discussion but also expand the characterizations of Shooter and Willie.

Shooter's marriage is one of the main topics of their conversations. He indicates his resentment of Sondra almost immediately. Informed by Willie that she has just called, Shooter replies, "Somebody did one helluva job teaching that girl to tell the time. Tells me the time to come home, tells me the time to eat, tells me the time to go to bed" (82). Shooter is even more angry about her spending habits. He tells Willie, "What she wants, my man, is everything there is. Sable coats, suede chairs, a Cuisinart and a cook to run it, trips to wherever-it-is Hong Kong, five-hundred-dollar shoes, and fourteen-carat gold fingernails" (86).

Furthermore, when Shooter bought himself a recliner, she gave it away because it did not match the rest of her furniture. Willie tries to defend her: "She's doin' what she can. Makin' you look good, and makin' your house look good. You quit work, she'll make poor look good. So you shut up about you have to work to pay her bills" (93). Because Shooter and Sondra are the children of his best friends, Willie is absolutely determined to help make their marriage work: "And you are going to stay married to her or you are going to have to answer to me. . . . And you are going to keep her happy or you are gonna stay outta my sight. You gonna grow up if it kills you" (86). His devotion is indicative of his character; he is also old-fashioned in his disapproval of Shooter's mild flirtation with Deedee. Stubborn and fierce, he repeatedly tells Shooter to go home, and he makes pointed references to "your wife."

Willie also encourages them to have children, but this is another sore spot because Shooter wants children and Sondra does not. He tells Willie she has said, "I'm gonna blow up like a whale? Not this body, baby. Uh-uh, honey" (94), and she uses every form of birth control available. Willie shifts the responsibility back to Shooter, saying that if he would stay at home more, she might be more receptive. With an offstage character like Sondra, the question might arise as to how fair or accurate her depiction is because she is not there to speak for herself. There is only what the other characters say about her, yet Shooter's sincerity is convincing enough to give credibility to his description of her shallowness.

A final indication of Sondra's character is her reaction to another offstage character—her father, George. George's health is failing, and Shooter has bought him a motorized wheelchair. When Willie tells him how George appreciates it, Shooter replies, "Sondra said he wouldn't even know it was real leather, but I figured, what the hell, it's only money" (83). Although Willie admits she does call her father, she has been reluctant to visit George, saying he has been "smelling funny" (102). Shooter treats Sondra's father better than she does. Willie has similarly let George fill the jukebox with his favorite oldies, although George likes "real crap" like Tennessee Ernie Ford and Pat Boone (102).

Shooter's realization of Willie's kindness and love helps to bring them close together at the end of the act. But before their final embrace, they must come to terms with the third offstage character, Shooter's father. Shooter, whose real name is Gary Wayne, has been using his father's name, but Willie pointedly calls him G.W. Shooter tries to imitate his father's moves and speech habits, but he does not have the pool skills of his father. Shooter confides to Deedee how close his father, Willie, and George were: "I ever needed anything, lunch money, rubbers, anything, didn't matter which one I asked. Seemed like it all came out of the same pocket" (97). Willie repeatedly reminds Shooter that he paid the costs of Shooter's birth and that he took care of the arrangements after Shooter's father committed suicide. The suicide is another troubling topic for Shooter. He wants to know why his father killed himself and why he leaped from the salvage-yard side of the bridge rather than into the water. Willie explains that his father jumped because he knew he was losing his legendary pool skills and chose the junkyard side because he was a good swimmer and did not want to be able to back out (88–89). At last they reach some understanding of a man they both loved. When Willie and Shooter have finally said everything they need to say, they begin playing pool, reciting in unison one of Shooter's father's favorite expressions: "Give me a break" (103).

Although not as dependent on offstage characters as is *Third and Oak*, Norman's next play, *The Holdup*, still concludes some use of this technique. In *The Holdup*, set in 1914, the last legendary outlaw has come to a watering hole in New Mexico to meet his former sweetheart, Lily. They find a cookshack set up for a wheat-threshing crew and currently being guarded by the Tucker brothers, Henry and Archie. Henry is a mean, bitter man obsessed with outlaw legends, whereas Archie is an innocent seventeen-year-old. The Outlaw shoots Henry and tries to commit suicide with morphine but is saved by Archie and Lily. By the end of the play, the Outlaw and Lily will marry, and Archie is ready to face whatever adventures life can offer him. Richard Wattenberg has shown how Norman has transformed the "frontier myth":

> The old frontier myth which revolves around a climactic "marriage" of male/West/savagery with female/East/civilization gives way to a more

realistic vision of the frontier experience as a growth-process pointing toward some nebulous future climax or resolution.[8]

The key action is Archie's initiation to adulthood, and one of the significant offstage influences is his dominating mother. He reveals that he has not signed up to participate in the budding war effort, because "Mother would *kill* me" (110), and Henry later snidely remarks, "Archie would shoot a good horse if Mother told him to" (115). But by the end of the play, he makes love to Lily on his mother's quilt, and Lily promises to write his good-byes to his mother (155). This change signals his passage to adulthood (Wattenberg, 514).

One offstage character, a rancher who had proposed to Lily, is a catalyst in Lily's development. The Outlaw rode across the country to shoot him, revealing the depth of the Outlaw's feeling for Lily. Shot by the jealous Outlaw, the rancher left his money to Lily, who built a school with his money and in his name, thus associating herself with the education of the West (Wattenberg, 510).

Two additional offstage characters—the Outlaw's brother and nephew, Bill and Fred—were killed in an attempted robbery after the Outlaw fled the scene. Henry tells the Outlaw what had happened, having read about it in one of the outlaw magazines in the barbershop. Henry delights in rubbing in the gory details of their deaths:

> The shot blew Bill right out of the saddle, but Fred's body kept riding around till somebody plugged the horse in the belly. Damn strong horse though. Made it all the way to the post office hitching post where it finally fell down in a big mess of blood, squashed Fred's body underneath, flat as flat. And where were you? (129)

Henry's meanness prepares the audience to accept the Outlaw's killing of him. The Outlaw's guilt over the deaths of Bill and Fred also make his character more sympathetic.

It is in Norman's best known play, *'night, Mother,* however, that offstage characters gain even more prominence. This tense drama features only two people onstage as Jessie Cates seeks to rationalize her impending suicide to her mother Thelma ("Mama"). Their discussions bring to life several additional characters who have influenced their lives and contributed to Jessie's decision: Jessie's father, her brother Dawson and his wife Loretta, her son Ricky, her ex-husband Cecil, and Mama's friend Agnes Fletcher.

At the beginning of the play, Jessie is searching for her father's pistol. She has one of Cecil's but wants to use her father's, indicating the closeness of the relationship. Jessie knew her father loved her. He had made pipe cleaner creatures for her, and they had carried on private conversations of which Mama was jealous. In contrast, Jessie's father did not have much to say to Mama, even on his deathbed: "It was his last chance not to talk to me and he took full advantage of it."[9] Mama is finally able to admit that she did not love him, and Jessie desires this kind of honesty on this last night of her life. She wants answers, for herself and Mama. Jessie learns that her father also had suffered epileptic fits, as she does, giving Mama someone to blame besides herself (although she does that, too).

As Jessie searches for her father's pistol, she comments that Dawson had better not have it (8). Her resentment of him is obvious in her complaints: "He just calls me Jess like he knows who he's talking to" (23), but he does not know her. He buys her slippers that fit his wife's feet, not hers. That they have never been close is underscored when Jessie reports that after she asked him what kind of bullets she should buy (not telling him for what purpose), "He said we ought to talk like this more often" (15). She enjoys the joke of his unwitting participation and later enjoys the power she will have because he will follow the instructions she is leaving on what to buy Mama for Christmas.

Jessie feels Dawson does know things about her that she does not wish him to know. She is adamant about keeping him out of her last evening. She instructs Mama to let the police into her room first after she is dead, not Dawson, and also tells her not even to share any of the funeral food with Dawson and Loretta. As Jenny S. Spencer points out, "Dawson's deliberate exclusion from this evening protects Jessie's already violated sense of privacy and thereby thwarts his only power over her" (Spencer, 368). At least Jessie gives him credit for being able to take care of their mother. She keeps telling Mama to call Dawson to take care of problems—if she has a mouse, if the lights go out, if the police call to tell her Ricky has done something serious.

Jessie's son Ricky is another source of pain for her. He is becoming a serious juvenile delinquent. Jessie is completely honest, however pessimistic, in assuming what Ricky is capable of doing:

> Those two rings he took were the last valuable things *I* had, so now he's started in on other people, door to door. I hope they put him away sometime. I'd turn him in myself if I knew where he was. (11)

She later says it is "only a matter of time" before he kills someone (25) or is doing time: "five years for forgery, ten years for armed assault" (60). But she identifies with him:

We look out at the world and we see the same thing: Not Fair. And the only difference between us is Ricky's out there trying to get even. And he knows not to trust anybody and he got it straight from me. And he knows not to try to get work, and guess where he got that. (60)

Throughout the play, whenever Jessie comments on Ricky, Mama springs to his defense, always expressing the hopes that he will change, find a job, marry, be "nice" again. This action reinforces Mama's blind optimism, her desire not to see the truth. But by the end of the play, when Jessie tells her that she is leaving Ricky her watch, Mama admits he will sell it to buy dope—she is finally on the road to understanding.

In seeking to understand Jessie's decision, Mama wants to know whether it is anyone's fault. One person to blame might be Cecil, Jessie's ex-husband. Cecil, a carpenter who builds things to last, could not make his marriage last, despite Jessie's love and her efforts to please him. Jessie does not blame him, saying that his departure was "a relief in a way. I never was what he wanted to see, so it was better when he wasn't looking at me all the time" (61). Not only does this comment reflect Jessie's intense need for privacy, but it also echoes Mama's earlier comment that she did not have anything Jessie's father wanted (46). Sally Browder has written that "women's lives are embedded in relationships," and sometimes women determine their value in terms of what they have to offer others.[10] Both Mama and Jessie feel they have been inadequate in their relationships with the offstage characters as well as each other (see also Spencer, 375).

Cecil is also part of Mama and Jessie's honesty, an essential element of the evening. Mama admits she maneuvered the relationship, and Jessie admits she wrote Cecil's good-bye note. Both finally acknowledge that he left because he was having an affair, not because he made Jessie choose between him and cigarettes, or because her fits made him sick, or because he simply did not know how to hold on (56–57).

The woman with whom Cecil has an affair is the daughter of the last significant offstage character—Mama's friend Agnes. In a segment that provides some comic relief, Mama exaggerates Agnes's eccentricities in an effort to entertain Jessie. She says that Agnes has "burned down every house she ever lived in," even setting out chairs and serving lemonade once; that Agnes has a house full of birds; that Agnes eats okra twice a day (38–40). But Jessie finally wrings the truth from Mama and emphasizes that the truth is what she wants. She also needs to know why Agnes will no longer visit their house and is amused to learn that Agnes is afraid of her.

Mama informs Jessie of one of Agnes's sayings: "You gotta keep your life filled up." Mama adds, "She says a lot of stupid things" (40), yet this is how Mama lives—keeping her life filled with candy, TV, and crocheting, as Norman herself points out.[11] Mama also has friends like Agnes, and Jessie does not—a key difference between them. Jessie knows that Agnes will be there to comfort Mama after she is gone, helping with funeral details and perhaps even staying with her. Jessie had earlier suggested the possibility of Agnes's moving in, but Mama was quick to deny the friendship so Jessie could not use that thought to ease her conscience. Like the other offstage characters, Agnes serves multiple functions and is part of the complex patterns Norman skillfully weaves under the play's surface simplicity (Harriot, 142).

Norman's next play, *Traveler in the Dark,* also revolves around offstage characters. Brilliant surgeon Sam has returned home for the funeral of his devoted friend and nurse, Mavis, who died of cancer despite Sam's efforts to save her. Mavis's death forces Sam to come to terms with the other major crisis in his life—the death of his mother, Mary, when he was young. These two losses have caused a tremendous crisis of faith.

A minor offstage character is Sam's mother-in-law. She is rich and enjoys displaying her wealth. She is a snob (Glory, Sam's wife, has not brought "the right clothes" to suit her, [195]) and has a new "boy toy." She serves mainly as a comic foil to Glory, who is warm and caring, but the bulk of the play belongs to Mary and Mavis.

Mary and Mavis are depicted almost as fully as the characters onstage. Sam remembers his mother's nurturing: she read him fairy tales and nursery rhymes, and would show him things "like dragons' teeth, witches' fingers and fallen stars." He thinks of her in terms of sweets:

> She was the gingerbread lady. Curly red hair and shiny round eyes and a big checked apron. Fat, pink fingers, a sweet vanilla smell, and all the time in the world. Sing to you, dance with you, write your name on the top of a cake. (171)

Everett, Sam's preacher father, recalls his wife's humor. She would bake cookies for someone, eat them herself, and then send the wax paper she baked them on with a note to the recipient. Her homespun wisdom is seen in her comment that marriage

> was like your favorite shirt. You could wear it day after day, and you could try to keep it clean, but sooner or later it was going to have to go

in the wash. But as soon as it was clean, you could press it fresh, and put it back on, looking good as new. (179)

Mavis also is made vivid by what the characters say and remember about her. In love with Sam, she was proud of his accomplishments and sent Everett clippings about Sam's successes. Despite her unrequited love, she could also be a good friend to Glory; she borrowed money from Everett so that Glory could have cosmetic surgery on her eyes. She had a cat named Peaches, to whom she made Everett talk on the phone. She was self-sacrificing at every opportunity, and Glory tells Sam that she died unafraid (198).

Mavis is a source of tension between Sam and Everett. Everett had wanted Sam to marry Mavis and resents the way Sam treated her, accusing Sam of taking everything Mavis had (179). Sam, in turn, resents his father for not paying attention to his mother: "You even loved Mavis more than Mother" (191). Mavis's death has caused Sam to confront not only his feelings about her and his mother but also those about Everett. Mavis's death also causes Sam to panic about his marriage, and he tells Glory he wants a divorce. By the end of the play, he realizes that this was only a knee-jerk response, made because he did not want to hurt Glory as he thinks he had hurt his mother and Mavis, or because he feared losing her, too (203).

His mother's death affected Sam as much as Mavis's did. Everett says Mary's death is the reason Sam became a doctor (183). It is also the reason he lost the faith that made him a child preacher, and he blames God as well as his father. He is angry at her, too, for leaving him. He expresses this by explaining to his son, Stephen, why Humpty Dumpty fell off the wall:

> His . . . mother . . . laid him there. . . . She told him he was a man. See? She dressed him up in a little man's suit. He didn't know he could fall. He didn't know he could break. He didn't know he was an egg. (164–65)

Mary's death taught Sam he could break. He later says he should have known Mavis would die, because his mother died (170). Mary's death started the process that Mavis's death completes. By the end of the play, he has worked through his guilt and pain until he understands that faith is like the geodes his mother collected but would never break open: "It was better for it to be safe than for you to know what it was, exactly" (201). Sam and Everett eventually reconcile their differences with each other, and Everett's speech about Mary at the end of the play could apply to Mavis as well:

I guess you can be a real big part of somebody else's world without ever understanding the first thing about it. Somebody can give you their life and you'll never know why. Never know what they wanted from you, or if they ever got it. Then when they die, well, knowing so little about these people makes it real hard to lose them. (200–201)

This is the lesson Everett and Sam learn through the deaths of Mary and Mavis, and it is a key theme of Norman's—people learning to understand each other.

Everett and Sam join Arlie, Deedee and Alberta, Shooter and Willie, the Outlaw and Lily, and Jessie as complex characters who come to terms with themselves and whom Norman shapes by her use of offstage characters.

Notes

1. Mel Gussow, "Women Playwrights: New Voices in the Theater," *New York Times Magazine* (1 May 1983), 26.
2. Marsha Norman, *Four Plays* (New York: Theatre Communications Group, 1988). All quotations from these four plays are from this edition and are cited parenthetically in the text.
3. Lisa J. McDonnell, "Diverse Similitude: Beth Henley and Marsha Norman," *Southern Quarterly* 25 (Spring 1987), 95–104.
4. Leslie Kane, "The Way Out, the Way In: Paths to Self in the Plays of Marsha Norman," *Feminine Focus: The New Women Playwrights*, ed. Enoch Brater (Oxford: Oxford University Press, 1989), 257, 268–269.
5. Lori Miller, "Writing Was the Only Choice," *New York Times Book Review* (24 May 1987), 10.
6. Esther Harriot, *American Voices: Five Contemporary Playwrights in Essays and Interviews* (Jefferson, N.C.: McFarland, 1988), 134.
7. Jenny S. Spencer, "Norman's *'night, Mother*: Psycho-Drama of Female Identity," *Modern Drama* 30, no. 3 (1987), 365. See also C. W. E. Bigsby, *Modern American Drama, 1945–1990* (Cambridge: Cambridge University Press, 1992), 316.
8. Richard Wattenberg, "Feminizing the Frontier Myth: Marsha Norman's *The Holdup*," *Modern Drama* 33, no.4 (December 1990), 513.
9. Marsha Norman, *'night, Mother* (New York: Hill and Wang, 1983), 53. All further citations from this play are parenthetical within the text.
10. Sally Browder, "'I Thought You Were Mine': Marsha Norman's *'night, Mother*," in *Mother Puzzles: Daughters and Mothers in Contemporary American Literature*, ed. Mickey Pearlman (New York: Greenwood Press, 1989), 111.
11. Kathleen Betsko and Rachel Koening, *Interviews with Contemporary Women Playwrights* (New York: Beech Tree Books, 1987), 328.

Murder Most Civilized:
The Stage Thrillers of Frederick Knott

ARTHUR NICHOLAS ATHANASON

LESS sophisticated and more melodramatic than mystery stories, "thrillers" emphasize swift, suspenseful action and the excitement of very ordinary persons caught in dangerous situations from which it seems impossible to extricate themselves. Writers of this popular genre have been called "thriller merchants." Unquestionably one of the most entertaining "thriller merchants" of the postwar stage is Anglo-American playwright Frederick Knott, whose London and Broadway success, not only with *Dial M for Murder* but also with *Write Me a Murder* and *Wait until Dark*, has proved, at least at the box office, that crime can often pay very well.

Born in Hankow, China, on 28 August 1918, Knott spent much of his early childhood in the Orient, where his British parents, Cyril Wakefield and Margaret Caroline (Paul) Knott, were both stationed as missionaries. The year he was born, his father was employed as a science teacher at Griffith College near Hankow. Until age ten, Knott attended school in China and thereafter was educated in England, first at Oundle School and then at Cambridge University, where he received a degree in law. Like Tony Wendice, the charming ex-tennis-player protagonist of *Dial M for Murder*, Knott himself was a tennis star while at Cambridge. In fact, when he first visited the United States in 1937, it was as a member of the Oxford-Cambridge tennis team to compete against Harvard and Yale at Newport, Rhode Island. By 1938, when he graduated from Cambridge, he was captain of the university tennis team.

From 1939 to 1946, Knott served as an officer in the Royal Artillery, rising to the rank of major. The following year, after being demobilized, he began writing screenplays for the J. Arthur Rank Organization and then for Grendon Films. During this time he became a member of The British Screenwriters' Association, whose members elected him chairman in 1950. On 10 November 1953, Knott married British actress Ann Hillary (née Ann Margaret Francis), emigrating with her in 1954 to the United States, where their son, Anthony Frederick, was born in 1959. Knott currently holds memberships in The Dramatists Guild, The Writer's Guild of America, Mystery Writers of America, The Dramatists Club, and The Players.

In 1950, inspired by Anthony Armstrong's 1933 detective play *Ten-Minute Alibi*, Knott wrote his first stage thriller, *Dial M for Murder*, the story of a young Englishman who plots the "almost perfect" murder of his wealthy wife. Knott first prepared *Dial M for Murder* as a half-hour television play, but the firm for which he wrote it went bankrupt before it could be produced. During the next year and a half, he expanded the script into a full-length stage play, but after six London producers turned it down, he decided to return to screenwriting. Then, at the outset of 1952, the BBC proposed giving the script a telecast on its Sunday night series, and in only two days, Knott adapted it into a ninety-minute television play. When it was aired live on 23 March 1952, *Dial M for Murder* received unanimously enthusiastic reviews although no interest was shown by London stage producers. As a result, Knott eventually sold the film rights to Sir Alexander Korda, the head of a London film company, for a modest £1,000. A few days after the purchase negotiations had been finalized, James P. Sherwood, a London stage producer currently leasing the Westminster Theatre, had to withdraw the production of a previously scheduled play and decided to replace it with *Dial M for Murder*. Under the direction of John Fernald, the play opened (after only two and a half weeks' rehearsal) on 19 June 1952, to high critical praise, and ran for 425 performances.

The Anglo-American actor Maurice Evans was in London at the time to appear in a feature-length film, *Mr. Gilbert and Mr. Sullivan*, produced by Korda. While *Dial M for Murder* was in rehearsal at the Westminster Theatre, Evans had a chance to read the script and was so taken by it and its virtuoso lead role of Tony Wendice that he immediately began negotiations for its American stage rights. He believed *Dial M for Murder* more suitable to American tastes than most of the British stage thrillers of the previous few years, and when he attended the play's triumphant opening night in London, he was more eager than ever to play the leading role of Tony Wendice on Broadway.

A clause in Knott's contract with Korda, however,

> prohibited the play from being staged anywhere in the world for a full year after the release of the film [version, and] plans were already underway to make the film, with Knott writing the screenplay. Finally Sher-

wood and Evans managed to negotiate an agreement lifting this restriction [at least, on Evans's proposed Broadway production], and *Dial M for Murder* [under the direction of Reginald Denham] began its run of 552 performances on Broadway on October 29, 1952 at the Plymouth Theatre.[1]

In his *New York Times* review of the production (30 October 1952), Brooks Atkinson praised the play as "original and remarkably good theatre—quiet in style but tingling with excitement underneath" and Evans's performance as "marvelously expert." Atkinson further remarked that *Dial M for Murder* was the "sort of suave make-believe [that] an actor might be willing to pay a small fee to act in on the stage." Walter Kerr, in his *New York Herald Tribune* review of the production (30 October 1952), praised the play as "a holiday for whodunit fans" and summarized it as "one of those happy cat-and-mouse melodramas which establishes [such] a wonderfully innocent belief in its macabre and complicated goings-on [that] no matter how many hollow footsteps are heard to pound along the hallway, no matter how many garden windows are bashed in, the play's sleek surface of credulity never cracks."

In his memoir, *All This . . . and Evans Too!* (1987), Evans divulged that for the Broadway production of *Dial M for Murder,* he had requested certain changes in the script, to which Knott had readily agreed, that might insure that the play's characters and their motivations would be more credible and comprehensible to American audiences. For example,

> The letter "M" in the title is a reference to the villain's Maida Vale telephone number and would be quite meaningless in America. This was overcome by changing the name of the wife ["Sheila"], from what it had been in the London production, to "Margot." While we were about it, and because the writing emphasized the wife's helplessness, we thought she would gain more sympathy if she spoke with a foreign accent. . . . I was also bothered about the implausibility of the villain's former schoolchum agreeing to throttle the wife simply because of a threat that, if he refused to cooperate in the mayhem, a crime committed in their schooldays would be exposed. The outrageous felony occurred when the chum had sunk to the depths of stealing a trifling amount from the cash box of the school's football club—a revelation that would make him a social outcast for the rest of his life. That anyone could dream of such a dastardly act seemed to raise the hair of English audiences, but we couldn't envisage it disturbing any coiffures on Broadway; so a new form of blackmail, involving drug peddling, was suggested in the interest of believability.[2]

For Evans, one of the most gratifying pleasures of performing a stage thriller such as *Dial M for Murder* is the strong "bond it creates between the actor and the audience even when, as in the case of *Dial M*, the husband's guilt is known to the spectator right from the start. Whether or not [Tony Wendice] will get away with the crime causes everyone 'out front' to become a self-appointed detective."[3] In fact, at one performance of the play at the Plymouth Theatre, Evans recalls that

> This spirit of audience-involvement almost caused a riot. A man in the audience had obviously worked out in his mind exactly how the perfect murder plan was going to succeed and had boasted to his wife that he had it all down pat. However, just before the final curtain when [Detective Inspector Hubbard] reveals the true solution of the puzzle (making a pause for dramatic effect), the amateur sleuth, his infallible solution torn to shreds, was heard to say in a voice loud and clear: "Well, I'll be a son of a bitch!"[4]

The anticipation of such spontaneous audience reactions as this contributed immensely to the mischievous delight Evans took in carrying out his advance preparations for *Dial M for Murder*'s Broadway production. In his memoir he recalls a significant, but entirely unplanned, bit of stage business employed in the London production that he shrewdly reemployed in the Broadway production:

> It was a freak success that we succeeded in creating the right atmosphere of tension in the play's final scene, and this was thanks to the low scenery budget allotted the London production. The [Wendices' London] flat was a rehash of scenery from another production stored in the basement [of the Westminster Theatre]. With a new coat of paint it served its purpose, except that the main door to the outside passageway had a three-inch gap at its bottom panel. This became apparent only when the lighting rehearsal was in progress. With the living room in total darkness, the electricians were rigging the lights in the passageway, whereupon a stagehand's feet could clearly be seen through the slit of light under the ill-fitting door. In both the London and New York productions this fluke effect was way beyond anything the author had envisaged and had everyone in the audience holding their breath. Would the villain fall into the trap awaiting him in the darkened room? The street door was heard to slam. Footsteps were heard in the passageway and a pair of feet seen under the door. They hesitated, then retreated slowly towards the street door. A change of mind and the footsteps returned to the flat entrance. That time and with a change of keys, I [Tony Wendice] entered. The inspector switched on the lights, picked up the telephone, and said, 'Give me Scotland Yard.' *Curtain!*[5]

Visual moments such as these, Evans notes, can "create a tension that in its special fashion cannot be duplicated in the movies."[6] Furthermore, Evans contends, "Even such a master as Alfred Hitchcock in his film of *Dial M* entirely missed that tense moment. He followed the villain with his camera in the passageway, even had him leaving the house, then changing his mind, thus destroying the 'will he, won't he?' excitement of the stage business caused by that strip of light under the door."[7]

During the ensuing five years, *Dial M for Murder* was translated into more than twenty languages and successfully performed in more than twenty-five countries, including the U.S.S.R., where the play was titled *Telephone Call.* Soon after the play's Broadway premiere, Korda, who had never succeeded in getting Alfred Hitchcock to direct for his studio, sold the film rights, which he had purchased originally for £1,000, for £30,000 to Warner Brothers who, in 1953, filmed it in Naturalvision, their version of 3-D, with Hitchcock both producing and directing and Knott writing the screen adaptation under Hitchcock's close guidance. Hitchcock's light but deft treatment of Knott's classic five-character stage thriller starred Ray Milland as the villain-husband, Grace Kelly as his rich and victimized wife, Robert Cummings as her American boyfriend, and John Williams re-creating his stage role as Detective Inspector Hubbard.

Knott's second stage thriller, *Write Me a Murder,* premiered on Broadway at the Belasco Theatre under the direction of George Schaefer on 26 October 1961 and ran for 196 performances. The following year it opened in London at the Lyric Theatre on 28 March and enjoyed a considerable run. The play, which concerns a professional writer's attempt to concoct an "almost perfect" murder to save his family's English estate, "won Knott a special Edgar Allan Poe Award from the Mystery Writers of America in 1962, just as *Dial M for Murder* had in 1953."[8] Howard Taubman, in his *New York Times* review of the production (27 October 1961), praised both Knott's craftsmanship as a "fresh fillip in murder mystery practice" and the overall play, which "assembles people a cut more interesting than the usual puppets of the species, builds steadily, amusingly and suspensefully, and reaches a swift and convincing climax." Walter Kerr, in his *New York Herald Tribune* review of the production (27 October 1961), praised Knott's craftsmanship and also his fidelity to a genre that takes "delight in preposterous puzzles, so long as they can be discreetly conducted alongside glowing fireplaces in shadowed rooms, with an automobile's headlights piercing the half-dark now and then, and once—just once—the rustle of an unidentified figure upon the curving stairs." Overall, however, Kerr found the play to be "utter foolishness [but,] for afficionados whose tastes have been little catered to of late, splendid fun."

Knott's third and most recent stage thriller, *Wait until Dark*, premiered on Broadway at the Ethel Barrymore Theatre under the direction of Arthur Penn on 2 February 1966 and ran for 373 performances. Norman Nadel, in his *New York World-Telegram* review of the production (3 February 1966), summarized it as

> a tense thriller [that passed the test] only minutes before the final curtain fell. . . . At a sudden, violent movement on the darkened stage, every man and woman in the audience gasped audibly, exclaimed, screamed, shouted a warning, or at least gulped air. . . . Bull fighting has its moment of truth, and suspense drama its moment of forgiveness, because if you are sufficiently scared, you are willing to shrug off any tedium you might have endured while the play was building toward that climax.

Stanley Kauffmann, however, in his *New York Times* review of the production (3 February 1996), was much less forgiving: "There are some pretty good scares in the final scene. . . . But Frederick Knott, the author, makes us pay for the chills in that scene with a slow start, unnecessarily complicated action and some weak motivation. As his title promises, we do a good deal of waiting for the dark."

In spite of the mixed critical press that *Wait until Dark* received, it became very popular with audiences, running for 373 performances on Broadway and for two years in London and also earning for Lee Remick, its Broadway star, a Tony Award nomination for Best Actress. The film version, its rights purchased by Warner Brothers for a record sum prior to the Broadway premiere, was also extremely successful, opening in November 1967. Produced by Mel Ferrer and directed by Terence Young, the film starred Audrey Hepburn, who received an Academy Award nomination for Best Actress for her portrayal of the blind Susy Hendrix, who is menaced by a sinister trio of small-time criminals (Alan Arkin, Richard Crenna, and Jack Weston) trying to recover, by deceit or by force, a heroin-stuffed doll that they suppose is concealed in her Greenwich Village apartment.

All three of Knott's stage thrillers are "inverted" murder mysteries, the audience knowing at the outset the villain's identity and motive, but in some doubt as to whether or not he will be clever enough to carry off his perfectly planned crime. Also, the action of all three is confined, almost claustrophobically, to one room, whether the living room of the Wendices' London flat in *Dial M for Murder*, the library and study of five-hundred-year-old Rodingham Manor (situated about two hours from London) in *Write Me a Mur-*

der, or the living room of the Hendrixes' Greenwich Village basement apartment in *Wait until Dark*. Knott's confinement of stage action to one setting not only is sound theatrical economics but also elevates the physical chase to a mental exercise as the audience follows the diligent efforts of each villain to carry off a perfect murder or to deceive a blind adversary. The limitation of the action to one setting has at least one other function as well: it serves to demarcate the private space or world of the defenseless young women, who are literally and figuratively confined to their domestic situations. This private space, representing intimate security, is then savagely violated by the intrusion of hostile agents whom each must outwit without the help of any personal defender. In *Dial M for Murder*, the hostile agent is Margot Wendice's own husband, Tony, whom she loves and trusts despite her brief affair with Max Halliday. In *Wait until Dark*, Susy Hendrix's husband, Sam, is conveniently lured away on a bogus photography assignment, leaving his wife defenseless against the tactics of a ruthless gang of petty thugs determined to get their hands on the heroin-stuffed doll that Susy does not know she has. Such intrusion and violation of these women's psychological privacy successfully arouse a primal terror in the audiences of both plays.

Knott's use of this violation motif is more apparent in *Dial M for Murder* than in his two later works. *Write Me a Murder* relies heavily on actual mechanical time-delay devices and gimmicks that, although clever, reduce the characters to stereotypical pawns who are in themselves nothing but facilitators of the ingeniously contrived murder. *Wait until Dark*, on the other hand, minimizes clever plotting and maximizes a *grand guignol* situation by having Suzy, defenseless and blind, extricate herself by her own cunning and survival instinct.

Dial M for Murder best exemplifies Knott's unique brand of stage entertainment, both in its ingenious plot and its proven grip on audiences. Tony Wendice, a retired English tennis pro, has quite blatantly married his wife for her money and now plans to murder her for the same reason. When it becomes apparent that the attractive Margot is in love with Max Halliday, an American television mystery writer, Tony fears that she will divorce him, depriving him of his luxurious lifestyle. To prevent this, he carefully begins to plan her murder, blackmailing a former Cambridge acquaintance, Captain Lesgate, into strangling her while he himself establishes a perfect alibi. According to plan, Lesgate enters the Wendices' flat unseen while Tony and Max are attending a stag party nearby. The scheme goes awry, however, when Margot defends herself so ably that she kills Lesgate. Quick to seize an opportunity, Tony plants evidence to suggest that Margot has killed Lesgate, not merely in self-defense, but because he has been blackmailing her about her affair with Max. She is tried and convicted, but Detective Inspector Hubbard of Scotland Yard, who is in charge of the case, continues his investigations and proves Tony's guilt, barely in time to save Margot's life.

Central to *Dial M for Murder* is the vulnerable female terrorized by a hostile adversary. Like Emlyn Williams's *Night Must Fall* (1935), Edward Chodorov's *Kind Lady* (1935), Patrick Hamilton's *Angel Street* (1938), and Lucille Fletcher's *Sorry, Wrong Number* (1948), *Dial M for Murder* is a classic "woman alone" thriller in which no one but the threatened woman herself is able to rescue her from her desperate plight. This victimization motif seems to indicate a general fear implied in all Knott's scripts: a belief that ultimately we cannot trust anyone, not even close friends and marital partners with whom we think we have established inviolate bonds of intimate trust and openness. The plights of characters such as Tony and Margot Wendice dramatize repeatedly the existential truth of individual isolation and forlornness and the need for constant vigilance against menace from unexpected directions. No one is to be trusted. The power of this communicated fear may explain why audiences seem to put aside normal skepticism and overlook minor discrepancies in plot craftsmanship. This might explain why the audience in *Wait until Dark* does not expect Susy Hendrix to contact the police or leave her apartment to seek help, or why it may also accept as credible that Sam Hendrix chooses to wait patiently for more than two hours for a nonexistent celebrity to show up for a photo-shoot, or why Tony Wendice and his wife, worth a crucially significant fortune, live in a small, nondescript two-room-and-kitchenette flat without even a part-time maid. The moral values, too, in *Dial M for Murder* are so confused that an audience is expected to regard the unfaithful Margot Wendice and her illicit lover as sympathetic and even heroic, while Tony, the offended husband, is cast as a scoundrel before there is any evidence of his villainous treachery. It is also illogical that Margot, while awaiting hanging for murder, freely moves between jail and her living room whenever Detective Inspector Hubbard thinks he may have uncovered some new evidence. Such discrepancies never seem to shift the audience's attention from riveting concern for a terrorized female victim whose plight represents the worst of personal fears, that is, isolation and defenselessness.

Although Frederick Knott's stage thrillers neither elevate an audience nor purport to be other than contrived make-believe, there is no question about their gripping power. It is as if author, actors, and audience sit on both sides of the footlights, cordially suspending disbelief as they engage vicariously in homicide. The murder may be gruesome, the villain horrifying, but the audience enjoys the crime. Is that because it knows that this is a stage game, only its costumed characters mystified, or that all its action is vicariously only in the mind, or because the playwright stands aside with relish while his clever contrivances defy each other? Or is it because the phenomena of blackmail, deception, the punctilio of a detective, and the stamina of the stalked collectively cue in to primal impulses and criminal proclivities, perhaps latent in us all?

Notes

1. "Knott, Frederick M. P." *Encyclopedia of Mystery and Detection*, eds. Chris Steinbrunner and Otto Penzler (New York: McGraw-Hill, 1976), 236.
2. Maurice Evans, *All This . . . and Evans Too: A Memoir* (Columbia: University of South Carolina Press, 1987), 215.
3. Ibid., 216.
4. Ibid., 216–17.
5. Ibid., 217.
6. Ibid.
7. Ibid.
8. *Encyclopedia of Mystery and Detection*, 236.

On Military History

Memoirs, Fiction, and Paradox: A Reflective Essay on the Memory of War

ROBERT C. DOYLE

WAR has an insatiable appetite for minutiae, and the proverb, "The devil lies in the details," is nowhere more applicable. There is no lack of recorded statistics for modern wars, but as Stanley Weintraub's *Last Great Victory* (1995) and *Long Day's Journey into War* (1991) show very clearly, war's human, and often mysterious, details lie well hidden from prominent view.[1] Because these details form individual perceptive truths in the human memory, there is no lack of paradox and controversy.

As I sifted through Civil War records held at the Andersonville Historic Site in Georgia, the horrid Confederate prison camp that set the standard for inhumanity in America during the summer of 1864, I realized why former Union POWs wanted compensation from the federal government for their injuries. The federal government asked each man to write his narrative in order to receive a few dollars a month, not much really. Many supplied photographs of themselves as visual evidence of their incarceration because they feared that their readers would refuse to believe them. I imagined the sound of their voices as I read their applications for compensation. Knowing that each handwritten document represented the experience of real sufferings in their own time, my impartial historical sense weakened and gave way to feelings of compassion, shock, and horror. I forgot about time; I was in Andersonville.

Not far from Andersonville, dedicated now to the remembrance of all American prisoners of war in our history, I managed to jump eighty years, from 1864 to 1944, when I sat a day and interviewed Carl Nash, a ground soldier who was captured in the Philippines in 1942. Nash marched with thousands of others on Bataan, spent three years as a prisoner of the Japanese army, and lived to tell his story. As Carl and I talked, my mind wandered to a bus ride I took in the Philippines in 1968, one that took me unwittingly along the path of the Bataan Death March. It was April then. I remembered the road signs that resembled the Stations of the Cross, and the Island of Luzon was not beyond my imagination. When Carl spoke of tortures, my mind wandered again, this time to my experience with Giles Norrington, different war, longer captivity. Giles spent five years in a North Vietnamese prison and learned to endure torture much as Carl had. In each of these experiences, one with written documents and two with living informants, I discovered that chronological time began to melt into a kind of timeless universal experience of suffering behind barbed wire. Arthur M. Schlesinger Jr. was correct: "History is to the nation as memory is to the individual."[2]

For POWs at least, the act of writing about or narrating the experience of war not only served as a form of personal history but also as a catharsis for their personal feelings, an ethical forum to tell the world what happened to them and why, and, in the end, functioned as a kind of psychological closure to an experience that often generated more questions than answers. The problems I wish to address concern the nature of paradox in American wartime memoirs: why former soldiers wrote them; why some memoirs often ultimately failed to come to terms with the experiences that they attempted to reconcile; why some memoirs' interpretations were essentially unsatisfying to both writer and reader; and why subsequent generations either took issue with the memoirs or failed to apply them to later generations.

John Stoessinger noted in *Why Nations Go to War* (1990) that in both victory and defeat, war introduces its own illogical truth and brings catastrophic reality to the leaders through the terror experienced by a country's soldiery and civilian population.[3] No one author can possibly tell the whole story about any aspect of war, and few authors agree about its meaning. From Moses to Caesar, and from St. Augustine to Clausewitz, at its very core, the understanding of war has evolved into vast networks of competing, often paradoxical, interpretations that fall considerably short of clarity. Millions of pages seek answers to why and how the American nation so often put its young in harm's way, yet when they were called, millions of Americans put on uniforms of various colors, carried flintlock muskets or M-16 assault rifles, and came home when it was over. Most were touring part-timers; some were professionals. Some came home whole; many were disfigured or maimed for life. Well over two million lost their lives. Every night we hear about another war on the evening news; every day we read about war in the newspaper. Despite the efforts of reasonable people who know the costs of war and who make every effort to stop it, the act of public war persists around the world, always a crisis with overwhelming human suffering.

My little wars began when I grew up in Southwest Philadelphia; the big one took place in South Vietnam, first in 1968, then again from March 1970 to March 1971. I saw my father, a seasoned veteran of the bloody Pacific campaigns between 1942 and 1945, cry for the first time when I left the Philadelphia airport bound for Travis Air Force Base in California, our departure point for flights to South Vietnam. He had mistakenly thought that his war was the last war, and he knew the tragic dangers of harm's way very well. During my war, I was an intelligence officer who spooked the bad guys so that we, the good guys, could win and go home. Although 2.7 million of us did our duty in Vietnam, we didn't "win" our war in the classic sense because we were part of the Cold War that was far more complex than a one-year tour in a combat zone. Most of us survived and came home quietly with no parades, bands, or ritualistic expressions of national gratitude, just a passionate desire to get on with our lives. We earned our degrees with GI Bill money, married, had children, and became about as middle class as people could become.

When I came home, I was a different person, determined to study war no more. I thought that my war went away, that it disappeared into my personal past much as bad dreams did. I was wrong. John Keegan commented in *A History of Warfare* (1993) that "Soldiers are not as other men."[4] He was right. The experience of war threw me and many other Vietnam veterans into what Keegan called "the spell of an entirely different world," one that had enormously powerful invisible arms that reached out and clutched many of us long after we took off our uniforms. We found one another in odd places at odd times, and it mattered little about gender, race, or class. What mattered was that we formed a community, perhaps a unique kind of tribe that shared a relatively common history, even if that history consisted of the memory of one year in Vietnam. We discovered back in "the world" that we had endless numbers of stories to tell. Some were hilariously funny; others were too painful for audiences who had never shared a similar experience. Some were believable; others were too far-fetched or outrageous to accept at face value. Some salved the conscience; others exacerbated guilt. In the end, regardless of what audiences decided to accept or reject, telling what happened, or in some cases inventing what could have happened, returned soldiers as writers and tellers of tales to their entirely different world, not the real battlefield, but a new and lonely one of words.

Few wars have left the committed participants of one generation in agreement with the involved historians of another. Historian Barton R. Friedman commented that what we construe as history depends on the interactions that take place, first, between the historian and the evidence and, second, between the narrative built from the evidence and the readers.[5] Culture historians concerned with war search for the processes that influenced the decision-making of individuals and institutions that led to continuity and change, and it becomes imperative that one generation of scholars dismantle propaganda and probe deeply into the events of war to tell the next generation what it was about, comment on the mistakes that were made, and redefine both the heroes and the villains. In *Wartime: Understanding and Behavior in the Second World War* (1989), for example, Paul Fussell enlivened his memory and took a critical look at how his fellow soldiers behaved during World War II. Using personal narratives, poetry, advertising, and popular propaganda, Fussell examined SNAFU (Situation Normal, All Fucked Up) culture in the military, which, in his view, thrived in an organization of nameless amateurs on the lowest levels and pseudo-event creators on the highest. Enemies were as bad as or worse than the Allies, and he argued that World War II was a horror because its makers were horrors; that is, they were self-aggrandizing psychopaths who did it only for the sake of their own careers at the expense of the soldiers who fought it. Fussell, of course, never served with British POWs on the Kwai Railway, with Carl Nash on the Bataan March in the Philippines, or with Giles Norrington in Hanoi, and he fails to show any reasons that could have generated a willingness to endure pain, sacrifice, and loss.

Often veiled behind the wartime memoir lies another paradox: the unsettling fact that war itself became a narcotic for many soldiers. It took them away from the dull and sometimes boring lives they led in peacetime, and it gave existence real meaning. Graham H. Greenwell, a British World War I veteran, shocked the critics in 1935 when he published the war letters he wrote to his mother. He commented that,

> For my own part I have to confess that I look back on the years 1914–18 as among the happiest I have ever spent. That they contained moments of boredom and depression, of sorrow for the loss of friends and of alarm for my personal safety is indeed true enough. But to be perfectly fit, to live among pleasant companions, to have responsibility and a clearly defined job—these are great compensations when one is very young.[6]

In combat, every nerve woke up, and the adrenalin flowed. In Vietnam, I saw "War is hell, but actual combat is a real bitch" painted on a bulkhead of a United States Coast Guard river patrol boat. Before my first combat experience, I found those words unsettling and scary. By the end of that day, I knew what they meant. We waited in silence for an attacking enemy. It was a bad day, and I remember that seconds felt like hours. Ambrose Bierce, a front-line Union officer from 1862 until 1865, would not have found those feelings unusual. In 1891, he wrote, "An army in line-of-battle awaiting attack, or prepared to deliver it, presents . . . precision, formality, fixity, and silence."[7] He surely described the handful of American sailors clutching their weapons on a river patrol boat that April day in 1970.

Bierce's fiction shows readers that reflections of war are full of irony and tragedy; Kurt Vonnegut Jr. takes us a step further. Vonnegut had his bad days, too, as one of the 23,554 American soldiers captured between 16 and 25 December 1944, by German forces during the Battle of the Bulge in the Ardennes. On 13 February 1945, when Vonnegut was a POW in Dresden, British and American aircraft fire bombed the city and killed about 135,000 people, mostly civilian refugees escaping from the onslaught of the Red Army. Subsequent generations of the world's citizens still ponder the event and ask, Why Dresden? Vonnegut was spared and liberated by the Russians, and his novel, *Slaughterhouse-Five* (1966), became an imaginative reflection on his own POW experience. According to Vonnegut, the central character, Billy Pilgrim, was based on Army PFC Joe Crone, a "stockpiled college kid" who died in captivity of malaise.[8] Paradoxically, Vonnegut acknowledged plainly that in his case, war and its horrors formed the watershed event of his life. More importantly war became the seed bed for works of many World War II-era military veterans on all sides, such as James Clavell, Norman Mailer, Irvin Shaw, Pierre Boulle, David Westheimer, Heinrich Böll, Alfred Andersch, and others who turned into world-class writers.[9]

Joseph Heller's novel *Catch 22* (1955) captured the spirit of the grand paradox correctly: one is sane only if one is crazy, and crazy only if one is sane. In Vietnam, the grand paradox became more real when I saw a navy gunner's mate wearing a Pennsylvania hunting license on the back of his flak jacket. On another occasion, I asked a Navy Corpsman (medic) who served with a SEAL Team why he decided to become a SEAL (acronym for Sea, Air, Land: the navy's Special Warfare Unit) when he might have served in an air-conditioned naval hospital. He replied, "I hate sick people." There is also a part of war that no one talks about because words are difficult to find for unresolved emotions of sacrificial love or unbridled hate. Both live side by side in the world of war because near the prospective battlefields, the notion of a war in principle gives way to the individual's war in a landscape where red badges of courage become Purple Hearts in short order. Perhaps human suffering, from time to time, needs to be separated from the politics of war.

It is no wonder that the experience of war acted as a watershed for writers like Vonnegut, and it should be expected that many memoirs carry strong doses of polemic intent, sometimes far beyond the simple goal of telling what happened to individual soldiers. Diaries and simple chronicles do that. Narrative truth in the wartime memoir serves a different purpose: not only did memoirists reveal what happened to them, they reminded the public in graphic terms what could happen. Thus many memoirs function as stories that bear witness to the horrors of war, and a strong point of view is evident from the first page to the last. Some are factually accurate, some are only partially accurate, and some are filled with personally interpreted fantasies. If there has to be some assumption that sets the tone, it is that wartime memoirs are perceptually true and as accurate as one person's memory can be over a long period of time. Some memoirs were created from diaries; others synthesized the author's personal experience with historical facts and recollections from others. This is not to argue that every word in thousands of American war memoirs, especially the dialogues, was recorded with videotape accuracy; rather, this corpus of material contains images so vivid that they can never pass from the human memory. Evelyn Cobley was correct when she stated, "the memoir acts as a commemoration . . . a memorial, monument, or memento to the dead and as a warning or reminder for the living."[10]

The heart of the issue about memoirs remains the question of believability: Are they honest personal histories of time past, or are they simply statements full of overblown antipathies, propaganda, and vindictive diatribes? Acting as documents, not documentaries, and with enough witnesses telling similar stories about similar events, the weight of the narrative evidence, especially from World War II, becomes overwhelming and in effect believable within limits. If memoirs of wartime events are written with this kind of conviction, the kind that can be generated only by experience, then Gene Wise's comment that "experience is a more existentially grounded term than reality" has found a wholly new application.[11] With the kind of accuracy that can be compared with the revelations of other participants in the same or similar circumstances, some may be mistaken from time to time, or caught up in popular myth systems, but it is very difficult to call them liars.

Veterans from the time of the Revolution have shown a consistent and seemingly insatiable appetite for laudatory memoirs about their own wars and often soak themselves in them long after their personal encounters in or near combat. As a result, many people spend a short time in a war and the rest of their lives reading or writing about it. Many literary and media productions that depict the experience of war rest on the fuzzy connection between history and fiction. Although the characters in any one particular work may be fictitious, landscapes, personal dilemmas, and characterizations of quirky human behavior most often stem from composites of very real people. Place names are often ones that popular audiences would either recognize or be familiar with, and ethical questions were those that real soldiers had to address. In the world of popular culture, history has, in effect, intermingled with the trifocal lenses of fiction, drama, and feature films, with the result that popular culture has produced an interpretive montage of competing, if not confusing, images. A good example of this problem is James Clavell's novel, *King Rat* (1962), which Brian Forbes turned into a classic film noir in 1965.

Clavell, a British serving officer and POW during World War II, examined life in Changi Prison, Singapore, through the action and philosophy of an American corporal, Sam King, known in camp as "the King." With the Japanese army remaining in the distant background, the action centered on the traditional clash between officers and enlisted ranks common in all armies and a triangulated culture clash between the British, Australians, and Americans thrown together in Changi. King symbolized the traditional American myth of individual entrepreneurial success: he is restless and determined not only to survive but also to live as well as possible through his wits and the exploitation of others. Although they suffered from a severe sense of class even in a prison camp, the British officers symbolized the soldierly values of duty, loyalty, honor, and rank. The Australian sergeant represented the stereotypical Aussie revulsion toward military rank, authority, and order except, of course, in his service to his "mates." Competing with an Australian sergeant for business, King acted as a classic middleman, buying and selling contraband goods to the guards and prisoners alike for profit and personal comfort. Clavell ignored the captors, who acted only as customers. Nearly everyone in camp became one of King's customers or found himself on the payroll except Grey, a socialist British captain and camp provost who played cat-and-mouse with King until he discovered that the entire camp, from the senior British ranking officer to the lowest private, participated in the "business." Well past the trading, the real business in Changi was survival.

What James Clavell showed in his novel and Brian Forbes in the film was that this prison community was perhaps united against its captors, the Japanese, but was badly divided against itself. Only Corporal King, taking the role of Clavell's Mephisto, stood in the middle as the mediator of nearly everyone's survival. In the midst of starvation and want, King surrounded himself with relative splendor. With his uniforms starched, he dined on eggs while other prisoners suffered from near starvation. After a chance meeting, King showed the aristocratic Malay-speaking British Flight Lieutenant Marlowe, whom King needed in the organization as an interpreter, that anything could be bought or sold for money or food, including power, even inside a major Japanese military prison. Along with Australian prisoner-entrepreneurs, King created an ingenious plan to raise rats and sell the meat to officers only. King enjoyed tricking the officers as an aside, but he wanted the cash. The Australians reveled in demeaning the officers and cared little, if anything at all, about the cash. The enlisted POWs enjoyed a good laugh over King's rat-meat scheme. King bribed guards and other prisoners with food, medicine, or access to decision-making officers. The ultimate indignity came when King bought temporary loyalty, personal service, power, and influence from others in camp, and his downfall only during liberation and repatriation, when camp relationships faded back into soldierly, rank-oriented precapture hierarchies. One of the armed British officers liberating the camp looked at King and wanted to know why he looked so good while the others looked so bad. King made no reply. After liberation, as they boarded trucks for their return to Allied military control, a quiet captive community nearly forgot about King's natural sense of organization, leadership, and determination to survive. Except for Flight Lieutenant Marlowe, whose life King had saved, the prison community members bathed themselves in shock and resentment rather than euphoria. In the end, only King walked away unaffected by life in Changi.

James Clavell wrote, "The happenings in the novel happened. At least as I remember them. . . . Not all . . . occurred in Changi, some in Java and elsewhere, most I saw, the rest came from eye witnesses, the living and the dead."[12] Clavell formed Sam King as a composite character consisting of elements from three Americans: Eddie MacArthur, a merchant seaman captured by a German raider in the South Atlantic and deposited in Singapore; Bob Martin, a crewman from the sunken cruiser, the USS *Houston;* and Albert L. "Buttercup" Carpenter of Battery F of the New Mexico National Guard.[13] Remembering that Carpenter was the deal-maker and a dominant force in Changi, Air Vice Marshal Sir Thomas Howell, RAF (Ret.), a former Changi inmate with Clavell, recalled, "He was by no means so sinister or selfish" as Clavell's character in the novel, but "he became a 'skillful operator' and, as a result of using profits for the benefit of other prisoners, he was an instrument in saving many lives at risk."[14] According to other prisoners, what the screen depicted as an indictment of uncontrolled American entrepreneurism was more accurately a representation of unique trading skills that led to both physical and emotional survival for many Allied POWs in the camp. James Clavell's memory, although it translated actual experience into a major piece of postwar fiction, was only one of many, and several fellow prisoners were far from satisfied with his vision.

Why do subsequent generations either take issue with the memoirs or fail to apply them to later generations? Looking at the transition of Indian captivity narratives to popular entertainment gives a clue. Remaining traditionally conservative, the captivity narrative described a chaotic hell on earth where normalcy was catastrophic and catastrophe was normal. Narrative style, especially in the Indian captivity narratives written in the seventeenth and eighteenth centuries, was usually simple and direct, full of anecdotal evidence of brutality, torture, stress, and moral outrage against the captors. Some were designed to generate a political change. Others reinforced the power of faith or called for a return to religious values and, in some cases, acted as propaganda by demanding a military response to a national crisis. Few, if any, were simple chronicles of suffering. They had distinct and readily identifiable purposes. When authors turned to fiction, however, intent began to change. Authors had to shift from education to entertainment. To do so they abandoned a strict adherence to the traditional narrative structure based on the chronology of events as they happened and focused on the dramatic lucidity of simplified synchronic interpersonal conflict. Throughout the nineteenth-century dime novels or "penny dreadfuls" and then the action thrillers created by POWs themselves in the twentieth century, an American artistic tradition was established that appealed to popular audiences hungry for escapist entertainment full of violence, terror, political and racial stereotypes, propaganda, and romance. Kathryn Zabelle Derounian-Stodola and James Arthur Levernier argue that this form of pulp fiction victimized Indians far more than their captives. That they were real or imaginary became irrelevant. The innumerable and substantially false images of torture, starvation, and murder created vicious but widely popular anti–Indian propaganda and intentionally not only served the expansionist politics of Manifest Destiny, but also helped create receptive cultural conditions for nineteenth-century wars of removal and genocide.[15]

Alfred Owen Aldridge noted that Benjamin Franklin used Jonathan Swift's popular *Gulliver's Travels* (1726) as a format to create a fictional satire, "Extract from the Account of the Captivity of William Henry in 1755 and of His Residence among the Seneka Indians six Years and seven Months til he made his Escape from them," published by the *London Chronicle* on 23–25 June and again on 26–28 June 1768. Aldridge noted that many Londoners accepted Franklin's work as a true narrative; however, it was a purely fictional work designed to satirize what Franklin believed was the cheating and greedy trade practices of colonial businessmen with the Indians in Pennsylvania.[16] Frightful images of Indian captivity also played a vital role in James Fenimore Cooper's *Last of the Mohicans* (1826), and captivity narrative finally degenerated into thoroughly popular, stereotype-oriented thriller fiction, the "penny dreadful" that achieved best-seller status in the nineteenth century with more than 3,000 titles from the 1860s to the 1890s, the bulk of which was published by Beadle and Adams of New York. In other words, the already strong polemic content of American captivity narratives expanded into realms of sensationalism and horror. Lack of truth never hampered the marketing of good stories.

With such processes afoot and with the heavy demand for captivity stories by a growing readership hungry for action and romance, the narrative style, once a mark of reportage based on unusual yet perceptively truthful personal experience, inevitably evolved into outright fictional thrillers, embellished to suit the tastes, stereotypes, and expectations of an active reading popular audience. The vast amount of this pulp, written and published in the last quarter of the nineteenth century, continued to focus on Indian captivities of the old Eastern forest frontier. In time, the genre went beyond the dark forests of New York, Pennsylvania, Virginia, and New England to the expanse of the great plains, Texas, and beyond. The representation of war, much like Indian captivities, went beyond experience and found a home as an important part of popular entertainment, and as some media scholars have commented, Hollywood reformulated and refought nearly every American war. In the movies, actors playing soldiers in blue, gray, brown, and green were often stand-up tough guys who embodied those values that we understand as representing the best, sometimes the worst, of ourselves. Beyond the movies, few of us were ever clearly heroes or villains, but there were some. War crimes trials attempted to bring many villains to justice. On the other hand, Congress has awarded 3,396 Americans the Medal of Honor. No one knows how many more should have been given for acts above and beyond the call of duty.

Despite the numbing effects of fear, some people really loved war; others hated it. Some soldiers went willingly into uniform; others refused altogether or went because they were forced into the military services by national conscription. Regardless of how they got there, the experience of war bound many men and women together into unique, nearly homogeneous unified communities driven by powerful ideas about how and why things ought or ought not to be. Memoirists do indeed study war, but they focus entirely on their war, which implies that they usually reflect their own value systems sharpened by the sting of experience. Modern historical empiricism requires accuracy of dates, places, battle tactics, and statistics that attempt to show causality through correlation. Memoirists and novelists are more interested in recording personal human suffering and individual survival with distinct, sometimes outmoded, points of view. If there is a common denominator to be found in wartime memoirs, it reveals itself in the form of moral judgment that tests one's ability to withstand the catastrophic nature of the unexpected by bearing witness to how and why one survived when others died.[17] In 1995, as the fiftieth anniversary of VE and VJ days showed around the world, historians and memoirists, from book-length authors to writers of simple letters to the editor, again made it ever clearer that human sacrifice and suffering, good and evil, and even questionable politics, need to be remembered. Stanley Weintraub's *Last Great Victory* (1995) showed the world yet again that concepts like justice and morality remain embedded in the hearts of humanity, imperfectly perhaps, even in a world beset by horror and terror.

I confess that upon hearing a helicopter, I always look up, and to this day I hate the sounds of fireworks and jackhammers. My mother once saw me look up at a helicopter flying by our home. I suppose I had a look that only a parent understands. "You think about the war [Vietnam] a lot, don't you?" she asked. "Every day," I replied. She knew that my father thought about his war, too. I also confess that I have not written a complete memoir of my own experiences, I suppose, not only because I hardly believe that anyone would be interested, but also for me, some experiences that disturb my memory still remain too painful to recount in print. That one should not speak ill of the dead remains an unbreakable rule. However, each time I open new files from new informants, my curiosity peaks, and I discover yet again that the human memory opens doors to an entirely different world, one where the human condition in conflict unfolds a drama with unique complexities and nearly endless paradoxes.

NOTES

1. See Stanley Weintraub's numerous books on war, including *The Last Great Victory: The End of World War II, July-August 1945* (New York: Dutton, 1995);

"The Christmas Truce," *MHQ: The Quarterly Journal of Military History* 5, no. 2 (1992): 76–85; *Long Day's Journey into War: December 7, 1941* (New York: Dutton, 1991); *A Stillness Heard Around the World: The End of the Great War, November 1918* (New York: E. P. Dutton, 1985); and *War in the Wards: Korea's Unknown Battle in a Prisoner-of-War Hospital Camp* (New York: Doubleday, 1964; 2d ed., San Rafael, Calif.: Presidio, 1976). All these books and articles on war separate propaganda from reality and show how difficult it is to make sense of human behavior in war.

2. Arthur M. Schlesinger, Jr., *The Disuniting of America: Reflections on a Multicultural Society* (New York: Norton, 1992), 45.

3. John G. Stoessinger, *Why Nations Go to War*, 5th ed. (New York: St. Martin's, 1990), 207–14.

4. John Keegan, *A History of Warfare* (New York: Random House, 1993), xvi.

5. Barton R. Friedman, *Fabricating History: English Writers on the French Revolution* (Princeton, N.J.: Princeton University Press, 1988), 9.

6. Graham H. Greenwell, *An Infant in Arms. War Letters of a Company Officer* (London, 1972), xxi. Quoted in Franz Karl Stanzel, "War and Literature," in *Intimate Enemies: English and German Literary Reactions to the Great War 1914–1918*, eds. Franz Karl Stanzel and Martin Löschnigg (Heidelberg: Universitätsverlag C. winter, 1993).

7. Ambrose Bierce, "'One Officer, One Man,' *In the Midst of Life: Tales of Soldiers and Civilians*," in *The Collected Writings of Ambrose Bierce* (New York: Citadel Press, 1946), 108.

8. Kurt Vonnegut Jr., *Fates Worse than Death: An Autobiographical Collage of the 1980s* (New York: G. P. Putnam's Sons, 1991), 106–7. See also Peter G. Jones, *War and the Novelist: Appraising the American War Novel* (Columbia: University of Missouri Press, 1976), 1. Jones discusses the significance of the American war novel as genre but deliberately excludes any discussion of the POW and Cold War novel in his study.

9. For war and survivor guilt, see Leon F. Seltzer, "Dresden and Vonnegut's Testament of Guilt," *Journal of American Culture* 4, no. 4 (winter 1981): 55–69.

10. Evelyn Cobley, "History and Ideology in Autobiographical Literature of the First World War," *Mosaic* 23, no. 3 (summer 1990): 35.

11. Gene Wise, *American Historical Explanations*, 2d ed. (Minneapolis: University of Minnesota Press, 1980), 51.

12. Personal letter from James Clavell, 22 February 1993. See also Clavell's opening remarks in *King Rat* (New York: Dell, 1962). See Gavin Daws, *Prisoners of the Japanese: POWs of World War II in the Pacific* (New York: William Morrow, 1994). Daws points out that Japanese POW camps were not homogenizing institutions but tribal societies of Americans, British, Australians, Dutch—and Japanese. Inmates did what they had to do to survive and afterward tried to live with their guilt.

13. Robert S. LaForte and Ronald E. Marcello, eds., *The Ordeal of American POWs in Burma, 1942–1945: Building the Death Railway* (Wilmington, Del.: Scholarly Research Press, 1993), 229.

14. Personal letter from Air Vice Marshal Sir Thomas Howell, RAF (Retired), 2 December 1992.

15. Kathryn Zabelle Derounian-Stodola and James Arthur Levernier, *The Indian Captivity Narrative 1550–1900* (New York: Twayne, 1993). See also Frances Roe Kestler, *The Indian Captivity: A Woman's View* (New York: Garland, 1990); Annette Kolodny, "Among the Indians: The Uses of Captivity," *New York Times*

Book Review 7 (31 January 1993), 25–26, 28–29; and Kolodny's "Review Essay," *Early American Literature* 14 (1979): 229–36.

16. Alfred Owen Aldridge, "Franklin's Deistical Indians," *Proceedings of the American Philosophical Society* 94, no. 4 (August 1950): 402–10.

17. Terrence Des Pres, *The Survivor: An Anatomy of Life in the Death Camps* (New York: Oxford University Press, 1976), 25. See also Robert C. Doyle, *Voices from Captivity: Interpreting the American POW Narrative* (Lawrence: University of Kansas Press, 1994), 259.

Stanley Weintraub: A Select Bibliography
COMPILED BY FRED D. CRAWFORD

BOOKS

An Unfinished Novel by Bernard Shaw (edited). New York: Dodd, Mead, 1958; London: Constable, 1958.

Private Shaw and Public Shaw: A Dual Portrait of Lawrence of Arabia and G.B.S. New York: George Braziller, 1963; London: Jonathan Cape, 1963.

C. P. Snow: A Spectrum: Science, Criticism, Fiction (edited). New York: Scribner's, 1963.

The War in the Wards: Korea's Unknown Battle in a Prisoner-of-War Hospital Camp. Garden City, N.Y.: Doubleday, 1964; revised as *War in the Wards: Korea's Unknown Battle in a Prisoner-of-War Hospital Camp* (San Rafael, Calif.: Presidio Press, 1976).

The Yellow Book: Quintessence of the Nineties (edited). Garden City, N.Y.: Doubleday/Anchor, 1964.

The Art of William Golding. New York: Harcourt, Brace & World, 1965; Bloomington: Indiana University Press, 1968. With Bernard S. Oldsey.

Reggie: A Portrait of Reginald Turner. New York: George Braziller, 1965; London: W. H. Allen, 1965.

The Savoy: Nineties Experiment (edited). University Park and London: Penn State University Press, 1966.

The Court Theatre 1904–1907: A Commentary and Criticism (edited). Coral Gables, Fla.: University of Miami Press, 1966; as *Desmond MacCarthy's The Court Theatre 1904–1907: A Commentary and Criticism* (London: University of Miami Press, 1966).

Beardsley: A Biography. New York: George Braziller, 1967; London: W. H. Allen, 1967; *Aubrey Beardsley: Eine Biographie,* translated by Christian Spiel (München: Winkler, 1968); *Biahzuri,* translated by Susumu Takagi (Tokyo: Bijutsu Shuppan-Sha, 1969); *Il prezioso perverso: Beardsley alle radici del Liberty,* translated by Anna Piva (Bari: De Donato, 1970); revised edition (Harmondsworth, Middlesex, England: Penguin, 1972).

"Bernard Shaw, Novelist." Ann Arbor, Mich.: University Microfilms, 1968. Ph.D. Dissertation, Penn State, 1956.

The Last Great Cause: The Intellectuals and the Spanish Civil War. New York: Weybright & Talley, 1968; London: W. H. Allen, 1968.

Biography and Truth (edited). Indianapolis and New York: Bobbs-Merrill, 1967.

Evolution of a Revolt: Early Postwar Writings of T. E. Lawrence (edited). University Park and London: Penn State University Press, 1968. With Rodelle Weintraub.

Cashel Byron's Profession by George Bernard Shaw (edited). Carbondale: Southern Illinois University Press, 1968; London and Amsterdam: Feffer & Simons, 1968.
Literary Criticism of Oscar Wilde (edited). Lincoln: University of Nebraska Press, 1968.
Shaw: An Autobiography 1856–1898 (edited). New York: Weybright & Talley, 1969; London: Max Reinhardt, 1970.
Shaw: An Autobiography 1898–1950: The Playwright Years (edited). New York: Weybright & Talley, 1970; London: Max Reinhardt, 1971.
Robert Hichens, *The Green Carnation* (edited). Lincoln: University of Nebraska Press, 1970.
Bernard Shaw, *Saint Joan* (edited). Indianapolis and New York: Bobbs-Merrill, 1971.
Journey to Heartbreak: The Crucible Years of Bernard Shaw, 1914–1918. New York: Weybright & Talley/McKay, 1971; revised slightly as *Bernard Shaw, 1914–1918: Journey to Heartbreak* (London: Routledge & Kegan Paul, 1973).
Bernard Shaw's Nondramatic Literary Criticism (edited). Lincoln: University of Nebraska Press, 1972.
Directions in Literary Criticism: Contemporary Approaches to Literature (edited). University Park and London: Penn State University Press, 1973. With Philip Young.
"Saint Joan": Fifty Years After—1923/24–1973/74 (edited). Baton Rouge: Louisiana State University Press, 1973; Charlottesville, Va.: Teleprint, 1986.
Whistler: A Biography. New York: Weybright & Talley, 1974; London: Collins, 1974; condensed as *Whistler*, with *Times to Remember* by Rose Fitzgerald Kennedy, *The Legend of Baby Doe* by John Burke, and *All the President's Men* by Carl Bernstein and Bob Woodward (New York: Newsweek Books, 1974); translated into Czechoslovakian by Alena Hartmanová (Prague: Odeon, 1987); revised (paperback) edition (New York: Truman Talley Books/Dutton, 1988).
Lawrence of Arabia: The Literary Impulse. Baton Rouge: Louisiana State University Press, 1975. With Rodelle Weintraub.
Aubrey Beardsley: Imp of the Perverse. University Park and London: Penn State University Press, 1976; translated into Japanese by Susumu Takagi (Tokyo: Chuokoron-Sha, 1989).
Four Rossettis: A Victorian Biography. New York: Weybright & Talley, 1977; London: W. H. Allen, 1978.
The Portable Bernard Shaw (edited). New York: Viking, 1977; Harmondsworth, Middlesex, England: Penguin, 1977; slightly revised (New York: Penguin, 1986).
The London Yankees: Portraits of American Writers and Artists in England, 1894–1914. New York and London: Harcourt Brace Jovanovich, 1979; London: W. H. Allen, 1979.
The Portable Oscar Wilde (edited). Revision of Richard Aldington's 1946 edition. New York: Viking, 1981; Harmondsworth, Middlesex, England: Penguin, 1981.
Bernard Shaw. *Heartbreak House: A Facsimile of the Revised Typescript* (edited). New York: Garland, 1981. With Anne Wright.
Dictionary of Literary Biography. Vol. 10: *Modern British Dramatists, 1900–1945* (edited). Detroit: Gale Research, 1982.
The Playwright and the Pirate: Bernard Shaw and Frank Harris: A Correspondence (edited). University Park and London: Penn State University Press, 1982; Gerrards Cross, Bucks., England: Colin Smythe, 1983.

The Unexpected Shaw: Biographical Approaches to G.B.S. and His Work. New York: Frederick Ungar, 1982.

Dictionary of Literary Biography. Vol. 13: *British Dramatists since World War II* (edited). Detroit: Gale Research, 1982.

A Stillness Heard Round the World: The End of the Great War, November 1918. New York: Truman Talley Books/Dutton, 1985; as *A Stillness Heard Round the World: The Silencing of the Guns of War, November 1918* (London: Allen & Unwin, 1986); in paperback (New York: Oxford University Press, 1987); in paperback (New York: Oxford University Press, 1988).

Bernard Shaw: The Diaries 1885–1897 (edited). University Park and London: Penn State University Press, 1986.

Benjamin West Drawings from the Historical Society of Pennsylvania, May 31 through September 17, 1987 (edited). University Park: Penn State University Press and Historical Society of Pennsylvania, 1987. With Randy Ploog.

Victoria: An Intimate Biography. New York: Truman Talley Books/Dutton, 1987; as *Victoria: Biography of a Queen* (London: Allen & Unwin, 1987); as *Queen Victoria: Eine Biographie*, translated by Christa Broermann and Wiebke Schmaltz (Zurich: Benziger Verlag, 1987); in paperback (New York: E. P. Dutton, 1988); in paperback as *Victoria: Biography of a Queen* (London: Unwin Paperbacks, 1988); as *Victoria: Une biographie intime*, translated by Béatrice Vierne (Paris: Robert Laffont, 1988); New York: Truman Talley Books/Plume, 1992; translated into Japanese by Midori Hiraoka (Tokyo: Chuokoron-Sha, 1993).

Bernard Shaw on the London Art Scene 1885–1950 (edited). University Park and London: Penn State University Press, 1989.

Long Day's Journey into War, December 7, 1941. New York: Truman Talley Books/Dutton, 1991; in paperback (New York: Truman Talley Books/Plume, 1991).

Bernard Shaw: A Guide to Research. University Park: Penn State University Press, 1992.

Arms and the Man & John Bull's Other Island by George Bernard Shaw (edited). New York: Bantam Books, 1993. With Rodelle Weintraub.

Disraeli: A Biography. New York: Truman Talley Books/Dutton, 1993; London: Hamish Hamilton, 1993.

Heartbreak House & Misalliance by George Bernard Shaw (edited). New York: Bantam Books, 1995. With Rodelle Weintraub.

The Last Great Victory: The End of World War II, July-August 1945. New York: Truman Talley Books/Dutton 1995.

Shaw's People: Victoria to Churchill. University Park and London: Penn State University Press, 1996.

Uncrowned King: The Life of Prince Albert. New York: Free Press, 1997; as *Albert: Uncrowned King.* London: John Murray, 1997.

ARTICLES, CONTRIBUTIONS TO BOOKS, REVIEWS, AND EPHEMERA

"Bernard Shaw's Boswells" (review of *George Bernard Shaw: Man of the Century* by Archibald Henderson and *Bernard Shaw: His Life, Work and Friends* by St. John Ervine). *Shaw Bulletin* 1, no. 10 (November 1956): 20–22.

"Bernard Shaw, Novelist." *Dissertation Abstracts* 17, no. 2 (1957): 369–70.
"Leaves from a Prison Diary" by Bernard Shaw (edited). *Shaw Bulletin* 2, no. 1 (January 1957): 1–3.
"Bernard Shaw, Charles Lever and *Immaturity.*" *Shaw Bulletin* 2., no. 1 (January 1957): 11–15.
"The Garnetts, the Fabians and *The Paradox Club.*" *Shaw Bulletin* 2, no. 2 (May 1957): 9–12.
"Shavian Dead Letter File." *Shaw Bulletin* 2, no. 2 (May 1957): 23–24.
"'Humors' Names in Shaw's Prentice Novels." *Names* 5 (December 1957): 222–25.
"Shaw's *Divine Comedy:* Addendum." *Shaw Bulletin* 2, no. 5 (May 1958): 21–22.
"Shavian Dead Letter File." *Shaw Bulletin* 2, no. 5 (May 1958): 23–24.
"Ibsen's 'Doll's House' Metaphor Foreshadowed in Victorian Fiction." *Nineteenth-Century Fiction* 13 (June 1958): 67–69.
"Shavian Dead Letter File." *Shaw Review* 2, no. 7 (January 1959): 16–18.
"The Metamorphoses of *The Shaw Review.*" *Modern Drama* 2, no. 2 (September 1959): 162–63; reprinted as "*The Shaw Review:* How It Grew," *Newsletter of the Shaw Society of Chicago* (September 1959).
"The Embryo Playwright in Bernard Shaw's Early Novels." *Texas Studies in Literature and Language* 1 (autumn 1959): 327–55; *California Shavian* 4 (November-December 1963): 2–17.
"Eliza's Prototypes?" (letter). *Times Literary Supplement* (13 November 1959), 668. With letter by Eric J. Batson.
"*Un Petit Drame:* G.B.S's First Play." *Esquire* 52, no. 6 (December 1959): 52–53.
"St. Pancras Manifesto" (edited). *Shaw Review* 3, no. 1 (January 1960): 21–31.
"Bernard Shaw—Aspects and Problems of Research." *Shaw Review* 3, no. 2 (May 1960): 18–26. With Arthur O. Lewis, Jr.
"Reviews and Essays Contributed by Shaw to *The Pall Mall Gazette*" (edited). *Shaw Review* 3, no. 3 (September 1960): 27–31.
"Bernard Shaw, Actor." *Theatre Arts Monthly* 44 (October 1960): 66–67.
"Apostate Apostle: H. L. Mencken as Shavophile and Shavophobe." *Educational Theatre Journal* 12 (October 1960): 184–90; *California Shavian* 3 (September-October 1963): 1–6; reprinted in S. Leonard Rubenstein and Robert G. Weaver, *The Plain Rhetoric.* Boston: Allyn & Bacon, 1964; 192–201.
"Translating Drama: A *Saturday Review* Debate" by Max Beerbohm, Aylmer Maude, and Bernard Shaw (edited). *Shaw Review* 4, no. 1 (January 1961): 2–10.
"Bernard Shaw—Ten Years After (1950–1960): A Transcript of the Second MLA Conference of Scholars on Shaw." *Shaw Review* 4, no. 2 (May 1961): 29–32. With Arthur O. Lewis, Jr.
"Shaw's Mommsenite Caesar." *Anglo-German and American-German Crosscurrents* 2. Edited by Philip Allison Shelley and Arthur O. Lewis Jr. Chapel Hill: University of North Carolina Press, 1962; 257–72.
"How History Gets Rewritten: Lawrence of Arabia in the Theatre." *Drama Survey* 2, no. 3 (winter 1963): 269–75.
"An English Academy of Letters: A Correspondence of 1897" (edited). *Shaw Review* 6, no. 1 (January 1963): 13–26.
"*Lord of the Flies:* Beelzebub Revisited." *College English* 25, no. 2 (November 1963): 90–99. With Bernard Oldsey.

"From Shaw to Shaw" (letter). *Times Literary Supplement* (21 November 1963), 956.

"Foreword" to B. C. Rosset, *Shaw of Dublin*. University Park: Penn State University Press, 1964; vii–x.

"*Castle Corner:* Joyce Cary's *Buddenbrooks.*" *Wisconsin Studies in Contemporary Literature* 5 (1964): 54–63.

"The Uneasy Adventurer—Lawrence of Arabia." *Carnegie Magazine* 38 (March 1964): 101–5.

"The Two Sides of 'Lawrence of Arabia': Aubrey and Meek." *Shaw Review* 7, no. 2 (May 1964): 54–57; reprinted in *Bernard Shaw's Plays*. Edited by Warren Sylvester Smith. New York: W. W. Norton, 1970.

"*The Yellow Book:* A Reappraisal." *JGE: Journal of General Education* 16, no. 2 (July 1964): 136–52.

"Two Edwardian Satires on G.B.S." [*Some Doctored Dilemma* by Robert Ross (?) and *Bruce's Play* by Ada Leverson] (edited). *Shaw Review* 7, no. 3 (September 1964): 87–94.

"Bernard Shaw's Other Saint Joan." *Shavian* (London) 2, no. 10 (October 1964): 7–13; *South Atlantic Quarterly* 64, no. 2 (spring 1965): 194–205.

"What Shaw Said to the Publishers." *Author* 76 (winter 1965): 33–37.

"Mr. Shaw's Method and Secret" (edited). *Shaw Review* 8, no. 2 (May 1965): 65–67.

"Life, Literature, and Political Economy" by Bernard Shaw (edited). *Shaw Review* 8, no. 3 (October 1965): 104–10.

"The Avant-Garde Shaw." In *Shaw Seminar Papers—65*. Toronto: Copp Clark, 1966; 31–52; reprinted in *Bernard Shaw's Plays*. Edited by Warren Sylvester Smith. New York: W. W. Norton, 1970.

"Wesker's Mint." *London Review* 1 (winter 1966): 27–34.

"The *Getting Married* Controversy" by Lord Alfred Douglas and Bernard Shaw (edited). *Shaw Review* 9, no. 2 (May 1966): 66–74.

"A Man Who Knew Lawrence of Arabia." *Trenton Review* 1, no. 1 (fall 1966): 45–50.

"Who Shall Be Laureate?" by Bernard Shaw (edited). *Shaw Review* 10, no. 1 (January 1967): 34–35.

"Biography and Truth." *JGE: Journal of General Education* 19, no. 3 (October 1967): 171–77.

"Four Fathers for Barbara." *Arena Stage* 67/68, no. 147 (1968): 8–9; *American Shakespeare Festival Theatre* (1972 season), 19–23; reprinted in *Directions in Literary Criticism: Contemporary Approaches to Literature*. Edited by Stanley Weintraub and Philip Young. University Park and London: Penn State University Press, 1973; 201–10.

"The Indefatigable Non-Correspondent: G.B.S." *Texas Quarterly* 11, no. 1 (spring 1968): 113–27.

"'The Stage as a Profession': An 1897 Controversy" (edited). *Shaw Review* 11, no. 2 (May 1968): 52–78.

"Mencken to Shaw: 'A Young Man in the Writing Trade' Writes to His Hero." *Menckeniana* no. 26 (Summer 1968): 9–10.

"Recent Shavian Criticism." *Éire-Ireland: A Journal of Irish Studies* 4 (1969): 82–89.

"George Bernard Shaw: An Enquiry" by Arnold Bennett (edited). *Shaw Review* 12, no. 2 (May 1969): 77–79.

"The Making of an Irish Patriot: Bernard Shaw 1914–1916." *Éire-Ireland: A Journal of Irish Studies* 5, no. 4 (1970): 9–27.

"Bernard Shaw's Last 'Irish' Play." *Irish Press* (1970), 6.

"Shaw's *Lear*." *Ariel: A Review of International English Literature* 1, no. 3 (July 1970): 59–68; as "*Heartbreak House:* Shaw's *Lear*," *Modern Drama* 15, no. 3 (December 1972): 255–65.

"Genesis of a Play: Two Early Approaches to *Man and Superman*." In *Shaw: Seven Critical Essays*. Edited by Norman Rosenblood. Toronto: University of Toronto Press, 1971; 25–35.

"Openings on the Campus." *Author* 82 (1971): 169–71.

"*Last Things:* C. P. Snow Eleven Novels After." *Mosaic* 4, no. 3 (1971): 135–41; reprinted in *New Views of the English and American Novel*. Edited by R. G. Collins. Winnipeg: University of Manitoba Press, 1973; 135–41.

"George Bernard Shaw, 1914–1918: Journey to Heartbreak." *Intellectual Digest* 2, no. 3 (November 1971): 29–36, 79–80.

"G.B.S. Borrows from Sarah Grand: 'The Heavenly Twins' and 'You Never Can Tell.'" *Modern Drama* 14, no. 3 (December 1971): 288–97.

"GBS on the Pre-Raphaelites: Two 'Art Corner' Reviews" by Bernard Shaw (edited). *Shaw Review* 15, no. 2 (May 1972): 76–80, 85.

"Cosas poco sencillas: 'Hemingstein' en la guerra." In *La Guerra de España* by Stanley Weintraub, Aldo Garosci, and Ernest Hemingway. Buenos Aires: Proceso, 1973; Buenos Aires: Corregidor, 1975.

"Aubrey Beardsley, *une grande ombre*." *Cahiers Renaud Barrault* 83 (1973): 55–69.

"Gleaning the Shaw Archives." *South Atlantic Quarterly* 72, no. 1 (Winter 1973): 149–53.

"*Don Juan:* A Timeless Play." *New York Sunday News* (14 January 1973), p. 14.

"Chapman's Homer." *Classical World* 67, no. 1 (October 1973): 16–24. With Rodelle Weintraub.

"Literary Biography and Autobiography." In *The Reader's Adviser: A Layman's Guide to Literature*. Edited by Sarah L. Prakken. Ann Arbor, Mich.: R. Bowker, 1974; 716–39.

"T. E. Lawrence." *Encyclopedia Britannica*, Macropaedia, 15th ed. Chicago: Encyclopedia Britannica, 1974; 10: 725–27.

"George Bernard Shaw." *Encyclopedia Britannica*, Macropaedia, 15th ed. Chicago: Encyclopedia Britannica, 1974; 16: 655–59.

"The Private Life of a Dead Poet." *New Republic* 170 (23 March 1974): 27–28.

"*Moby-Dick* and *Seven Pillars of Wisdom*." *Studies in American Fiction* 2, no. 2 (Autumn 1974): 238–40. With Rodelle Weintraub.

"Autobiography and Authenticity: Memoir Writing among Some Late Victorians." In *Sources for Reinterpretation: The Use of Nineteenth-Century Literary Documents. Essays in Honor of C. L. Cline*. Edited by Roger Abrahams and David Farmer. Austin: Department of English and Humanities Research Center, University of Texas, 1975; 1–21; *Cahiers Victoriens & Édouardiens* 2 (1978): 1–20.

"Exploiting Art: The Pictures in Bernard Shaw's Plays." *Modern Drama* 18, no. 3 (September 1975): 215–38.

"Comment and Response: Sexuality in Biography." *College English* 37, no. 1 (September 1975): 72–73.

"Shaw's Lady Cicely and Mary Kingsley." In *Fabian Feminist: Bernard Shaw and Women*. Edited by Rodelle Weintraub. University Park and London: Penn State University Press, 1976; 185–92.

"Bernard Shaw." In *Anglo-Irish Literature: A Review of Research*. Edited by Richard J. Finneran. New York: Modern Language Association of America, 1976; 167–215.

Contributor to "Bernard Shaw—Scholarship of the Past 25 Years, and Future Priorities: A Transcript of the 1975 MLA Conference of Scholars on Shaw" (edited by Charles A. Berst). *Shaw Review* 19, no. 2 (May 1976): 56–72.

"Shaw on 'Flagellomania': A Lecture and a Letter" (edited). *Shaw Review* 20, no. 2 (May 1977): 89–93.

"The Craft of Biography." *Dewan Bahasa* (November 1977), 718–33; reprinted in *Faculty Lecture 3, Faculty of Arts and Sciences*. Singapore: National University of Singapore, 1983.

"The Genesis of *Saint Joan*." *Literatur in Wissenschaft und Unterricht* (Kiel) 10 (December 1977): 259–74.

"Bernard Shaw" (letter). *Times Literary Supplement* (16 June 1978), 672.

"In the Picture Galleries." In *The Genius of Shaw: A Symposium*. Edited by Michael Holroyd. New York: Holt, Rinehart & Winston, 1979; 43–63.

"Orage on Shaw: An Unpublished Manuscript ['The Philosopher' by A. R. Orage]" (edited). *Shaw Review* 22, no. 1 (January 1979): 2–12.

"Bernard Shaw at Oxford: GBS's Lecture on Playwriting—A Reporter's Transcript" (edited). *Shaw Review* 22, no. 2 (May 1979): 92–96.

"Medicine and the Biographer's Art." In *Medicine and Literature*. Edited by Enid Rhodes Peschel. New York: Neale Watson Academic Publications, 1980; 128–39.

"Shaw's Other Keegan: O'Casey and G.B.S." In *Sean O'Casey: Centenary Essays*. Edited by David Krause and Robert G. Lowery. Gerrards Cross, Bucks., England: Colin Smythe, 1980; Totowa, N.J.: Barnes & Noble, 1980; 212–27.

"A 'Redbarn Wash' Adventure" by Bernard Shaw (edited). *Shaw Review* 23, no. 1 (January 1980): 27–30.

"Playwright Cut Playwright: Bernard Shaw on George Moore" by Bernard Shaw (edited). *Shaw Review* 23, no. 2 (May 1980): 90–94.

"The Queen's Speech" by Bernard Shaw (edited). *Shaw Review* 23, no. 3 (September 1980): 135–38.

Introduction to *Heartbreak House: A Facsimile of the Revised Typescript*. New York: Garland, 1981; i–xxvii.

"Bernard Shaw and 'The Unknown Soldier.'" *Times Literary Supplement* (13 November 1981), 1325.

"Bernard Shaw." *Dictionary of Literary Biography*. Vol. 10: *Modern British Dramatists 1900–1945*. Detroit: Gale Research, 1982; Part 2, 129–48.

"William Butler Yeats." *Dictionary of Literary Biography*. Vol. 10: *Modern British Dramatists 1900–1945*. Detroit: Gale Research, 1982; Part 2, 227–37.

"The Royal Court Theatre and the New Drama." *Dictionary of Literary Biography*. Vol 10: *Modern British Dramatists 1900–1945*. Detroit: Gale Research, 1982; Part 2, 297–307.

"David Edgar." *Dictionary of Literary Biography*. Vol 13: *British Dramatists since World War II*. Detroit: Gale Research, 1982; Part 1, 160–71.

"A Mutual Responsibility." *Literature and Medicine* 1 (1982): 38; *JAMA: Journal of the American Medical Association* 262 (July 1989): 3; reprinted in *Literature and Medicine: Toward a New Discipline.* Edited by Kathryn Allen Rabuzzi. Baltimore: Johns Hopkins University Press, 1992; 38.

"The Irish Playwright and the Irish Pirate: Bernard Shaw and Frank Harris, 1895–1931." In *Studies in Anglo-Irish Literature.* Edited by Heinz Kosok. Bonn: Bouvier Verlag Herbert Grundmann, 1982; 105–16.

"Joyce and His Fellow Townsmen Yeats and Joyce." *GBS* (Newsletter of the Bernard Shaw Society of Japan) no. 10 (December 1982).

"His Brother's Keeper: William Michael and Dante Gabriel Rossetti." In *Blood Brothers: Siblings as Writers.* Edited by Norman Kiell. New York: International Universities Press, 1983; 227–75.

"The Practice of Biography: An Interview with Stanley Weintraub." In *Dictionary of Literary Biography Yearbook: 1982.* Detroit: Gale Research, 1983; 34–46.

"Shaw, George Bernard." In *Funk & Wagnalls New Encyclopedia* (1983): 3:352–53.

"Bernard Shaw." In *Recent Research on Anglo-Irish Writers.* Edited by Richard J. Finneran. New York: Modern Language Association, 1983; pp. 66–84.

"Less Scenery Would Mean Better Drama" by Bernard Shaw (edited). *SHAW: The Annual of Bernard Shaw Studies* 3 (1983): 25–27.

"How Bernard Shaw Produces Plays, as Told to Lillah McCarthy," approved and revised by Bernard Shaw (edited). *SHAW: The Annual of Bernard Shaw Studies* 3 (1983): 163–68.

"Uneasy Friendship: Shaw and Yeats." *Yeats: An Annual of Critical and Textual Studies* 1 (1983): 125–53.

"Humanities Research Center: A Consumer's Report." Texas Humanist 5, no. 5 (May/June 1983); 6–7.

"Buchan's Heroes" (letter). *Times Literary Supplement* (11 November 1983), 1247.

"Shaw's Dramatic Criticism in *Our Corner*, 1885–1886" (edited). *SHAW: The Annual of Bernard Shaw Studies* 4 (1984): 5–32.

"Lawrence of Arabia: The Portraits from Imagination, 1922–1979." In *The T. E. Lawrence Puzzle.* Edited by Stephen E. Tabachnick. Athens: University of Georgia Press, 1984; 267–92.

"Confessions of a Bookworm's Apprentice." *Town & Gown* 19, no. 9 (September 1984): 24–54.

"J. B. Priestley." *Dictionary of Literary Biography Yearbook: 1984.* Detroit: Gale Research, 1985; 191–94.

"Bibliography Panel" (panel member). In *Philadelphia Ink: A Literary Celebration.* Philadelphia: Pennsylvania Humanities Council, 1985.

"A High Wind to Jamaica." *SHAW: The Annual of Bernard Shaw Studies* 5 (1985): 37–44.

"Curiosity and Motivation in Scholarship." *JGE: Journal of General Education* 38, no. 3 (1986): 159–66.

"A Jennifer from Australia: Edith Adams, Her Husband, and *The Doctor's Dilemma.*" *SHAW: The Annual of Bernard Shaw Studies* 6 (1986): 77–80.

"Two Pieces from *The Star*" by Bernard Shaw (edited). *SHAW: The Annual of Bernard Shaw Studies* 6 (1986): 157–64.

"A Respectful Distance: James Joyce and His Dublin Townsman Bernard Shaw." *Journal of Modern Literature* 13, no. 1 (March 1986): 61–75.

"Reviewing Literary Biography: Apprehending the *Daimon*." *UNISA English Studies: Journal of the Department of English* 24 (May 1986): 18–23; reprinted in *Literary Reviewing*. Edited by James O. Hoge. Charlottesville: University Press of Virginia, 1987; 29–43.

"Shaw as an Actor." In *"Shaw 86"* (supplement), *Hershey Chronicle* (25 June 1986), 9.

"A Pennsylvania Yankee at King George's Court: Benjamin West." In *Benjamin West Drawings from the Historical Society of Pennsylvania, May 31 through September 17, 1987*. Edited with Randy Ploog. University Park: Penn State Museum of Art, 1987; 1–13.

"Introduction to Shaw." In *Modern Critical Views: George Bernard Shaw*. Edited by Harold Bloom. New York: Chelsea House, 1987; 27–45.

"Collecting the Quarrels: Whistler and *The Gentle Art of Making Enemies*." In *Twilight of the Dawn: Studies in English Literature in Transition*. Edited by O. M. Brack Jr. Tucson: University of Arizona Press, 1987; 34–44.

"Victorian in Name Only: The Queen Was Amused in the Bedroom and Elsewhere." Discussion with Leah Rozen. *People Weekly* 27 (22 June 1987): 58, 60, 62.

"Exasperated Admiration: Bernard Shaw on Queen Victoria." *Victorian Poetry* 25, nos. 3–4 (autumn-winter 1987): 115–32.

"Hanley's Collections" (letter). *New York Times Book Review* (11 October 1987), 20.

"Victoria of Ireland: A Tale of Too Little and Too Late." In *Anglo-Irish and Irish Literature: Aspects of Language and Culture*. Edited by Birgit Bramsback and Martin Broghan. Uppsala, Sweden: Acta Universitatis Uppsaliensis, 1988; 213–20.

"A Report from *The Star*" by Correspondents from *The Star*, including Bernard Shaw (edited). *SHAW: The Annual of Bernard Shaw Studies* 8 (1988): 1–11.

"Memoirs of an Old-Fashioned Physician" by Bernard Shaw (edited). *SHAW: The Annual of Bernard Shaw Studies* 8 (1988): 135–37.

"*Caesar and Cleopatra*—A Melbourne-Victorian Dimension." *Shavian* (London) 6, no. 6 (spring 1988): 6–8.

"Ballads by Shaw: The Anonymous *Star* Versifier of 1888–1889." *SHAW: The Annual of Bernard Shaw Studies* 9 (1989): 29–37.

"Bernard Shaw in Darkest England: G.B.S. and the Salvation Army's General William Booth." *SHAW: The Annual of Bernard Shaw Studies* 10 (1990): 45–59.

"Reviewer of Forgotten Novelists: Two Early Unsigned Notices from the *Pall Mall Gazette*" by Bernard Shaw (edited). *SHAW: The Annual of Bernard Shaw Studies* 10 (1990): 136–41.

"Having It Both Ways: *Getting Married* as Serious Farce." Program for "The Once and Future Shaw" Symposium, 20–22 April 1990. New York: Long Island Stage, 1990; 8–11.

"'The Seven Pillars of Wisdom'" (letter). *Times Literary Supplement* (20–26 July 1990), 775.

"The Trial of John Brown: Barrie Stavis and History." *Cardoza Studies in Law and Literature* 2, no. 2 (fall-winter 1990): 163–76. With Mark Bennett Weintraub.

"Victorian Poets and Physicians." *Literature and Medicine: Tenth Anniversary Retrospective* 10 (1991): 86–97.

"Bernard Shaw Besieged: Political Progresses to Oxbridge, 1888–1892." *SHAW: The Annual of Bernard Shaw Studies* 11 (1991): 37–46.
"Bernard Shaw and the American Theatre." *UNISA English Studies: Journal of the Department of English* 29, no. 2 (September 1991): 36–42; reprinted in *Cambridge Guide to American Theatre*. Edited by Don B. Wilmeth and Tice L. Miller. Cambridge: Cambridge University Press, 1993; 426–28.
"Bernard Shaw" (letter). *Times Literary Supplement* (27 September 1991), 19.
"Pearl Harbor in the Mind of Japan." *New York Times Magazine* (1 December 1991), 16, 18.
"Three Myths About Pearl Harbor." *New York Times* (4 December 1991), p. A27.
"Disraeli and Wilde's 'Dorian Gray.'" *Cahiers Victoriens & Édouardiens* 36 (October 1992): 19–27; *UNISA English Studies: Journal of the Department of English* 31, no. 2 (September 1993): 29–53.
"The Messages of Pearl Harbor" (letter). *New York Times Book Review* (29 November 1992), 35.
"Franklin D. Roosevelt" (letter). *Times Literary Supplement* (11 December 1992), 15.
"'The Hibernian School': Oscar Wilde and Bernard Shaw." *SHAW: The Annual of Bernard Shaw Studies* 13 (1993): 25–49.
"The Christmas Truce." *MHQ: The Quarterly Journal of Military History* 5, no. 2 (winter 1993): 76–85.
"That Notorious 14th Paragraph" (letter). *New York Times Book Review* (14 March 1993), 30.
"Disraeli" (letter). *Times Literary Supplement* (17 December 1993), 15.
"A Kid's War." In *Contemporary Authors Autobiography Series*. Detroit: Gale Research, 1994; 20: 297–317.
"Shaw Decides to Become a Playwright: July–December 1892." *SHAW: The Annual of Bernard Shaw Studies* 14 (1994): 9–23.
"Curtains Speech: A New Source for *Heartbreak House*." *English Literature in Transition 1880–1920* 38, no. 4 (1995): 497–500.
"Shaw's Diary Fragments: Some Additions." *SHAW: The Annual of Bernard Shaw Studies* 15 (1995): 203–9.
"The Three-Week War: The End of the War with Japan." *MHQ: The Quarterly Journal of Military History* 7, no. 3 (spring 1995): 86–95.
"GBS and Women" (letter). *Times Literary Supplement* (31 May 1996), 17.

Journal Editorships

Shaw Bulletin 1, no. 10–2, no. 6 (November 1956–September 1958); *Shaw Review* 2, no. 7–18, no. 3 (January 1959–September 1980); *SHAW: The Annual of Bernard Shaw Studies* 1–10 (1981–1990).
Comparative Literature Studies 24–25 (1987–1988), with A. Owen Aldridge; *Comparative Literature Studies* 26–29 (1989–1992), with Gerhard F. Strasser.

Note: Omitted from this list are literally hundreds of additional items, including reviews, short notices, and letters to the editor.

Contributors

M. D. ALLEN is associate professor of English at the University of Wisconsin-Fox Valley. His main research interest is the lives and writings of English travellers in the Middle East. He is the author of *The Medievalism of Lawrence of Arabia* (1991)—the book version of the dissertation he wrote under Stanley Weintraub's supervision—and of articles and book reviews in scholarly journals.

MELISSA WITTE ANTINORI has taught at The Pennsylvania State University, Juniata College, and Westmoreland Community College. Recently moved to New York City with her husband, John, a software designer, she teaches at Long Island University (Brooklyn) and is writing her dissertation on the author in Victorian fiction. Her paper in this volume grew out of a class with Stanley Weintraub.

ARTHUR NICHOLAS ATHANASON is professor of English at Michigan State University. Recipient of an Amoco Foundation Excellence-in-Teaching Award, he also directs plays in professional, university, and community theater. He has contributed essays on John Osborne and Agatha Christie to the *Dictionary of Literary Biography: British Dramatists Since World War II* and pieces on Francis Beeding, Thomas Burke, and Gaston Leroux to *Twentieth Century Crime and Mystery Writers*. His Twayne Masterwork Study, *Endgame: The Ashbin Play* (1993), was nominated by Twayne Publishers for the Joe A. Callaway Prize.

TRACY SIMMONS BITONTI has completed her Ph.D. at the University of South Carolina with a dissertation on selected twentieth-century American women writers and the literary marketplace. She received her B.A. and M.A. degrees from The Pennsylvania State University. She has edited *Yemassee*, a literary journal, and has published works on F. Scott Fitzgerald and Bernard Shaw. She is employed at the ublishing firm of Bruccoli Clark Layman.

FRED D. CRAWFORD, associate professor of English Central Michigan University, succeeded Stanley Weintraub as editor of *SHAW: The*

Annual of Bernard Shaw Studies. His books include *Mixing Memory and Desire: "The Waste Land" and British Novels, British Poets of the Great War,* and *Richard Aldington and Lawrence of Arabia: A Cautionary Tale.* He is currently writing a biography of Lowell Thomas and compiling a volume of Thomas' selected letters.

Robert C. Doyle, after his naval service and activity as a professional musician, earned his doctorate in 1987 at the Bowling Green State University. He taught American Studies at The Pennsylvania State University, at the Westfalische Wilhelms-Universitat-Munster as a Fulbright scholar, and as a Visiting Professor of American Civilization at the Universite des Sciences Humaines de Strasbourg II. His books include *Voices from Captivity, Interpreting the American POW Narrative* (1994) and *Escape into History* (1997).

KAY LI, formerly of the secretariat of the Hong Kong government, is a Ph.D. student at York University (Canada). She is the author of articles on Bernard Shaw, Virginia Woolf, and various translations. Stanley Weintraub served as her external examiner at the University of Hong Kong.

MIKE MARKEL is director of technical communication and professor of English at Boise State University. Early in his career, he wrote about Hilaire Belloc and other English poets but then he went astray and now focuses on technical communication.

MICHAEL PHARAND has published articles on Bernard Shaw, Tennessee Williams, Lawrence Durrell, Richard Aldington, and Robert Graves. He has taught at universities in Toronto, Canton (New York), Mosul (Iraq), and at The Pennsylvania State University. He was recently assistant professor in the Graduate School of Kansai Gaidai University in Osaka, Japan, and is now Research Fellow at the Robert Graves Project, St. John's College, Oxford.

JOHN R. PFEIFFER, professor of English language and literature at Central Michigan University, taught one of the first undergraduate courses in fantasy and science fiction at the U.S. Air Force Academy in 1971. He has been bibliographer of *The Shaw Review* and *SHAW: The Annual of Bernard Shaw Studies* since 1972. In addition to a number of articles on Octavia Butler, his work includes pieces on Lewis Carroll, William Morris, J. S. Mill, Sir Richard Burton, Friedrich Durrenmatt, Günter Grass, John Christopher, John Brunner, and Ursula LeGuinn.

KINLEY E. ROBY taught in the English Department at Northeastern University in Boston for twenty-four years, having served for a number of years as chair of the Department. He is the author of books on Arnold Bennett, Joyce Cary, T. S. Eliot, and Edward VII. For the past twenty years, he has been 20th-Century Field editor for G. K. Hall & Company, now Twayne Publishers.

SUSAN RUSINKO, retired professor and chair of the English department, Bloomsburg University, is the author of *Terence Rattigan; Tom Stoppard; British Drama, 1950 to the Present: A Critical History; The Plays of Benn Levy;* and *Joe Orton.* Her publications include articles and book reviews, mostly on modern British drama.

JULIE SPARKS is a Ph.D. candidate at The Pennsylvania State University, currently working under Stanley Weintraub on her dissertation, tentatively titled "Taking Our Own Measure: The Evolution of the Artificial Human in Victorian and Early Modernist Literature."

RODELLE WEINTRAUB's books include *Fabian Feminist: Bernard Shaw and Woman* and *Captain Brassbound's Conversion* in the series, *Bernard Shaw Early Texts: Play Manuscripts in Facsimile.* With Stanley Weintraub, she is coeditor of two Bantam edition pairings: *"Arms and the Man" and "John Bull's Other Island"* and *"Misalliance" and "Heartbreak House."* She has served as assistant editor of *The Shaw Review* and as editor for special topics issues of *The Shaw Review (Shaw and Women),* and of *SHAW: The Annual of Bernard Shaw Studies,* 5 *(Shaw Abroad).* Her numerous articles have appeared in journals such as *Cahiers Victoriens & Edouardiens, The Shaw Review, SHAW,* and *Ritual Remembering History, Myth and Politics in Anglo Irish Drama.* Currently she is working on a study of Shaw's "problem solving" dream plays.

MILTON T. WOLF has published over seventy articles on a variety of subjects, in works ranging from the *Encyclopedia of Science Fiction* to *Library Journal.* As director of collections at the University of Nevada, Reno, where he also teaches science fiction, he is best known for editing (with Bruce Miller) *Thinking Robots, An Aware Internet and Cyberpunk Librarians* and the December 1995 special issue of *Information Technology and Libraries* devoted to "The Information Future." He was also coeditor of *Visions of Wonder,* a science fiction anthology (TOR Books, 1996) and editor of the 1996 special topics issue of *SHAW and Science Fiction.*

Index

Albert, Prince, 10, 25
Albert, Sidney, 31; "Reflections on Shaw and Psychoanalysis" (1971), 31
Aldridge, Alfred Owen, 199–200
Allen, Grant, 95; *The Woman Who Did* (1895), 95
Allen, M. D., 11, 214; *The Medievalism of Lawrence of Arabia* (1991), 11, 214
Andersch, Alfred, 195
Antinori, Melissa Witte, 11, 214
Archer, William, 35, 41, 57, 124, 129; *The Life, Trial, and Death of Francisco Ferrer* (1911), 129
Aristophanes, 91; *The Clouds* [432 B.C.], 91
Armstrong, Anthony, 181; *Ten-Minute Alibi*, 181
Asimov, Isaac, 133, 138
Asquith, H. H., 55, 56
Asquith, Mrs. Raymond, 124
Athanason, Arthur Nicholas, 12, 214
Atkinson, Brooks, 182
Augustine, Saint, 134, 192

Baker, John F., 28
Baring, Maurice, 121, 124, 128; *The Russian People* (1911), 128
Barras, Vicomte Paul François de, 42, 43
Barrie, Sir James, 58
Beardsley, Aubrey, 10, 25
Beatles, 155, 156, 161
Beerbohm, Max, 80
Beeton, Isabella, 127, 130; *The Book of Household Management* (1861), 130
Begum, Zohra ("Lady Venus"), 11, 110–18
Bell, Quentin, 87
Bellamy, Edward, 11, 64–66, 73–76; *Looking Backward* (1887), 64
Belloc, Hilaire, 11, 121–30; *On Nothing & Kindred Subjects* (1908), 123
Bennett, Arnold, 9, 11, 23, 53–61; *The Author's Craft* (1914), 53, 54; *The Bright Island* (1925), 54–55, 59, 60; *Buried Alive* (1908), 54, 56; *Cupid and Commonsense* (1908), 58, 61; *Don Juan de Marana* (1914), 60; *The Great Adventure* (1913), 53–54; *Judith* (1918–19), 57; *Liberty—A Statement of the British Case*, 55; *The Love Match* (1922), 60; *The Pretty Lady* (1918), 56, 57; *Mr. Prohack* (1927), 60; *The Return Journey* (1928), 60, 61; *The Roll-Call* (1918), 56, 57; *The Title* (1918), 57
Bennett, Dorothy Cheston, 60
Bentley, Eric, 67, 80
Berst, Charles A., 41, 42, 44
Bertolini, John A., 83
Besant, Walter, 95; *All in a Garden Fair* (1883), 95; *The Revolt of Man* (1882), 95
Bezalel, Judah Loew b., 136
Bicknell, Herman, 113, 115
Bidwell, Robin, 112
Bierce, Ambrose, 195
Bitonti, Tracy Simmons, 12, 214
Böll, Heinrich, 195
Bonaparte, Napoleon, 11, 41–46, 48, 49, 50–51
Boulle, Pierre, 195
Browder, Sally, 176
Bulwer-Lytton, Edward, 11, 64, 67–68, 69, 76, 77, 78, 81; *The Coming Race* (1871), 67
Burne, Lt. Col., 116
Burton, Sir Richard, 115–16; *A Personal Narrative of a Pilgrimage to El-Medinah and Mecca* (1855), 115
Butler, LaFayette, 22
Butler, Octavia, 12, 140–52; *Adulthood Rites* (1988), 148; *Bloodchild and Other Stories* (1995), 140; *Clay's Ark* (1984), 141, 144–46; *Dawn: Xenogen-*

INDEX

esis (1987), 148; *Imago* (1989), 149–50; *Kindred* (1979), 141, 146–48; *Mind of My Mind* (1977), 141–42; "Near of Kin" (1979), 140; *Parable of the Sower* (1993), 140, 148, 150; *Patternmaster* (1976), 141, 142; *Survivor* (1978), 141, 142, 146; *Wild Seed* (1980), 141, 143–44, 148
Butler, Samuel, 138
Byron, George Gordon, Lord, 162

Campbell, Sr., James L., 68
Capek, Karel, 137; *R.U.R. (Rossum's Universal Robots)* (1921), 137
Carpenter, Albert L., 198
Cary, Joyce, 11
Charteris, Evan, 125
Chesterton, Cecil, 129
Chesworth, Jo, 28
Churchill, Winston, 124, 128, 161
Clavell, James, 195, 197–99
Clough, Arthur Hugh, 125; "The Latest Decalogue," 125
Cobbold, Lady Evelyn, 110, 119; *Pilgrimage to Mecca* (1934), 110
Cobley, Evelyn, 196
Cohen, Paula M., 97
Conlon, John J., 28
Conrad, Joseph, 15, 57
Cooper, James Fenimore, 200; *The Last of the Mohicans*, (1826), 200
Coustillas, Pierre, 96
Crawford, Fred D., 9, 10, 11, 15–18, 214
Crenna, Richard, 185
Crone, PFC Joe, 195
Cummings, Robert, 184

Dante, Aligheri, 157, 158
Darwin, Charles, 64, 66, 68, 69, 79; *On the Origin of Species* (1859), 64
Davies, A. Emil, 85; *I Wander*, 85
Delaroche, Paul, 43; *Napoleon at Fontainebleau* (1845), 43; *Napoleon at Saint Helena* (1852), 43; *Napoleon Crossing the Alps* (1848), 43
Denham, Reginald, 182
Derounian-Stodola, Kathryn Zabelle, 199
Dickens, Charles, 108
Digby, Lady Jane, 110
Disraeli, Benjamin, 24, 25

Douglas, James, 124, 128
Doyle, Robert C., 11, 191–95, 201, 215; *Voices from Captivity: Interpreting the American POW Narrative* (1994), 11
DuMaurier, Gerald, 54
Dyhouse, Carol, 98

Edward VIII, 11
Einstein, Albert, 49
Eliot, T. S., 11
Ervine, St. John, 58–59
Evans, Maurice, 181–84; *All This . . . and Evans Too!*, 182

Fagan, James Bernard, 58
Fernald, John, 181
Ferrer, Mel, 185
Ferrer y Guardia, Francisco, 124, 129
Fitzgerald, Zelda, 26; *Save Me the Waltz*, 26
Flameng, François, 43
Forbes, Brian, 197
Forster, E. M., 138; "The Machine Stops" (1909), 138
Franklin, Benjamin, 199
Frazer, Sir James George, 124, 128
Freud, Sigmund, 31–32; *Interpretation of Dreams* (1899), 31
Friedman, Barton R., 193–94
Friel, Brian, 33; adaptation of *Fathers and Sons* (1987), 33
Fussell, Paul, 194; *Wartime: Understanding and Behavior in the Second World War* (1989), 194

Galsworthy, John, 54, 57
Galton, Sir Francis, 76, 79
Ganz, Arthur, 47
Gissing, George, 11, 15, 95–108; *Born in Exile* (1892), 96, 103, 105; *In the Year of Jubilee* (1894), 96, 97, 101–03, 105, 107; *New Grub Street* (1891), 95, 96, 99–100, 106; *The Odd Women* (1893), 96, 97, 103–04, 108; *The Whirlpool* (1897), 96, 97, 106, 107
Goosens, Eugene, 60
Grand, Sarah, 96; *The Beth Book* (1897), 96; *The Heavenly Twins* (1892), 96
Greenwell, Graham H., 194

Gussow, Mel, 164, 166

Halliwell, Kenneth, 156, 157, 160
Hanley, T. E., 22
Hardy, Thomas, 15, 96; *Jude the Obscure* (1895), 96
Harriot, Esther, 167, 168
Harris, Frank, 10
Haynes, E. S. P., 128
Heller, Joseph, 195; *Catch 22* (1955), 195
Henderson, Archibald, 57
Henley, Beth, 166
Hepburn, Audrey, 185
Herbert, Frank, 138; *Destination: Void* (1981), 138
Hillary, Ann (née Ann Margaret Francis), 180–81
Hitchcock, Alfred, 184
Hitler, Adolf, 50
Hogarth, D. G., 115; *The Penetration of Arabia* (1904), 115
Holroyd, Michael, 80–81
Homer, 84, 134; *Iliad*, 83, 84, 88, 91, 134
Horne, Amelia, 118
Howarth, W. D., 47
Howe, Irving, 96
Howe, Tina, 166
Howell, Sir Thomas, 198
Hugo, Leon, 83
Hurgronje, Snouk, 113

Ibsen, 129, 166; *Ghosts*, 166

Jacquet-Droz, Henri-Louis, 136
Jacquet-Droz, Pierre, 136
Joan of Arc, 41, 43
Jonson, Ben, 160
Jones, Ernest, 31; "The Oedipus Complex as an Explanation of Hamlet's Mystery" (1910), 31
Joséphine, Empress, 42, 43, 44
Joyce, James, 157, 158, 160

Kaltenborn, H. V., 19
Kane, Leslie, 166, 171
Kauffmann, Stanley, 185
Keane, Elizabeth (née Thomas), 113
Keane, John Fryer Thomas, 110–18; *My Journey to Medinah* (1881), 118; *Six Months in Meccah* (1881), 110

Keane, William (Reverend), 113
Keegan, John, 193; *A History of Warfare*, (1993), 193
Kelly, Grace, 184
Kerr, Walter, 182, 184
Kiernan, R. H., 112; *The Unveiling of Arabia* (1937), 112
Knoblock, Edward, 53, 60
Knott, Anthony Frederick, 181
Knott, Cyril Wakefield, 180
Knott, Frederick, 12, 180–88; *Dial M for Murder* (1950), 180, 181–87; [also titled *Telephone Call*], 184; *Wait until Dark* (1966), 180, 185–86; *Write Me a Murder* (1961), 180, 184, 185, 186
Knott, Margaret Caroline (Paul), 180
Kropotkin, Prince Peter, 78
Korda, Sir Alexander, 181–82, 184
Korg, Jacob, 96, 98

Lahr, John, 156, 160
Lamarck, Jean Baptiste Pierre Antoine de Monet de, 69, 70, 71, 79
Laurence, Dan H., 22
Lawrence, A. W., 24
Lawrence, D. H., 9, 24
Lawrence (of Arabia), T. E., 9, 11, 23, 24, 25, 26
Lester, Richard, 156
Levernier, James Arthur, 199
Lévy, Arthur, 42; *Napoléon intime* (1893), 42; *The Private Life of Napoleon* (1894), 42
Lewenstein, Oscar, 156
Li, Kay, 11, 215
Limbaugh, Rush, 27
Linton, Eliza Lynn, 95; *The Girl of the Period* (1883), 95; *The One Too Many* (1894), 95
Logue, Christopher, 164
Lucas, Edward Verrall, 124, 128; *A Wanderer in London* (1906), 128
Lyons, James E., 125
Lyttelton, Alfred, 124, 129

MacArthur, Eddie, 198
MacCarthy, Desmond, 73
Macintosh, Miss. *See* Begum, Zohra
Magnus, Albertus, 134
Mailer, Norman, 195
Mann, Charles, 28
Marconi, Guglielmo, 121, 129

INDEX

Markel, Mike, 11, 215
Markow, Alice B., 96
Martin, Bob, 198
Martin, Mrs. W. T., 117
Martin, W. T., 117, 119
Massingham, Henry W., 54
Masterman, C. F. G., 124, 129
McCarthy, Lillah, 54, 57
McDonnell, Lisa J., 166, 167, 169
McDowell, Frederick P. W., 88
McGough, Roger, 164
Meissonier, Jean-Louis, 43; *Campaign of France* (1864), 43; *Napoleon in 1814* (1863), 43
Meyrink, Gustav, 137; *Der Golem* (1915), 137
Miles, Eustace Hamilton, 124, 129
Milland, Ray, 184
Mintz, Steven, 97, 98; *A Prison of Expectations* (1983), 97
Montagu, Samuel (Lord Swaythling), 124, 129
Monteith, Charles, 156
Moore, George, 15, 60
Moore, Mina, 48
Moravec, Hans, 138
Morris, William, 11, 64, 65, 73, 74, 78; *News from Nowhere* (1891), 64
Murray, Gilbert, 32, 45
Murrow, Edward R., 19
Mussolini, Benito, 18, 50

Nadel, Norman, 185
Nash, Carl, 191–92, 194
Nietzsche, Friedrich, 79
Norman, Marsha, 12, 166–79; *The Fortune Teller* (1987), 166; *Four Plays* (1988): 166; —, *Getting Out* (1977), 166, 167–70; —, *The Holdup* (1980–83), 166, 173–74; —, *Third and Oak* (1978), 166, 167, (*Laundromat* and *The Pool Hall*), 170–73; —, *Traveler in the Dark* (1984), 166, 167, 177–79; *'night, Mother* (1983), 166, 167, 174–77
Norrington, Giles, 192, 194
Nuttall, Harry, 124, 128

O'Malley, Ellen, 58–59
Orton, Joe, 12, 155–64; *Crimes of Passion* (1967), 164; —, *The Erpingham Camp* (1966), 155, 161, 164; —, *The Ruffian on the Stair* (1964), 155, 161, 164; *Entertaining Mr. Sloane* (1964), 155, 156, 161, 163–64; *Funeral Games* (1966), 155, 161; *The Good and Faithful Servant* (1964), 155, 161; *Head to Toe* [orig. *The Vision of Gombold Proval*] (1961), 155, 156–61, 164; *Loot* (1965), 155, 161, 162, 163, 164; *The Orton Diaries* (1986), 164; *Up Against It* (1979), 155, 156, 161–64; *What the Butler Saw* (1969), 155, 159, 161, 162, 163, 164
Orton, John, 158
Osborne, John, 12
Owen, Robert, 66–67

Peerboom, J. J., 80
Penn, Arthur, 185
Pfeiffer, John, 11, 215
Pharand, Michael, 11, 215
Pinter, Harold, 12, 155, 161, 164; *The Homecoming* (1965), 164
Pitts, Joseph, 110, 115
Playfair, Nigel, 58
Poole, Adrian, 108

Rabelais, François, 157, 158
Rader, Shirley, 15, 28
Ralli, Augustus, 112, 115; *Christians at Mecca* (1909), 112
Rattigan, Terence, 155, 161
Remick, Lee, 185
Roberts, David, 98
Roby, Kinley E., 11, 216
Roosevelt, F. D., 19
Ross, Jean W., 28
Roughead, W. N., 125
Rusinko, Susan, 12, 216
Ruskin, John, 78
Ryan, Sir Andrew, 110, 114

Sabean, Samuel, 21
Sahib, Nana, 117
Salisbury, Lord, 116
Sardou, Victorien, 46–47; *Madame Sans-Gêne* (1893), 46
Saunders, James, 164
Schaefer, George, 184
Schlesinger, Jr., Arthur M., 192
Scholem, Gershom, 136
Selig, Robert, 96

Sevareid, Eric, 19
Shakespeare, William, 74, 160, 162; *King Lear* (1606), 83; *Macbeth* (1606), 54; *Romeo and Juliet* (1596), 162
Sharp, Clifford, 55
Shaw, George Bernard, 9, 10, 11, 15, 17, 21, 22, 25, 26, 31–33, 36, 37–38, 41–50, 53–61, 63–73, 75–77, 78, 79, 80–81, 83–88, 90
—Works: *Annajanska, The Bolshevik Empress* (1917), 57; *Arms and the Man* (1894), 11, 33, 38, 58; *As Far as Thought Can Reach* (1921), 76; *Augustus Does His Bit* (1916), 57; *Back to Methuselah* (1921), 47, 49, 56, 57, 58, 64, 68–69, 77, 79, 80; *Common Sense about the War* (1931), 55; *Don Juan in Hell* (1903), 21, 32, 72; *Everybody's Political What's What?* (1944), 50, 63, 65, 80; *Farfetched Fables* (1949), 81; *Heartbreak House* (1917), 11, 56, 57, 58, 59, 83, 84, 85, 87, 88, 90, 91; *In the Beginning* (1921), 76; "The Illusions of War" (1915), 85; *The Inca of Perusalem* (1915), 57; *Jitta's Atonement* (1922), 58; *Man and Superman* (1903), 21, 32, 72, 77; *The Man of Destiny* (1895), 41, 43, 44, 45, 46, 47, 48, 49, 51; *O'Flaherty, V.C.* (1915), 57; "On Christian Economics" (1913), 87; *The Perfect Wagnerite* (1898), 84; *The Quintessence of Ibsenism*, (1891), 78; *Saint Joan* (1923), 32, 43; *Shakes vs. Shav*, (1949) 88; *Sixteen Self Sketches* (1949), 81; "The Sufferings of the Sane," 86; *Table Talk* (1925), 53; *Too True to be Good* (1931), 49; "Troilus and Cressida" (1884), 83, 88, 90; "War Delirium," 86
Shaw, Irvin, 195
Shaw, T. E. *See* Lawrence (of Arabia), T. E.
Shelley, Mary, 137, 138
Shenstone, Walter, 155
Sherwood, James P., 181–82
Shirer, William, 19
Six Million Dollar Man, The, 138
Skeat, Walter William, 124, 129
Sloane, William Milligan, 42; *Life of Napoleon Bonaparte* (1939), 42
Smales, Giedon, 113

Smith, Warren Sylvester, 65
Snow, C. P., 10
Sparks, Julie, 11, 216
Spencer, Jenny S., 175
Stead, William Thomas, 124, 128
Stewart, George R., 150
Stoessinger, John, 192; *Why Nations Go to War* (1990), 192
Stoppard, Tom, 155
Strindberg, August, 35, 38; *Dream Play* (1901), 35
Stubbs, Patricia, 96
Sutherland, Bruce, 22
Swift, Jonathan, 91, 138, 157, 158, 199–200; *Gulliver's Travels* (1721–25) 91, 138, 200
Swinnerton, Frank, 61
Synge, John M., 33; *Playboy of the Western World* (1907), 33

Taubman, Howard, 184
Taylor, A. J. P., 50–51
Terry, Ellen, 46
Thomas, E. B., 115, 116
Thomas, J. F., 113
Thomas, Saint, 134
Trebitsch, Siegfried, 58
Trench, Richard, 112; *Arabian Travellers* (1986), 112
Turner, Reginald, 9, 23, 25, 60

Unwin, T. Fisher, 42

Valency, Maurice, 31, 45, 47
Vaucanson, Jacques de, 136
Venus, Lady. *See* Begum, Zohra
Voltaire, (François Marie Arouet), 157, 158, 163
Vonnegut, Kurt, Jr., 195; *Slaughterhouse-Five* (1966), 195

Walkley, A. B., 57
Wapole, Hugh, 60
Watson, Barbara Bellow, 31
Wattenberg, Richard, 173
Waugh, Auberon, 161
Weintraub, Rodelle, 11, 216 (*see also* Weintraub, Stanley)
Weintraub, Stanley, 9–12, 15–28, 76, 83, 87, 91, 191, 201
—Family: Benjamin (father), 18; David

Andrew (son), 23, 25, 28; Erica Beth (daughter); 23, 25, 28; Gladys (sister), 18; Herbert (brother), 18, 21; Mark Bennett (son), 23, 25, 28; MaryAlison (granddaughter), 25; Ray Segal (mother), 18; Rodelle Horwitz (wife), 10, 21, 22, 23, 24, 25, 26, 28
—Works: *An Unfinished Novel by Bernard Shaw* (1958), 10, 23; *"Arms and the Man" and "John Bull's Other Island"* (1993), 10; *Beardsley: A Biography* (1967), 9, 26; *Bernard Shaw, The Diaries, 1885–1897* (1986), 24; *Dictionary of Literary Biography, Volume 10: Modern British Dramatists, 1900–1945; Volume 13: British Dramatists Since World War II* (1982), 12, 26; *Directions in Literary Criticism: Contemporary Approaches to Literature* (1973), 26; *Disraelli: A Biography* (1993), 10; *Evolution of a Revolt: Early Postwar Writings of T. E. Lawrence* (1968), 26; *The Four Rossettis: A Victorian Biography* (1977), 25; *Journey to Heartbreak: The Crucible Years of Bernard Shaw, 1914–1918* (1971), 9, 25, 26, 91; *The Last Great Cause: The Intellectuals and the Spanish Civil War* (1986), 25; *The Last Great Victory: The End of World War II, July–August 1945* (1995), 9, 10, 25, 26, 27, 191, 201; *Lawrence of Arabia: The Literary Impulse* (1975), 26; *The London Yankees: Portraits of American Writers and Artists in England, 1894–1914* (1979), 9, 25, 26; *Long Day's Journey Into War, December 7, 1941* (1991), 10, 26, 191; *The Playwright and the Pirate: Bernard Shaw and Frank Harris, a Correspondence* (1982), 26; *The Portable Oscar Wilde,* (1977), 16; *Private Shaw and Public Shaw: A Dual Portrait of Lawrence of Arabia and G.B.S.* (1963), 10, 24; *Reggie: A Portrait of Reginald Turner* (1965), 24; *Shaw Bulletin*, 10, 22, 23; *The Shaw Review*, 10, 23, 27; *SHAW: The Annual of Bernard Shaw Studies*, 10, 23, 26; *Shaw's People: Victoria to Churchill* (1996), 9, 10; *A Stillness Heard Around the World: The End of the Great War, November 1918* (1985), 10, 25; *The Unexpected Shaw: Biographical Approaches to G.B.S. and His Work* (1982), 26; *The War in the Wards: Korea's Unknown Battle in a Prisoner-of-War Hospital Camp* (1964), 10, 21, 28; *Victoria: An Intimate Biography* (1987), 9, 10, 25; *Whistler: A Biography* (1974), 26, 27

Wells, H. G., 15, 49, 50, 57
Westheimer, David, 195
Weston, Jack, 185
Wheeler, General, 118
Wheeler, Miss, 118–19
Whistler, James Abbott McNeill, 10, 25
Wilde, Oscar, 9, 10, 15, 24
Williams, Emlyn, 187; *Night Must Fall* (1935), 187
Williams, John, 184
Williams, Tennessee, 166; *The Glass Menagerie* (1948), 166
Willkie, Wendell, 19
Wise, Gene, 196
Wisenthal, J. L., 77, 80
Wolf, Milton T., 11, 216
Wood, Charles, 164
Woolf, Leonard, 87
Woolf, Virginia, 87

Young, Philip, 26
Young, Terence, 185

Zohrab, Consul James, 110, 114, 116